# CULTURESHOCK!

## A Survival Guide to Customs and Etiquette

JAKARTA

Derek Bacon
Terry Collins

**Marshall Cavendish**
Editions

This edition published in 2007 by:
Marshall Cavendish Corporation
99 White Plains Road
Tarrytown, NY 10591-9001
www.marshallcavendish.us

Other Marshall Cavendish Offices:
Marshall Cavendish International (Asia) Private Limited. 1 New Industrial
Road, Singapore 536196 ▪ Marshall Cavendish Ltd. 119 Wardour Street, London
W1F 0UW, UK ▪ Marshall Cavendish International (Thailand) Co Ltd. 253 Asoke,
12th Flr, Sukhumvit 21 Road, Klongtoey Nua, Wattana, Bangkok 10110, Thailand
▪ Marshall Cavendish (Malaysia) Sdn Bhd, Times Subang, Lot 46, Subang Hi-Tech
Industrial Park, Batu Tiga, 40000 Shah Alam, Selangor Darul Ehsan, Malaysia

Marshall Cavendish is a trademark of Times Publishing Limited

ISBN 10: 0-7614-5407-1
ISBN 13: 978-0-7614-5407-6

Please contact the publisher for the Library of Congress catalogue number

Printed in China by Everbest Printing Co Ltd

Photo Credits:
All photos by Derek Bacon except pages x, 20–21, 30–31, 95, 197, 212,
220–221, 232–233 and 246–247 (Photolibrary) and page 127 (Ian Viney)
▪ Cover photo: HBL Photo Network

All illustrations by TRIGG except pages 137, 151 and 213 (Derek Bacon)

# ABOUT THE SERIES

Culture shock is a state of disorientation that can come over anyone who has been thrust into unknown surroundings, away from one's comfort zone. *CultureShock!* is a series of trusted and reputed guides which has, for decades, been helping expatriates and long-term visitors to cushion the impact of culture shock whenever they move to a new country.

Written by people who have lived in the country and experienced culture shock themselves, the authors share all the information necessary for anyone to cope with these feelings of disorientation more effectively. The guides are written in a style that is easy to read and covers a range of topics that will arm readers with enough advice, hints and tips to make their lives as normal as possible again.

Each book is structured in the same manner. It begins with the first impressions that visitors will have of that city or country. To understand a culture, one must first understand the people—where they came from, who they are, the values and traditions they live by, as well as their customs and etiquette. This is covered in the first half of the book.

Then on with the practical aspects—how to settle in with the greatest of ease. Authors walk readers through topics such as how to find accommodation, get the utilities and telecommunications up and running, enrol the children in school and keep in the pink of health. But that's not all. Once the essentials are out of the way, venture out and try the food, enjoy more of the culture and travel to other areas. Then be immersed in the language of the country before discovering more about the business side of things.

To round off, snippets of basic information are offered before readers are 'tested' on customs and etiquette of the country. Useful words and phrases, a comprehensive resource guide and list of books for further research are also included for easy reference.

# CONTENTS

# INTRODUCTION

Viewed from a safe distance, it's easy to assume that these days it's just one bad thing after another in Indonesia. How terrible must this place be to actually live in? How on earth do people manage to live there? It's easy for the outside world to get a distorted view of life somewhere, when all that seems to come from there is bad news. But these are just events, little blips that get reported along the way. It's in the moments between these events where the real picture lies, where day-to-day life goes on, apparently as normal. If you want to stand any chance of knowing Indonesia at all, you'll need to be there at ground level, with it whizzing all around you.

Towering well over 1.83 m (6 ft) tall, my co-authoring friend Terry Collins is definitely at ground level. In this reworked version of *CultureShock! Jakarta*, Terry brings our picture of Jakarta bang up to date. With 20 years of Jakarta living under his belt, he is well qualified in shifting the story forward. And, crucially, he still has enthusiaism for the Jakarta life. He may of course completely deny this, but it's this very enthusiasm that has helped paint this much fuller picture of the city, and one too that helps guide us through the often confusing decade of change (or non-change) since President Suharto made his dramatic exit in 1998.

So here then is Jakarta today. It's big. It's frustrating. It really is a monster. Don't say we didn't warn you.

# ACKNOWLEDGEMENTS

The thousand thank-yous I gave the first time around are still valid. So, Eric Birn, Francis Windsor, Ian Betts, Bapak and Ibu Made Suandhe, Mary Cooksey, Ratna Astuti and Sarah Holland—here's another big wet one from me. I'd also like to firmly shake the hands of Gayatri, Ian, Jez, Justin, John, Michelle and Ron just for being my mates. Lastly though, the loudest slap on the back goes this time to Terry Collins for his work on this mighty rewrite. Cheers moosh.

Derek Bacon

# ACKNOWLEDGEMENTS

It is often the way of things in Jakarta to beg, steal and borrow ideas and information, so much of what you read here is available under the Creative Commons licence or is otherwise in the public domain.

That said, an enormous acknowledgement must be made to the *Living in Indonesia* website (http://www.expat.or.id). Much of the information we offer may appear to be the same as theirs, and it is—but the opinions are ours. For example, you may find the Indonesian Highway Code elsewhere. I wrote the version you read here in Chapter Five, circulated it to magazines but as it remained unpublished, in March 2004, I resorted to putting it online on my blog *Jakartass*. It has since been plagiarised but, hey, I don't mind if it makes the living easier.

For adding to my knowledge about the labyrinthe complexities of the visa regulations and the section on doing business in Chapter Nine, I owe lots of Bintang beers to Gary Dean of Okusi Associates (http://www.okusi.net). I'm happy that he's teetotal.

Simon Grigg in Bali (http://opdiner.blogspot.com/) and Leonardo Pavlovic in New York (http://www.moonjune.com/) added depth to Chapter Seven with their analyses of Indonesia's music scene.

Although the Internet is still in its infancy here, I have made a number of online friends; we share opinions on events and comment on each other's writings. Without their contributions, this volume would have been longer in the writing and shorter in the reading.

- Oigal—http://greenstump.blogspot.com/
- Patung—http://www.indonesiamatters.com/
- Indcoup—http://indcoup.blogspot.com/
- Java Jive—http://www.thejavajive.com/blog/
- Hera Diani—http://hdiani.blogspot.com/
- Treespotter—http://treespotter.blogspot.com/
- The Reveller—http://www.jakartablokm.com/
- Antony Casual—http://jakartaniteout.blogspot.com/
- Simon Pitchforth—http://metromad.blogspot.com/
- Ong Hock Chuan—http://theunspunblog.com/
- Dominic in Surabaya—http://aussieindonesia.blogspot.com/

For a jolly good read, check out *Jakarta Kid* (http://jakarta-kid.blogspot.com/) which may or may not be a fictionalised account of an expat's stay in Jakarta back in the early 1990s.

Miko and Mr Snag have enlivened the comments in *Jakartass* and are therefore to be thanked, even though at times I've wished they used their own blogs rather than mine.

And a big 'hi' to Jenny Q. (http://jenjenqld.blogspot.com/) who was experiencing culture shock in Jakarta throughout the rewrite of this book.

There are innumerable others who have made my twenty odd, very odd, years in Jakarta most interesting. Many thanks to you all, especially to DJ, and very especially to Derek and my family, Lily, Jesse and Sam.

Derek and I would like some royalties for our efforts, so please don't beg, steal or borrow this book.

Happy Travels.

Terry Collins
http://jakartass.blogspot.com/

Jakarta, a place of conflicting images where wooden shacks are seen right next to modern offices.

# MAP OF INDONESIA

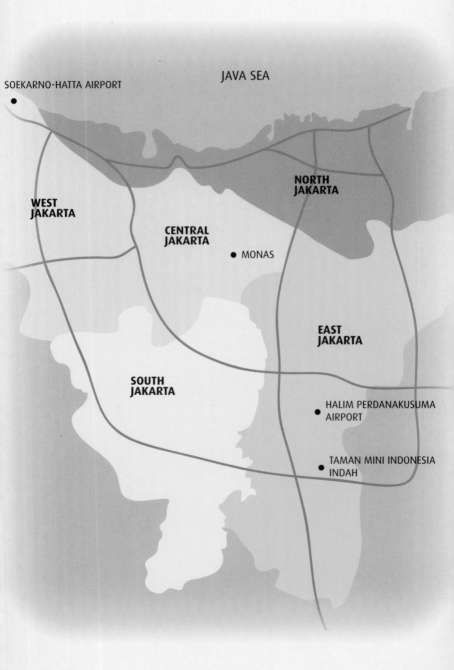

# MAP OF JAKARTA

JAVA SEA

SOEKARNO-HATTA AIRPORT

NORTH JAKARTA

WEST JAKARTA

CENTRAL JAKARTA

MONAS

EAST JAKARTA

SOUTH JAKARTA

HALIM PERDANAKUSUMA AIRPORT

TAMAN MINI INDONESIA INDAH

# FIRST IMPRESSIONS

'Journalists like to show my glamorous Indonesia
Hotel and behind it pictures of slums.'
—President Sukarno, *Sukarno: An Autobiography*
as told to Cindy Adams.

## TERRY

As a newly qualified Teacher of English as a Foreign Language (TEFLer), I was keen to get back into traveller mode. Because I'd heard horrific travellers' tales about Indonesia, I actually wanted to go back to Thailand but the offer of a return air ticket and an 18-month contract in Jakarta was too good to refuse.

I read up as much as I could in my local library. It wasn't that much. I bought a copy of Bill Dalton's *Indonesia Handbook* which seemed to be the best, but it had only eight pages about Jakarta, out of nearly 500 pages. I wrote to a few people and they told me that Jakarta was very green and that it was quite cheap to go sailing and play golf, neither of which particularly interested me.

I said my goodbyes the day after Boxing Day in 1987 and arrived in Singapore the next day to find that there was no pilot for my connecting flight to Jakarta. This being Singapore's Changi Airport, I soon found a seat on a later flight and was able to ring my sponsor to say I'd be arriving two or three hours later than anticipated.

It was dark in Jakarta's Soekarno-Hatta Airport, hot (what no air-conditioning?) and I couldn't find the driver who'd been sent for me. So I had to hunt for a money changer and make sure I had the correct coins for the phones. I was able to read the pictograms and the connection was made. The driver, I was told, had returned to the office. I was advised to come by taxi, BlueBird preferably. Ok, no problem: after all I'd not too long ago backpacked my way around the world—all by myself.

"So, what's Jakarta like?" I asked the Australian behind me. "Well, mate," he said, breathing in sharply, "it's no oil painting—I'll tell you that for nothing."
—Derek Bacon

"Taxi, mister?"

"Yeah, ok" (Thinks: I understand the language.) "Erm, where is it?"

"Parkir."

There in the car park was a beat-up first edition Kijang van and the driver was a woman. "Whoops!" I thought, as she paid the 'taxi' tout whatever and asked me for more rupiah (Rp) than, I found out later, it would have cost me in an air-conditioned BlueBird to get to my destination, Kebayoran Baru. But, hey, Endah spoke a little English and she was a single mother earning what she could to feed her five-year-old daughter and could she be my driver and where did mister live? And where are you from, mister?

We talked a lot so I remember little of what was dimly visible outside, even though we drove with the windows down to let in the breeze.

So we arrived at around 9:00 pm, I said goodbye to Endah, mentally wishing her well, and was greeted by my new boss, Phil. "What do you want to do, Terry?" "I'd love a beer, a shower and a beer," I replied.

I didn't get a shower that night but I've had a few in the 19 years I've been here since.

And a lot of beers.

### Beer and Ladies

One bar we went in that night was incredibly seedy. Alan, an Australian, young and handsome—pretty even, new colleague, sat with his beer in one hand and a girl on each knee with another around his neck.

"But, I'm gay", he cried.

"I'm not," I thought, "I'm not."

—Terry Collins

## PLANET JAKARTA

It is the worst place in Indonesia—and Indonesia is an amazing place. It is the biggest, most expensive, most

Jakarta's synopsis is a fragmented one; its map is vast. It doesn't have a centre as such. With nothing to grab hold of, everything hurtles past in a random rush of snapshots. First-time visitors will feel perpetually lost in a maze of never-ending back-streets, broken only by the occasional scrawny patch of grassland, bubbling river, festering rubbish pile and a sudden, surprising area of high-walled real-estate. It seems at times to be deliberately hiding itself. And people are absolutely everywhere.

polluted, most corrupt, most Westernised, most crowded, most lurid, most worldly city in Indonesia. It is the worst you will see of Indonesia. Oh dear.

It's so big, it's in danger of imploding. It can't quite seem to cope, but somehow, despite all overwhelming odds, it always seems to manage. It looks like it ought to work—on the surface that is. It's all there: gloss, fashion, technology, machinery, attitude, but...something's not quite right.

Look closely and see that everything is slightly broken, slightly chipped and cracked, slightly skew-whiff. On paper, it shouldn't really work at all. City planners would have given up at the drawing board had someone given them the plans for the city that exists today. It's wonky, lopsided. It's a mutant. It's the wrong shape. There's no apparent logic behind its design—it seems to have just happened this way.

It's a city under constant revision. The signs are everywhere: hopelessly struggling transport systems with endless traffic jams, the super-rich living opposite the very poor, a suffocating confusion of red tape and an increasingly restless yet apathetic young generation.

It has been said before, and it's true: Jakarta is all of Indonesia concentrated into a single fat Mother City—*Ibu kota kita*. Some 10–13 million people call it home, although nearly every one of them originates from somewhere else.

Construction work goes on day and night. The scaffolding and cranes, hills of red earth and continuous migration of cheap labourers, all confirm that Jakarta is by no means finished. From the air, it is still surprisingly green. This is the tropics and it doesn't take long for plant life to claim squatters' rights on land unclaimed or awaiting the developers. Apart from a tight area of skyscraping office towers and blocks of apartments in the centre and along a few major roads, the city is still a dishevelled mass of red residential *kampung* roofs.

The worst, most poverty-stricken slums are now fewer and further between, but the struggle to make basic ends meet goes on. The railway lines and river banks are still home to some of the worst indications of poverty, but in today's city, much of the urban poor live in brick or part-brick houses with running water and electricity. And every home has a television. The city has come a moderate way from the 'Jakarta' depicted in *The Year Of Living Dangerously*, but it is still mostly *kampung*.

There's always something going on—always a *warung* open. It may be incredibly frustrating, it may seem like The Last Place On Earth or The End Of The World or The Town Where No-one Got Off or The Land That The West Forgot or .... It's an entire planet of its own. It isn't boring but it does depend on what you find interesting. People seem to sit about, hang around, play cards, strum guitars and watch the world at every hour of the day. You see, in this city, there's always something going on—always something slightly shocking to see. It never sleeps. Every day brings a 'what-the-expletive?' moment.

When you consider Jakarta, you consider the 'problem' of Jakarta. The 'problem' of the overcrowded city, the 'problem' of what is an impossible city and the 'problem' of trying to live here. It's certainly not an easy place. Indonesians themselves go into culture shock when they come here. On the face of it, it doesn't appear to make any concession to being sympathetic to anyone. But given time and patience, and a certain understanding, Jakarta will lodge itself in the heart of anyone who has lived there. Part of you will hate it, part of you will love it. And part of you will hate yourself for loving it. Ultimately, however, you shouldn't have to gripe about Jakarta—it can't help it after all. It didn't mean to be like this.

For some, those coming from the West, where clean streets, freedom of speech and equal opportunity are taken for granted, it may seem nothing less than the end of the world. For rural Indonesians, it is only the start—the land of apparent plenty. People flood Jakarta all the year round in search of work. They bring with them a little piece of their

home, a little something from the 17,000 or so islands of the world's largest archipelago. This city's personnel is a constantly changing one.

For an Indonesian, Jakarta is the surest place to find work. It's obvious: with so many people concentrated in one place, there's always going to be something to sell; always some kind of service to provide. Unemployment is not necessarily the problem; it's more like underemployment for the most part. But still, there's always the chance of making that extra rupiah in Jakarta.

They might open a food stall. They might spend the day giving people lifts on their *ojek*, or cleaning people's houses or driving a taxi or *bajaj*. They might find work in a massage parlour or hawking the streets selling something: food, *jamu*, individual cigarettes, kitchen utensils, furniture, paintings or a particular regional variation of a drink. They might offer a service of some sort: sharpening knives, cutting hair, refilling disposable lighters, repairing broken things, unjamming stuck things, weighing and measuring things and re-soling shoes. They might get work operating a photocopier all day, or paying other people's bribes, or polishing shoes, or working the night market, or running errands in an office, or carrying bags of shopping for people, or digging holes for a construction company, or lending out umbrellas when it rains. They might end up begging for a living.

A great many, however, find the returns much less lucrative than they might have anticipated. And when they do eventually leave the teeming, steaming metropolis that is Jakarta, and '*pulang kampung*' (go home), most find they are no richer than when they had started—though not necessarily dejected by the experience.

The main benefit for those who stick it out is the prospect of being able to send regular money to their families back home. The returns may be small in comparison to some of the Big Money being made in Jakarta, but *uang* (money) goes further in the villages—everyone agrees on that. This system of sharing-alike is a widespread and unspoken obligation throughout Indonesia. For a country with very little in the way of an effective welfare system, it must be taken for granted that parents will provide for their children, no matter what difficulties arise. And the children, usually the eldest but not always, will be responsible for bearing the burden of the parents in old age. This unwritten agreement extends far beyond the nuclear family. An example of this would be if a particular member of the extended family had attained a certain degree of prosperity. It's quite possible that a distant (and poorer) relative would send one of their children to live with the well-off family, to run errands and generally be an unpaid servant on condition that the family provide an education for the child.

The person coming from the 'developed' world will find a world where a contradiction occurs with every other step. A world of improbable extremes. A world where any notion of apparent 'logic' is out the window; where saving face outweighs any other obvious course of thought. A world where individual opinions are blurred into a single collective mentality. Where people will actually 'lie' rather than risk offending you with what might be the truth. A world where, for the most part, people are forced to accept all manner of conditions, without even a murmur of protest. Where glaringly corrupt policies are implemented and labour forces exploited. Where imported technology is, apart from the latest handphones, three years behind everywhere else. Where human error runs high.

Where breakfasts are spicy. Where cats have no tails. Where brothels operate opposite mosques. Where every 'respectable' home has a servant. Where pineapples are salted. Where men hold hands. Where courting couples shouldn't. Where cough sweets are small change. Where mosquitoes are hungry. Where endangered species are on sale. Where a glass of beer is expensive. Where hormone-loaded snake blood is drunk. Where the police are bribable. Where the women outnumber the men. Where the days and nights are equal length. It's a place where the people are always smiling.

It's no oil painting, but as the people who live there will usually tell you; "*tidak apa-apa*"—it doesn't matter.

## DEREK

SLAM! It's the last time I make this journey; last time I take a taxi across this hot mad city—tomorrow I'm gone. Well-rehearsed, I'm saying hello and winding up the window as the driver turns the air-conditioning on. His name is Budi. He's Javanese, brown, glowing and married with six children. We talk. Well, I'm from England actually. No, I'm not married. Yes, I quite like rice. This is what it's been like: Jakarta. Home. Hmm. We stop at our first traffic lights. Three cars ahead, I spot a man in lipstick shaking a tambourine. To avoid fatal eye contact, I sink down, but it's too late—he (or she) has made a beeline for us. I'm almost invisible but the stares from the other vehicles and Budi's laughter soon blows my cover and I end up pushing a thousand-rupiah note through the window. And so, we are mobbed by a hundred other people performing impossible human tasks: children selling cakes, boys selling themselves and lepers begging for release. A man with a gaping hole for a nose slides past on a trolley. I wish the lights would change. The lights change.

I suppose I might come to miss all this.

By the time I get home, I will have grimaced through 26 sets of traffic lights and acquired the following: a hefty woodcarving of a horse; a censored girlie calendar; an inflatable Power Ranger; a chess set; nine boiled sweets; two slices of salted pineapple; a fake Rolex; three *kretek* cigarettes and a blowpipe.

> Keep your eyes glued to the road at all times and never assume you are going the right way. This road changed overnight recently from a two- to a one-way street and, a week later a bus lane appeared, running in the opposite direction.

It's nearly 6:00 pm and the sun is about to go down. It's prayer time: I'm journeying across this great wobbling thug of a city in a Koperasi taxi; my driver is Budi and I'm not invisible. We pick up speed on a stretch of dual carriageway still whitewashed from some VIP's visit. An orange bus, tilting dangerously to one side, tries to overtake us from the inside. For a while, we are neck and neck: old folks, pregnant women and knee-high schoolchildren elbowing around with the same blank abandon. Sometimes repairs are made with the bus still in motion. Sometimes the passengers have to get out and push. You see that too.

I ask Budi to be *hati-hati* (careful) on this road. But then again, not too careful—we wouldn't want to get pulled over.

Past air-brushed promises of malls-to-be, we zoom into the home straight; aiming for the middle of the road and swerving only when necessary. Random oil drums and funeral processions are two such necessities.

We arrive. He overcharges me; I overpay him. Thanks. See you again, maybe.

SLAM.

## AIRPORT

An uncertain time is had by most first-time visitors to Jakarta, but this need not be the case. One of the major characteristics of Jakarta's Bandara (airport) Soekarno-Hatta International is the incorporation of the local vernacular architecture into the design, and the presence of tropical gardens in between the waiting lounges. Soekarno-Hatta is a modern, spacious, air-conditioned airport, tastefully built in red brick. It was designed by a French architect Paul Andreu, who also designed the collapsed Terminal 2E at Charles de Gaulle airport in Paris. It has sufficient amenities, adequate information services, money changing facilities (in the baggage hall) and clean-ish toilets.

Terminal 1 is for domestic passengers and Terminal 2 for international arrivals and departures. By the time you read this, there may well be a Terminal 3 for passengers on low-cost no frills airlines, unless efforts to save the planet's climate have drastically reduced these people carriers.

Still, in 2006, over 30 million passengers used the facilities at an average of about 100 per plane. There were 49 airlines, but we aren't going to list them as they come and go. We assume that the near bankrupt national airline Garuda Indonesia will continue to be bailed out. Other international airlines are busy forming alliances to stave off bankruptcy, as are domestic low-price airlines. It's up to you to contact your travel agent or use the Internet to plan your route here. You may well find that a stopover and transfer in Singapore or Kuala Lumpur is your best option.

The madness starts when you leave customs. If you are being met, here is where your driver will be, hopefully holding up a card sign with your name on. Porters are available to help you, but you will have to pay them. Expect repeated offers of transport to Jakarta centre ("taxi, mister?"), which might well be genuine, but no guarantees can be made. Post-flight, you are probably in no mood for much debate should the deal turn out to be less than fair, and you are much better off taking a taxi from the taxi queue. If possible, wait to catch one of the more reputable firms, like BlueBird or Kosti Jaya. In theory, you are safe from rip-off drivers at the airport, as all taxi passengers are given a card detailing the taxi's make and number, as well as toll-road charges the passenger must pay.

The airport is 25 km (15.5 miles) to the north-west of the city centre along the coast linked by fast toll roads. In the rainy season (November to April), the access toll road can be flooded. From the airport to Blok M, for example, including the airport surcharge and a couple of toll-road fees, you are looking at paying around Rp 90,000. A far more cost-effective way to the city centre is the Damri bus service which leaves every half an hour for Blok M, Kemayoran, Gambir, Pasar

Minggu, Rawamangun and, less frequently, to the city of Bogor, some 65 km (40.4 miles) to the south. The fare is around Rp 15,000 per person.

Jakarta's Soekarno-Hatta Airport is significant because soon after leaving it, you lose any illusion that you are in the 'mystical east'. Once past the two immense red Balinese Hindu-style gates, you see your toll road circles above the sprawl of low rise dwellings, boring concrete shop-houses and mushrooming high-rises, all which seems to go on forever without any rhyme or reason.

In the next few chapters, we offer you some rhymes. We can't always find the reasons, but then that's because hardly a day goes by without something else making us blink and ask the question, "What the ...?"

# HISTORY, GEOGRAPHY AND POLITICS

**CHAPTER 2**

'I've just got back from Mumbai (Bombay);
it makes Jakarta look like Palm Beach!'
—Scott Buckman

## WEATHER

Jakarta is situated on an alluvial plain on the north coast of the island of Java. It lies just south of the equator, so it is generally hot. There are two hot seasons, one of which is wetter than the other. In the *musim hujan* (wet season), it's actually a bit cooler, but Jakarta is nothing less than hot and tropical all the time.

From time to time, however, strange weather does occur. Brief but intense falls of hailstones have been recorded several times in Jakarta, while at the other extreme, the notorious El Niño weather phenomenon forced the season's rains to move in the opposite direction in 1997, plunging the region into its worst drought for 50 years and leaving forest fires burning uncontrollably for months on end. These are exceptional weather conditions, however, and although it's true that long-term inmates do become sensitive to subtle variations in the weather, no one need go to Jakarta expecting a variable barometer.

The *musim kering* (dry season) is not without its drawbacks. When rain hasn't fallen for months on end, water supplies get scarce as wells begin drying up. If you don't have air conditioning, the nights are hot and sticky, although you are welcome to try your best with a carefully-angled fan. *Nyamuk* (mosquitoes) are never much fun at the best of times, not least than in the dry season when their quantity and ferocity is at a peak.

The dry season runs from about May to September and is influenced mainly by the Australian continental air masses. The wet season's tendencies are attributed to Pacific Ocean air masses and the Asian continent. But let's not pull any punches: Jakarta is HOT and that's that. Yet it would be hotter if Java wasn't an island or was bigger. The warm seas surrounding Java keep temperatures a touch less extreme than they could be. Something to be almost thankful for perhaps.

The surrounding hills, mostly to the south and east of the city, are the main water catchment areas, but rain can be quite phenomenal in the city—a monsoon no less. On an average day in the middle of the wet season, the sky is heavy with great swollen cumulonimbus clouds. By early afternoon, many of them have already greyed and things start to look ominous. An early indication of impending doom is a vibrating ripple in the water-dispenser, accompanied soon after by the far-off rumble of *guntur* (thunder). You know there's a monster coming and there's nothing you can do about it. Then the *halilintar* (lightning) starts: the

sky flashing in one giant Polaroid photo. Several flashes occur on top of one another and the sky goes bright white for a few long seconds. Everyone holds their breath and then says "*aduh*"

Try watching a storm from the highest storey of a Jakarta skyscraper. While you enjoy the fireworks display, you can play spot-the-biggest-lightning-rod and place bets on which area will blackout next.

(blimey). It's cartoon weather, with everything turning to X-ray. Bolts leap from cloud to cloud, before forking violently groundwards. Every building that values its future, not to mention the occupants within, needs to be grounded against lightning.

By now it's dark and the rain is all around you. What sounds like a bomb goes off above your head as a bolt hits home. You know the time has come. The rain is heavy and the noise tremendous. Conversation, phone calls and TV are put on hold, all other sounds obliterated by the roar. Then leaks start appearing. All round the building, the ceiling starts to weep—little drips, dribbles and drops appearing from nowhere. The rain finds its way through ceilings on every floor of a high-rise building. After cooking in the daytime heat, Jakarta's slap-quick skyscrapers are nothing but gap-toothed cavities waiting to be filled when the afternoon rain finally comes. The walls start trickling while inexplicably, a light bulb starts filling with water. A mass exodus of evacuating ants begins to chug its way down one side of one wall, re-enacting a scene from the Old Testament. The floor is cluttered with pots, pans and *ember* (buckets). The toilet belches before the electricity finally gives out.

Outside, the street has become a river. Sewers overflow and street-children start swimming. As any normal concept of 'traffic' is out of the question, the street becomes an open-market war. Taxi drivers wholeheartedly refuse to go anywhere near the *banjir* (flood) without hefty payment. Public transport is a free-for-all. People are left to wade single-file through the knee-high slush with everything balanced on their heads, hoping not to fall down a pot hole. Whole areas of *kampung* disappear, submerged by the sudden gush of water, much of it rushed downhill from nearby Bogor which is one of the wettest places in the world. Household guttering struggles to cope with the deluge, great fountains arching upwards from downpipes, evacuation pipes spouting like geysers on an oil field.

And every five years, boats are seen in Jakarta's streets as clogged drainage canals and rivers spill over. Refugee camps are set up in school playgrounds, the few stadiums, mosques and otherwise empty houses. The media focuses its lenses, politicians criticise bureaucrats and other politicians, celebrities are photographed handing out boxes of instant noodles, and then the rain clouds pass, the sun comes out and everything quickly dries out.

But sometimes the rain is a relief. When it hasn't rained for months on end, when it seems all the air has run out, everyone breathes a sigh when the skies finally let rip. And as the season draws to an end, the rain bursts get less irate. By the beginning of the dry season, the rain is infrequent; isolated cloud bursts appear, sometimes so small only a couple of houses are hit. Getting drenched in Jakarta then becomes as simple as turning the wrong corner.

## HEAT

The heat is ever present all-year round and rarely lets up. It hits you the instant you leave the airport and stays with you. With an average day and night temperature of around 30°C (86°F), you need to learn either to get used to it, or find your own way of keeping cool. If you can't find a parasol big enough, don't be *malu* (shy) about investing in a large umbrella for your outdoor activities. Often the hottest days in Jakarta are the ones with the most umbrellas.

The daytime heat in Jakarta is probably no hotter than other cities in Indonesia; it's the combination of pollution, population and frustration which makes it seem that much hotter. You become particularly aware of Jakarta's heat if you leave and return to the city. With every passing kilometre, there comes the realisation that you are approaching a cauldron.

The coolest time of the day is between 4:00–6:00 am when an awful lot of people are already up and about, doing exercises or hanging about. Since the sun hasn't fully risen, it's a relatively pollution-free, quiet, dusky time of the day, not unlike an English summer evening. And then the sun comes up.

It shoots up directly to the centre of the sky and sits there for 12 hours, bleaching out all colours, stripping shadows to the bare minimum and being nothing but HOT. By 9:00 am, everything is as hot as the sun. Then later at 6:00 pm, the sun, as if under government instruction, suddenly drops from the sky. Yet the heat remains. Big cities like Jakarta are good at trapping heat, so it may feel even hotter after dark.

In Jakarta, you definitely sweat. While air conditioning (AC) is present in most modern buildings, even this is not without disadvantages. AC is something you may come to rely on, especially if it's installed in your home and most definitely if you sleep with it. And when your AC breaks down, you can only accept the fact that you have become dependent on it as you despair. You have developed a disorientated concept of the climate, fighting a losing battle against the heat, much of which is, of course, caused by the millions of air conditioners working as heat exchangers.

At the height of the dry season, the air is still—there's no wind. Sometimes, the heat is so intense you cannot stand up. All you can do is lie down and try not to move. The heat holds you in its grip. This is called flat-out heat, and unless you stay inside with AC on all day and all your windows closed, sooner or later you are going to experience it. For everyone, things become '*besok aja*' (do it tomorrow). There is no hurry for Indonesian's construction workers—many of whom sleep on site—to finish a building before the season changes. For people from colder climes, it can be hard.

### Driven to Extremes

One man working in Jakarta found himself cracking up after six months of the heat and had to spend an evening standing in cold water with blocks of ice pressed all over him.

This is rather extreme; he could, after all, have just climbed into the *bak mandi* (water tank) for an hour or so. Yet it is indicative of the discomfort Caucasians may experience in the Jakarta heat.

On a more serious level, there are a number of heat-related illnesses: heat-cramps, heatstroke, exhaustion and sunburn.

Of these, the most serious is heatstroke, for which immediate medical help must be found. Victims of this horrible condition are unable to sweat, and thus the body temperature is allowed to rise unhindered. Convulsions, coma, permanent brain damage and even death can follow. A less serious form of heatstroke is heat-exhaustion caused through dehydration and salt depletion, coupled with strenuous activity.

With an average humidity of around 90 per cent, you feel continually sticky and damp. You may like to follow the Indonesian example of bathing twice or more a day. Bathing cools you down, cleans off the salt deposits left by your sweat and generally maintains healthier skin. Use a high-factor sunblock; your skin can start to burn in only 15 minutes in Indonesia. Above all, drink a lot of water and don't overeat.

Tempers are tested to the limit in this heat. When things are not working and you can't seem to get anything done and all the time the heat is screaming down on you, it's all too easy to lose your composure and 'flip out'. Other than drawing attention to yourself, this will get you nowhere. Indonesians do not readily relate to open displays of frustration. And it's not that they feel any cooler either—they simply have more self-control than you.

## NATURAL DISASTERS

Perhaps because it is spared many of the disasters possible elsewhere in Indonesia, Jakarta is a relatively safe place to be. Earthquakes and typhoons are common to South-east Asia but rarely afflict regions as far south as Jakarta. The rest of Indonesia gets its fair share of disasters; after all, it is situated within the 'Ring of Fire' so volcanic eruptions and earthquakes are frequent. Tremors are occasionally felt in Jakarta, particularly on upper floors of high-rises, but you don't need to keep tabs on the latest seismographic readings before going out. For the most part, you need worry more about things like leaking roofs, flooding floors and never-ending traffic jams than being sucked up into a tornado.

The waters around Jakarta Bay are slow and sluggish and, the risk of poisoning aside, nothing to fear. On the south coast of the island upon which Jakarta sits, the story is markedly different. A dynamic undertow and shores that drop like cliffs a few feet into the water make for impressive waves but genuinely dangerous swimming. The waters around Pelabuhan Ratu and Parangtritis are infamously perilous and held in great suspicion by locals. Dozens of stories exist of people disappearing into the water because they are wearing something green or have heard the siren's call of the Queen of the South Seas.

> Being something of a concrete jungle, the risk of death by a falling coconut or the spiky monster-fruit, durian, is considerably lower in Jakarta than elsewhere in the country.

### Volcanoes

If you live in Indonesia, you live near a volcano. The country sits on one gigantic chain of volcanoes, their very presence a welding point for two continental plates. Indonesia has approaching 200 active ones. In Java alone are about 30 volcanoes, of which most are quietly active. As a result, the soil in Java is among the world's most fertile, happily

Anak Krakatau Island, Indonesia.

supporting some 40,000 species of plants. The tremendously high iron content means it's a deep red colour, and continuous volcanic activity means the land is regularly replenished with a fresh layer of nutrient-rich volcano innards. True, the soil isn't evenly fertile throughout Indonesia, but when it is fertile, it's really fertile. Next time you pass some Jakarta road works, marvel at the rich, red colour.

Although Jakarta is an area unaffected by volcanoes, there are three nearby: Pangrango, Halimun and Gede. They are situated in a national park and you can get permission to climb them from the park's office. Start very early in the morning and take plenty of water; these require strenuous efforts but the view of the sun rising is truly stupendous. Then there's the most famous of them all, Krakatau. Officially, the casual visitor is not allowed to land on Krakatau—or rather 'Anak' Krakatau ('child' of Krakatau) as it's more accurately known—since the original blew itself up in 1883, and some 44 years later, a new one began to emerge. This is excellent advice. On the morning of 13 June 1993, an American woman was killed when the volcano erupted shortly after her group had climbed the crater.

It can be admired from the Carita Beach Resort, a four-hour drive from Jakarta, particularly at night when it looks like someone smoking a cigarette in the dark. More adventurous folk can journey over to the other side of the Sunda Strait to South Sumatra for an alternative view.

## HISTORY

In the beginning, Jakarta's plot would have been primeval rainforest and swampland—today it's more like Pizzaland. Earlier still, some 140 million years ago, Borneo, Sumatra and Java were still part of mainland Asia—itself the result of volcanic eruptions when the world began. (Incidentally, there are marsupials on the eastern half of Sulawesi because it drifted apart from what is now Australia).

Evidence of primitive human life in what is now Indonesia exists in the shape of the much-hyped discovery of one very old skull—the so-called missing-link that is Java Man. The skull is reputed to be that of *homo erectus*, a primitive version of the now-standard *homo sapiens*. But nothing is ever certain; the skull itself having undergone much speculation of late. Using more advanced dating methods than before, it is now accepted that the skull is probably several thousand years younger than originally thought. The implication of this is enormous: that in far-off places like Java, the outmoded *homo erectus* and the superior *homo sapiens* lived side-by-side for a few thousand years.

### Strange Beginnings

A few years before the publication of this book, anthropologists and archaeologists discovered the skeleton of a very short woman in a cave on the island of Flores. Debate has ensued about whether she belonged to a pygmy race which co-existed with homo sapiens or was a victim of dwarfism. Some people say that if isolated pockets of homo erectus and pigmy people managed to resist evolutional substitution in what is now Indonesia, this explains an awful lot.

Once boats and navigation became possible, after landmasses had roughly reached their present locations, Indonesia became a strategic place to settle. It was between India and China, on a major shipping thoroughfare and the fertile soil of the Spice Islands way off to the east had loads of valuable crops. This would have been an intriguing time to be in Indonesia: no colonial rule and no Jakarta either. What is now one very large republic was a disparate collection of mini-kingdoms. Some say it still is.

By the 12th century, Sunda Kelapa, just one of many shelters, was a reasonably-sized, functioning port governed from the relatively distant of the then more important Bogor. Traders who came to the area at the time included Indians, Arabs, Chinese and Portuguese. The last of these were befriended by the Hindus of Java and persuaded to join forces against the rising number of Muslim states gaining ground in Java. The Muslims, however, were the winners, first taking Banten and then Sunda Kelapa in 1527. They renamed the area Jayakarta. The history books give the exact date of this 'Great Victory', which is what Jayakarta means, as 22 June 1527—Jakarta's birthday.

But Sunda Kelapa, or rather Jayakarta, was still nothing special. At best, it was a place for the ruler of Banten, one Prince Jayawikarta, to store his stock of pepper reserves. Newer customers for Indonesia's spice trade changed all this. The Dutch and the British were determined to be the sole European distributors of spices but neither quite managed to monopolise it. Each was, however, able to set up a trading company. These newcomers were noticeably more violent than previous customers to the area, and from the very start it was obvious they had their sights set on more than just a few cloves from here and there.

Everyone knows about the Dutch: they came and stayed for 300 years and then left for a bit, still calling it their own. When they came back, they found nobody wanted them back and trouble ensued. They took away the power of Jayakarta's sultanate. They razed the original *kraton* and mosque that had coexisted in old Batavia. They split the empire of Mataram in two. They wiped out almost the entire population of the Banda islands. And in old Batavia, as they renamed the city, they held almost everyone as slaves.

The Dutch made Indonesia famous to the rest of the world. For the Europeans, they popularised the myth of the 'mystical east' with their souvenirs: *gamelan* music, rubber, spices and feathers from exotic birds. When the trading company ran out of money in 1799, the project was bailed out by the Dutch government, and the real colonisation began. They built posh houses in the Menteng area of Jakarta. They made Merdeka Square, Lapangan Square, and, when the Suez Canal opened for business, they re-worked Tanjung Priok into the strapping great port it is today. Towards the end of their stay, they introduced a few schools, which taught the Dutch curriculum in Dutch and seemed to be halfway towards encouraging autonomy.

The start of the end came when France went to war with the rest of Europe. The Dutch government, forced to keep a low profile in London, had no one to keep an eye on things down under. Britain sent Stamford Raffles to run the place for five years, where, after a shaky start fighting the French who had set up premature shop in the country, he and his crew achieved some positive things for a change. Raffles was embarrassed by slavery and encouraged Indonesian 'independence'. Nothing much came of it, and even though he left a lot of ideas in the suggestion box and the smelliest plant in the world named after him before popping over to Singapore, the Dutch were to begin a period of evermore blatant exploitation upon their return.

Unsurprisingly, feelings of unrest grew and grew in the country, and just as things were about to boil over, the last ones (and widely considered the worst of all) arrived—the Japanese. It seems Japan had big ideas at the time about being the big fish in Asia, just as Hitler had wanted in Europe. They even scared the Dutch away and initially made themselves out to be a 'friend' of Indonesia. But as we know, it wasn't to last, and Japan was left to bow one final bow before going home.

When the Dutch came back, again, they found a place which was already calling itself 'independent'. They didn't like this and did the logical thing of putting provocateurs like Sukarno and Hatta in jail in remote places. The idea of an independent Indonesia, however, refused to go away, and by 1950, the Dutch had to call it a day.

Even under Dutch rule, total administrative control had never been attained. Now things were different. Indonesia was free at last to do what it wanted, something the country is still trying to decide.

## KAMPUNG

Take the time to wander beyond the confines of the skyscraper and you'll enter the world of the *kampung*. Village life in the middle of a capital city is a world away from the shiny office blocks that are meant to be the 'real' face of Jakarta. *Kampung* is what makes up most of Jakarta. A *kampung* is where most people live—small houses, low-rise, red roofs, thin walls, village dwellings, narrow alleys and ramshackle rundown shanty-land.

Jakarta's *kampungs* are not readily apparent. Hidden behind the bigger, newer buildings and big roads, they are tucked out of sight so they may be partially forgotten about. But if you stroll down almost any narrow *gang* (alley) off a main road, you will soon find yourself in a densely populated area; with your arms out-stretched, you can touch both facing houses.

You will know when you are in a *kampung*; it feels different—all secular and self-sufficient. Washing stretched between houses and children hurtling everywhere, chickens, *dangdut* music, men in skirts, undervests and black hats sitting on rattan-mats—these are the hallmarks of the *kampung*. Religion and unity are well rehearsed. And so they should be, for these are the defining areas of the city. Everyone comes from a *kampung* somewhere along the line, regardless of where in Indonesia they came from.

The origins of Jakarta's *kampungs* lie in migrations to the big city at different times from different regions. The first Ambonese immigrants, for example, once they had unpacked their bags and put their feet up with a cup of *teh manis* (sweet tea), would have invited their friends to join them in Jakarta. As would the first Batak settlers, the first Balinese settlers and so on. The evidence is found all over the city in areas with names like Kampung Melayu and Kampung Ambon. The Javanese and Sundanese, however, were not welcome to set up *kampungs* until fairly recently; the Dutch ban on them was not relaxed until the end of the 19th century. Any gaps in these original *kampungs* are rapidly plugged by the continuing flow of young hopefuls to the capital, not to mention the offspring of the original first-comers.

*Kampungs* come in degree—not all are Third World shock-horrors. At the worst extreme, it means a bamboo and cardboard city constructed over an open sewer. Over the years, however, many of the worst slums have mutated into semi-decent (albeit cramped) accommodations, with semi-decent amenities and a price-tag attached. But either way, *kampung* means a lot of people living together in a small area. In Jakarta, money usually only buys two-dimensional space; high-rise housing is still being looked into. The best investment in Jakarta is land. Many areas of *kampung* refuse to disappear simply because they are built on such prime real estate—paying them off would be too expensive.

A typical *kampung* where everyone knows everyone, and where a strong sense of community binds all together.

But the *kampung* of Jakarta continue to irritate the authorities. They think the *kampung* let the side down, rather, that they don't fit what they think the modern face of the city should be. They think that everywhere in the city should resemble modern real-estate areas like Bintaro Jaya and Bumi Serpong Damai. Rumours abound of fires being deliberately started in a bid to clear areas of particularly stubborn *kampung*, and thus hasten the transfer of the poorer citizens to the outskirts.

## ARCHITECTURE

Despite guidebook claims about old Batavia—the present day area of Kota—resembling a European city at the turn of the century, people rarely go to Jakarta to admire the architecture. True, the oldest and most historical buildings are found in the north of the city, and the area of Menteng is a partially-preserved Dutch suburb of bungalows, gardens and mansions. But there's little confusion whether or not this is Amsterdam when you see the *bajaj*, smell the sewers and get bitten by another mosquito. The tropical heat doesn't lend itself to the European illusion too well either. These days, the city is characterised by the kind of high-rise you find in

Singapore, but this is only a tiny part of the picture. From the air, the city is a mass of red roofs, proof that Jakarta is still mostly residential and low-rise. Even the glossy skyscrapers look odd in Jakarta—all plush, neat and mirrored but only as far as the plot of land stretches. Anything outside this area is characterised by the rubbish piles and general impression that it has yet to be finished.

Architecture is big business in Indonesia and major construction work goes on everywhere. Experts claim Jakarta will look very nice when it's finished. Buildings are knocked up almost overnight here—shopping plazas definitely being among the most common. Big name outlets and businesses are huge investors in the Indonesian economy, and although the slump of 1997/1998 saw things slow for a while, Jakarta's frantic construction work continues, even at the expense of safety regulations. Completion work on Blok M Plaza was prolonged when the developer suddenly demanded two extra floors of shop space to make room for a fast food outlet and a cinema, prompting several architects to wash their hands of the project.

For examples of modern architecture, see Plaza Indonesia, built in the early 1990s, and compare it with the flat, post-colonial building next door that is Hotel Indonesia—and at the time (mid-1960s) one of the grandest buildings in Jakarta. The first president, Sukarno, was an engineering student and keen to re-engineer Jakarta: witness the period-piece sports stadium Senayan, an intimidatingly large building reminiscent of the mother-ship at the end of *Close Encounters*, only with fewer light bulbs. Some of the embassies along Jl. (Jalan) Rasuna Said and the office blocks that stretch from Jl. Sudirman to Monas are quite impressive, although very 'Singapore' in their layout.

The illusion and similarity with Singapore is confined to these few square kilometres, however, for behind almost every mirrored skyscraper is the inevitable sprawling *kampung*. In fact, this glaring contrast between rich and poor is partly what gives

Jakarta has yet to suffer the disaster of collapsing buildings that Bangkok and Manila have suffered in recent years, but look closely and you will see large cracks running through a lot of the modern buildings.

Jakarta its lopsided charm. Witness the *warung* and *kampung* along the river that runs behind Plaza Indonesia. A city in search of an identity? Not necessarily, but perhaps Jakarta should build itself a very tall building like Kuala Lumpur did with its Petronas building.

## MONAS

In front of the Presidential Palace stands the Monumen Nasional, Monas. Visible all over Jakarta, Monas is a 137-metre high obelisk based (apparently) on those old Javanese-Hindu symbols of fertility, linnga and yoni, which has prompted some to cite Monas as Sukarno's last great erection. It was built to the proportions of 8, 17 and 45—the date when Sukarno proclaimed Indonesia's independence. He designed and initiated many of the architectural landmarks that define Jakarta, including Hotel Indonesia and the Sarinah Department store in Jalan Thamrin. However, although its construction begun in 1961, it wasn't until 1975 that it was finished and officially opened by the second president, Suharto.

Lampangan Merdeka (Freedom Park), later to be renamed Monas, used to be the focal point for some of the cheapest dates in Jakarta. *Pembantu* (servants), *sopir* (drivers) and *tukang* (sellers) made up the majority of cooing couples who sat there in the dark. Perhaps it was the overwhelming symbolism of unflagging potency that attracted them there, or merely the fact that it was one of the last, and largest, open spaces in Jakarta. And you didn't have to pay to be there.

Unfortunately, Governor Sutiyoso (1997–2007) decided to 'beautify' the area. Itinerants were cleared out and deer moved in. A fence was erected around the entire site to make access extremely difficult. 'Open daily from 08:00 to 17:00, the monument offers unparalleled views of Jakarta!' If you can find a gate for the public to use, please contact the authors.

Once in, there is more to Monas than meets the eye. If you go in the day time, then do make the effort to ride up to the top and gaze at the view. Choose a day without haze if you want to see the hills to the south and the sea to the north.

The Monas stands proud against Jakarta's skyline.

If you go at night, then you are invited to dance along with the fountains modelled on those found in Las Vegas. Critics describe them as another monument—to Sutiyoso's ego.

The basement is home to a museum offering a series of 48 slightly eerie 3D dioramas, which apart from the obvious Java Man to Modern Java Man story, includes a vivid example of historical whitewash. The story is told of Indonesia's long struggle for independence: the anti-Dutch uprisings are depicted in garish detail, yet scant attention is paid to the events that led to the attempted coup of 1965 and subsequent inauguration of President Suharto.

President Sukarno had always been something of an eyebrow-raiser, but when the flamboyant leader began flirting with Communist China, while making threats in the direction of Malaysia, many believed he had, politically, lost the plot. And when six of Indonesia's top generals were murdered in what has gone down in official history as an attempt by Communists to seize power, a young General Suharto took his cue to step in and take the reins. Calling his government the 'New Order', Suharto condemned Communism outright, sparking a wave of fear and hatred between 1965 and 1969 which left hundreds of thousands of known Communists, suspected Communists and anyone vaguely Chinese, dead. The spontaneous execution of some half a million people was a shocking chapter in the country's modern history—*Time* magazine reported rivers 'clogged with bodies'—and, for a new leader keen to make a good impression on foreign investors, best air-brushed from the history books.

In Indonesia, Communism became the Big Fear, i.e. to blame every time something untoward happens in the country. As recently as July 1996, some 30 years after Suharto's ascension to the presidential throne, high-profile rioting in Jakarta against his New Order government was blamed on that oldest of scapegoats, Communism. In this case, the violence was attributed to a new and particularly vicious strain which had arrived in the shape of the Partai Rakyat Demokrasi (PRD) (People's Democratic Party). Its members were immediately arrested and blamed for inciting the riots. That, said the papers, was the end of the matter.

And Jakarta's military chief at that time became Governor of the city one year later so he could fence off Monas...

Although the passing of time and blatant rewrites of history—like that witnessed in the basement of Monas—do much to blur the events of Suharto's initial presidency, there remained the lingering fear that at any moment, it could happen all over again. And it did. In 1998, that same sense of anger returned in an explosion of rioting, looting and mayhem. But for the generations which had been raised and educated under Suharto, the idea that Communism could again be blamed for the country's social and economic problems didn't work. Instead, it was Suharto himself who was held responsible.

## WESTERNISATION

Indonesia is a new country rich in natural resources, so it is natural that foreign exploiters of those resources leave their mark on the capital city, and Jakarta shows all the stress of a city trying its best to cope with an assault of Western ideals. Where America once reigned, its popularity and power to influence has diminished in the population due to its War on Terror and the perceived occupation of Iraq. American influences, therefore, predominate through the entertainment industry and consumerism. But then this is mirrored throughout Asia: Hollywood films, TV shows, fast food and consumerism have given the urbanised middle classes a lifestyle to emulate. Each country adapts its influences; one of the most popular TV shows is *Indonesian Idol*.

Driving through the so-called 'Golden Triangle' area comprising Jl. Thamrin, Jl. Gatot Subroto and Jl. Rasuna Said on, say, a Sunday afternoon when the offices are shut, you might be fooled into thinking you were in Singapore. For this is the modern face of Indonesia; the bit they want you to see and write home about. At first sight, you might well believe Jakarta is just another South-east Asian city 'made good' by foreign investment and the plundering of natural resources. This is as modern as it gets. Here, standing tall are mirrored skyscrapers, five-star international hotels and Singapore-style shopping centres.

But this is only a tiny part of the picture that Jakarta is in real life. When viewed in the entire context of Indonesia, the Golden Triangle and its 'important' people are practically invisible. Lying low behind each office block are the bits you are not supposed to notice: the sprawling *kampung* of Jakarta where basic Indonesian village life goes on unabashed and where, more than likely, most of the skyscraper's employees live.

### Ooo! I Found 'Dirt' Under the Carpet!

When President Bill Clinton came to Jakarta for the 1994 APEC conference, he was driven on a very specific route through the city. Many of the city's eyesores were strategically avoided. Prior to his arrival, *kampung* areas and the like had been boarded up and the major thoroughfares given a complete whitewash. What the organisers hadn't anticipated was Clinton's unscheduled stop-off at a south Jakarta *kampung* to fulfil his apparent desire to shake hands with the 'real' people of Jakarta. What were the organisers trying to hide from the visiting President? Poverty? Beggars? Massage signs? Open sewers? Piles of rubbish? Sweat shops? Rust buckets masquerading as public transport? Jakarta itself?

There has to be a high degree of conflict in the lives of Indonesians as their country, especially its capital, is flooded with Western influences and ideas. Many Indonesians today walk with one step in the past and the other in the future— one half turned on by the attraction of being up with the times, the other half desperate to stay loyal to the past.

Some of that conflict is expressed in the lyrics of Husein Bawafi who, singing in 1955, had this to say about the changing times in Indonesia:

*Funny Style*

*The world spins*
*The times change*
*The period now*
*Is very trendy*
*With girl's things*
*And boy's too*

*And trousers so tight*
*You can't get your feet in*
*Hey! Look at that ...*
*Make no mistake*
*The one with white foundation*
*Wearing low cut dresses*
*Hair in curlers*
*And all powdered up*
*She wanders aimlessly around*

*Girls these days*
*Really like chatting*
*Gossiping and arguing*
*Wearing lipstick*
*Hair in rollers*
*They say they're anti-West*
*But they like rock 'n' roll*

---

### McDonalds in Jakarta

In 1991, McDonalds arrived to great fanfare in Jakarta. It was an immediate success with the young public, but it wasn't to everyone's taste or pocket, with meals costing the proverbial week's wages. The surrounding car park had more than its share of Mercedes. During the fasting month of Ramadan, curtains were drawn across the large windows so as to not offend passing Muslims: Ronald McDonald bowing down to Mecca.

---

The decades since independence have been much like Europe in mediaeval times, witness to the rise of a number of dynasties, rich, powerful families who are destined to be rich and powerful long into the future. Recent years in Jakarta have also seen the emergence of a materialistic middle-class who seem prepared to do anything to make their 'fortune'. The attitudes that accompany such material pursuits are at fantastic odds with the traditions of politeness, self-control and communality that are so typical of Indonesia. It might be assumed that these people are all too ready to disregard their heritage for the sake of a pair of designer shoes. Fortunately, this isn't quite the case.

While notions of self-opinion and self-expression are certainly taking root, these influences needn't be considered quite so corruptive. For the most part, Western ideals are absorbed into mainstream ways of thinking. Just as Islam, when it was first brought to Java, underwent a gradual transformation that was distinctly Javanese, so the great majority of Western ideals are woven into the larger Indonesian scheme of things. The traditions of 200 million plus people are, after all, a lot to compete with.

As the dominant religion in Indonesia, Islam has never been over-impressed with the West and its ways. The rise in fundamentalist thinking in Jakarta has only added to the conflict of Westernisation. This uncomfortable way of living, this duality of conflicting attitudes, modern and traditional, came to a head in 1991 during the Gulf War. When Indonesia was called on to show its support, it was reluctant to show allegiance to either the USA or Saddam Hussein. Although Indonesia has the world's largest Muslim population, it's categorically not an Islamic state. It was expected that Indonesia would show its support for Iraq. (Indeed, Muslim militants planted a bomb, which was later diffused, at the American ambassador's residence). At the same time, it had to be remembered that Indonesia depended on America for its foreign aid, which was an awful lot of money as much of it was used to arm the military.

The chance to afford those items advertised on TV every day is something everyone deserves, yet only a minority of the population is able to do so, apart from the soap powders that is. As ex-President Suharto explained in 1997, imbalances between those who have been able to profit from the country's development drive and those who have been left behind are a fact of life: "Sometimes, some people are able to make the best use of the opportunities earlier than others." he said. "Development activities in any country usually open new opportunities which some people can take better advantage of." Yet the fact remains: there are some immorally rich people in Jakarta.

Not all exploitation is bad, however. The land that makes up Indonesia, being so rich in natural resources, has a lot to offer: gold, diamond, silver, mercury, manganese, phosphate, nickel, tin, coal, oil and gas are all found in fantastic proportions. The problem, however, is getting at them. Cue foreign investors. This is the real reason Indonesia has remained in the West's good books. For despite worldwide coverage of a seemingly never-ending abuse of civil rights, foreign investors just can't wait to get their hands on the wealth that is under the ground. Foreign mining companies supply the required technology and the deal is a certain split of the winnings. In this way, all sides are kept happy, providing jobs and racking up profit.

Western workers, however, command Western salaries, and uncomfortable situations can arise where Westerners are working alongside locals, doing the same job yet receiving vastly different salaries. Ten times the difference might be a conservative estimate. It can't be good for an Indonesian's self-esteem to get a comparatively lousy salary, after having studied for it. It's a genuine cause for concern, particularly when expatriate workers have no formal qualifications. But then, if the work-visa granting bureaucrats weren't so corruptible, perhaps the official line 'if it can be done by an Indonesian, then it must be done by one' wouldn't be so openly abused.

## Sweat Shop Horror!

This massive financial imbalance has been highlighted by, among others, American civil rights leader Jesse Jackson who, in July 1996, drew world media attention to the Reebok shoe factory in West Java. Clearly bewildered at the way designer sports-shoes were being manufactured in what he accurately described as 'sweat shop' conditions, he called for something to be done. How, he argued, could a billion-dollar multinational company possibly justify selling its products at top price after manufacturing them at such low cost? He described this exploitation of Indonesia's cheap labour as nothing less than immoral; a living outrage. More depraved still is the truth that such misuse of people is merely indicative of all developing countries. And among the biggest employers of local workers are fellow Asians, the Koreans who constitute the largest group of expats in Indonesia.

## THE CENDANA CLAN

When President Suharto relinquished power after 32 years, he retired to his family home in Jalan Cendana in the upmarket Menteng area of Central Jakarta, where he is regularly visited by his cronies. He was, by Indonesian standards, an old man, and in many ways he had done tremendous things for Indonesia. He was there as the country blossomed in its first flushes of independence and under his leadership, Indonesia became self-sufficient in food, the population explosion imploded and literacy flourished—although literature didn't. It was under his leadership that Indonesia remained stable—up to a point anyway.

But he was also there when a number of terrible things were brushed under the carpet. Suharto was there when Indonesia was still fighting the Dutch; he was one of the 'old brigade', a man with a history. The first thing he did after stepping in to assist the ailing Sukarno led to the death of several hundred thousand people.

Having instilled a level of fear in the populace which was to last three decades, his second big move was less bloody, though no less ambitious: to take out a massive mortgage on the country in the form of foreign loans, mainly Yen and US dollars. It took nearly ten years following his 'abdication' for the country to get out of debt, years when some 40 per cent of Indonesia's annual earnings were put aside for the repayments. By the end of his marathon length in office, Suharto had seen some amazing changes occur, whilst simultaneously amassing a personal fortune for himself and his family.

While there are other wealthy, well-connected families in Indonesia, none have been afforded the privileges that the Suharto family afforded themselves. At the peak of their powers, they seemed to actually own Jakarta—so plainly were their names written over the nation's economy. The country's toll-roads, for example, belonged to the eldest daughter, while the youngest son had the Timor, the country's first 'all-Indonesian' car (except it was actually completely Korean). In addition, they also controlled the country's petrol supplies, an airline or three, TV stations, a taxi company, the Hyatt Hotel complex, besides virtual monopolies on plastics, paper, timber, banking, shipping, fishing, mining, telecommunications and cloves. They seemed to have at least 10 per cent on every business transaction in the country, and it was common knowledge that without the nod of approval from one of the Suharto family, foreign businesses could make little headway in Indonesia. Perhaps the most amazing fact was that they had managed to get away with it for so long. They couldn't have done it without outside help.

## TIME OF CRISIS

But then, in 1998, it all went pear-shaped as they say. It all seemed to happen at once for Indonesia—everything bad that could happen happened. Everything an ageing President Suharto had accomplished over three decades seemed to unravel in a few short months. Forecasters had long been predicting a 'crash' of some sort, a payback for the spending of borrowed funds. The process was a gradual one and had a number of seemingly disparate events; together they served to remove Suharto's aura of invincibility.

The previous years had certainly been touch and go in a number of respects. There was the 'problem' of East Timor with the United Nations' refusal to accept it as an Indonesian province, and the West's obligation to be appalled, while struggling with the dilemma of honouring escalating arms requests. But on the whole, scenarios like these (like the sporadic street violence, or the embarrassment of the Busang fiasco—what had been touted as potentially the world's biggest gold mine, attracted investments from the Cendana Clan but turned out to be a complete hoax) were viewed as localised problems which could be partially forgotten about by most of the world.

But there was an international outcry when it was revealed that various parts of Indonesia, as well as certain parts of Malaysia, were burning out of control. The resulting smog at one point affected Indonesia, Malaysia, Brunei, Singapore, Thailand, Philippines, and seemed poised to affect the whole planet. The international fire fighters were called in, and the traditionally imperious Suharto government had to admit that yes, there was a problem—they declared a national disaster, and Malaysia, a state of emergency—and yes, they would appreciate a hand in solving it. And by the way—sorry.

Jakarta was almost embarrassingly unaffected by the choking smog. As a diversion, the capital suddenly found itself hosting Pekan Olahraga Nasional 1997 (National Sports

Week) to great fanfare and, when the wind was blowing in the right direction, pretending that the trouble was somewhere else entirely. But no matter, Jakarta had trouble of its own brewing.

Indonesia had become a demon of all things anti-environmental. With the continuing spread of the fires and the realisation that they couldn't so easily be extinguished, came accusations that Indonesia was going for broke. Its developers were accused of monumental greed: for example, in order to catapult Indonesia to the rank of number one rice producer, vast areas of Kalimantan peat forest were cleared to be turned into paddies. That the land turned out to be totally unsuitable for rice production only added to the irony of their over-ambition. Rainforests in Sumatra and Kalimantan were also cleared, ostensibly for palm oil plantations but more likely for access to the profitable hard woods.

In defence, Suharto's business crony, Mohammed 'Bob' Hasan, appeared on TV saying that perhaps Western countries were jealous of Indonesia's breakneck economy, and asking why, for example, they didn't go and look at countries in Africa if they wanted to criticise developing nations' affairs. Few were convinced. The focus of the blame was pointed at the Suharto family; allegedly, most of the companies responsible for the land-clearance which had resulted in the fires could be linked back to a member of the Suharto family, or at least to one of the Cendana Clan—such as Bob Hasan. Meanwhile, orang utans, long a favourite of ecological documentary makers, were filmed rolling out of the blazing forests, confused and smouldering—and straight into the hands of the poachers.

To rub salt into the wound, three major accidents were then attributed, though of course never officially, to the smog. A Garuda Airbus flying from Jakarta to Medan lost visibility and flew into a mountain-side, killing all 234 aboard and making this Indonesia's worst ever air disaster. Days later, two cargo ships in the Malacca Straits collided, killing 28, and then, soon after leaving Jakarta, a Silkair plane bound for Singapore went down (although this was later found to have been caused by a failure of a rudder component).

So with eco-disasters, the horrors of the East Timor atrocities still fresh in the mind, plane-crashes, outbursts of rioting, drought and starvation in Irian Jaya, and the increasingly worrying question of what would happen after Suharto, the last thing the administration wanted was for the economy to crash. But that is exactly what happened.

## 'DOLLAR NAIK, RUPIAH TURUN'

Thailand, Japan and Korea experienced it first. And then it happened to Indonesia. At first, prices appeared to be doubling and tripling on a weekly basis, then daily. There was panic buying of the most fundamental things like rice, oil and powdered milk. Realising this potential, many suppliers withheld the *sembako* (staples, foods) and held out for the highest bidder. Bus, train and plane services were slashed. Banks were closed, and the bankers ordered not to leave the country. The airport fiscal was raised from Rp 250,000 to Rp 1,000,000. Imported goods tripled in price. Debts went unpaid. Work on construction sites halted. Great expanses of land which had been ear-marked for real-estate development lay empty, while the folks displaced from their land were left to stare back in confusion. Jobs were lost—millions of jobs.

Those hardest hit were those who had to struggle hardest to make ends meet. *Kaki lima* (street-vendors) began offering two prices: one for their regulars and one for non-regulars. The number of *pemulung* visibly increased—those who pick over the city's rubbish in the hope of finding something worth recycling. Unicef stepped in, advising people of ways to give children nourishment when food and money were so scarce. *Tajin*, the thick water from boiled rice, was reluctantly accepted as a poor substitute for milk.

Those fortunate enough to be paid in dollars, however, were less affected. And tourists coming to Indonesia suddenly had more rupiah than ever. But for the middle class Jakartan family, this was a nightmare they had hoped would never come true. The threat of poverty had always been two steps away for such a family—perhaps a couple in their 30s with the proverbial 2.4 children who both worked diligently 50 hours a week in an office to bring home just enough

The rupiah was renowned for its tendency to reflect the general state of affairs in Indonesia. Indeed, the mere mention of a presidential illness was enough to see it drop a few points, but few really expected it to crash so completely. People were genuinely confused by the new terminology emerging: CBS, ADB, IMF, debt rescheduling. For most people it was simply expressed as *'dollar naik, rupiah turun'*—'dollar up, rupiah down'. A strange sense of denial set in—disbelief that the city was being eaten from the inside out.

to sustain the illusion of being middle class. Now they had to drop down a few rungs of the social ladder, while the poor had to be content with a meal or two less. The corporate élite, on the other distant hand, continued limping by on borrowed time. But with their empires tied up in the massive debts that had caused the crash, theirs was an uncertain future too.

With morale so low, the government embarked on another of its famous propaganda campaigns. TV and billboard slogans this time implored the population: *'Saya cinta rupiah, saya cinta produk Indonesia'* (I love rupiah, and I love Indonesian products) and *'Mari, pakai rupiah di dalam bisnis anda'* (Come on, use the rupiah in your business). In addition, TV coverage was of government ministers donating gold, dollars, and even entire year's salaries, although it was the private sector and not the state which was bankrupt. The notion was that if the country stuck together, it could pull through. If there was ever a time for national consciousness, it was now.

Loans were promised, outstanding debts put on hold, and the government cornered into a bargaining liaison with the International Monetary Fund. Help would be given, it transpired, but only on certain conditions. Here was perhaps a chance for the long-standing corruption that defined much of the system to be swept away. But the government was obviously reluctant to comply with any reform measures and, despite some half-hearted attempts, much of the reform package was rejected on 'unconstitutional' grounds.

On the street level, this didn't translate so well. With powdered baby milk costing a week's wages for the poor of Indonesia, the protesters now had what seemed like a valid excuse for protesting. They suddenly had good reason to prove right what they had been saying all along was a rip-off.

Even with the government providing subsidised foods for the poor, exploding violence, as a consequence of the crash, had never seemed closer.

## ACTS OF REBELLION

Student protests were the headache that the Suharto government couldn't get rid of. They had a tried and tested method of containing any outbursts, however, in the shape of several hundred tons of military hardware purchased from the West. This time around though, it wasn't just the youngsters who were brave enough to stand up and make a stand. It was like the scene in *2001: A Space Odyssey* when the first ape-man dares to reach out and touch the monolith from outer space. When he realises it can be done without instant reprimand, the others one by one follow suit, and before they know what's happened, they have become a force of their own.

Their mood was infectious. TV celebrities came out to make their protests public. Letters to the newspaper called for Suharto to step down. Comparisons were made with Sukarno's presidency; that it had been good at the beginning, but tired and worn out at the end. There were, however, three distinct strands of opposition which eventually culminated in the downfall of President Suharto. The most vocal were the middle-class students—mostly educated, middle-class kids with hopes and career plans suddenly on the line. The most violent were the urban masses of *orang kampung*, those who did most of the looting. But the most significant were the ones from within—Suharto's own ministers and ex-ministers.

In the very short time since independence, the gap between rich and poor has widened beyond everyone's imagination. Dissatisfaction had grown, and corruption seemingly permeated every aspect of the Indonesian way of life. Yet for the older generation, a generation still reeling from the massacres of the late-1960s, it had always been too painful to contemplate questioning why their land was not theirs, or why they didn't earn enough money. But not for this new generation.

The widespread thinking of those over the age of 40, those who remembered that life hadn't always been so rosy, was that people in Jakarta would simply have to find a way to manage. It was Jakarta's Coca-Cola generation that was up in arms; for them, there seemed no excuse. Things had been going so well for everyone: a slice of the riches of an accelerating economy was seemingly available to everyone if they only worked at it. This new generation, the one born under the gaze of an ageing but still revered godfather, felt especially cheated. The promise they had been taught to believe was that Indonesia had so very nearly caught up with the 'developed' world. All the relevant technologies were in place, all the right attitudes had been practised—all that was left was to tidy up the edges a bit. It seemed so unreasonable that the country's veneer of apparent gloss and modernity could be wiped clean away so abruptly.

And so with a master plan that was apparently failing and large cracks appearing throughout the entire system, those who weren't prepared to keep their fingers crossed and hope it would get better soon took to the streets and began ripping the place apart. Or rather, threatening to rip the place apart. For most of the time, the legendary iron-rule of the Indonesian military was sufficient to contain most of the trouble. But not for long.

Perhaps everyone knew that they had too much foreign media interest to back them up should the government decide to jail everyone. Perhaps they just wanted what everyone, secretly or not, had been wishing for all along—a change for the better.

"Morally they are right. Whether politically they are right, they don't seem to care."
  –Sarwono Kusumaatmadja, former Environment Minister

## The Week That Was

The Week That Was began on a Tuesday when four students from Trisakti University were shot dead, and ended nine days later on a Thursday when President Suharto relinquished power. The days in-between saw unbridled anarchy sweep through Jakarta and the rest of the country. The man himself, however, the man who was ultimately to blame, was out of the country when the chaos erupted. Would he come back, they wondered? Some believed Suharto had written the country off and had left for good. There were strong rumours that he had stashed his cash in Austria. Or South America.

Thursday and Friday saw the worst of the mayhem. Anything remotely connected to the authorities was attacked; anything of any value was stolen or destroyed; and places worth looting were looted. The rioters singled out their Chinese half-cousins again, and almost the entire area of Glodok was destroyed, as well as Chinese-owned businesses such as Bank Central Asia. To cries of *"Hidup* Indonesia!" (Long Live Indonesia!), they ended up killing one another when they set the shopping malls on fire, unaware that shop staff and other looters were still inside.

Suharto flew back to a capital city, his reputation in tatters. The overwhelming calls for his resignation were met with the vague response that he might, after all, consider stepping 'aside'. The mayhem continued. The international press descended en masse, most to be encamped in the Mandarin Hotel. In a desperate measure to calm the situation, local TV was instructed to broadcast only the 'official' news, and food and petrol prices were cut. But still the mayhem continued. Those who could, began to leave. Those who couldn't, stayed

> "They have come to a point of no return. They will stage their demonstrations daily if necessary, until the old man goes forever."
>
> —Amien Rais, Head of Muhammadiyah, 20 May 1998

at home glued to their TV sets, hoping a truckload of looters wouldn't stop outside.

By Saturday, the atmosphere had calmed a little. A feeling of uncertain quiet came over Jakarta, as people stopped to assess the damage of their burnt-out city. The worst part was that they were still broke, still hungry and still under the rule of someone they had decided they no longer wanted.

The students headed for the parliament building. There was a peculiar sense of paranoid confidence, knowing that the world was watching, and that they could be killed at any moment. They put up banners in English and handed out flowers to the soldiers. Then they climbed on the roof of the parliament building and sat there, protesting. They were to occupy the parliament building for the next five days.

They called for Suharto to stand down, they called for Suharto to stand trial—even for Suharto to be executed. As the days progressed, the cries for "*reformasi*" grew louder, although precisely what they had in mind was never fully detailed. All they knew was they wanted 'the old man' out—a man who had come to symbolise the reason the country was in economic despair.

Riding high on the roller-coaster of support for Suharto's resignation was a vocal little man called Amien Rais, who had come to represent the heroic opposition to a dictatorship. It was Amien who, having been advised that the situation could turn into another Tiananmen Square, cancelled what was to be, in front of the Presidential Palace, the biggest demonstration yet. But as fate would have it, it was the government itself which actually came to the rescue. One by one, Suharto's ministers, past and present, began to publicly turn against him. Suharto appeared unworried, even chuckling, as he announced that he would be holding elections within six months—elections in which he would not be standing. This was not enough. They wanted him out now.

And so the next morning, Thursday, 21 May 1998, in a live televised broadcast to the nation, it was a shuffling old man who, clearing his throat, acknowledged that he had lost the trust of the nation. He begged for forgiveness for any mistakes he had made, said that he hoped to spend more time with his children and, after 32 years, stepped down as the President of Indonesia. There was a rapturous response from the students, and then a kind of stunned disbelief that the father of the nation, the Big *Bapak* himself was gone. The next day, after trying to barricade themselves in one final time, the students decide to vacate parliament and go home. The job had been done.

It was a week of madness that saw the true power of the Indonesian people expressed for the first time in three decades.

## THE ELECTORAL SYSTEM

Under the system that ex-President Suharto established, Indonesia's leader had the final say every time. The country's first president, Achmad Sukarno, however, began his office with a far more democratic parliament, but rapidly grew dissatisfied with it, believing it inherently *tidak cocok* (unsuitable) to the Indonesian way of things. Hence, the introduction of the state ideology *Pancasila* and a system of reaching agreement on a small scale through general consensus—as traditionally achieved in the *kampung*.

With general elections held to great fanfare every five years in Indonesia, there was always assumed to be a certain degree of democracy in play somewhere. Yet this façade belied the true restrictions of the New Order government. Under the system, only three parties were allowed: the ruling party Golongan Karya (Golkar), Partai Persatuan Pembangunan (PPP) which represents Islamic politics, and Partai Demokrasi Indonesia (PDI) which had always been the political troublemaker. However, the politics and leadership of any party remained at the sole discretion of the government. When, for example, in 1996, the President thought PDI had become too vocal for its own good, he merely removed its leader, Megawati Sukarnoputri, daughter of the first president, Sukarno, and installed one of his own carefully-vetted subjects. Adding to the façade of democracy were the restrictions placed on political campaigning. Under the law, should more than ten people have gathered in one place to discuss politics, the meeting became a political rally, which was illegal and had to be stopped.

Vote-rigging was never a problem, mainly because the electoral process had been orchestrated to work in the President's favour every time. ABRI (the Armed Forces) had a block vote in every election, while the cabinet itself remained the sole choice of the President.

---

**Fascinatingly Accurate**

In the run-up to the elections of May 1997, government experts reckoned Golkar would win with a 70.02 per cent majority. When all the votes had been counted, it was found Golkar had won with a 70.02 per cent majority.

---

This then was not democracy in any recognisable form, but a tightly-controlled pretence at it. Elections were solely about maintaining the status quo and changing as little as possible. And if things didn't go according to plan—which they always did—there was a caucus of non-elected representatives of various groups, functioned much like the House of Lords in the UK Parliament.

Throughout Suharto's regime, there was a system of proportional representation whereby electors voted for a particular party. Each party had a slate of potential members of Parliament and the percentage of votes cast for the party determined how many members would actually get to feed from the trough. Those at the top of each list were there by virtue of the size of their financial contribution to the party's coffers.

The system remains with slight variations. Firstly, there are as many as 20 political parties, with Golkar and PDI remaining as the wealthiest and with the most votes. Each must have offices and members in the majority of the nation's provinces. It has also been decreed, largely by those political parties which currently have some seats in the legislature, that at the next election, only those parties which garnered 5 per cent of the votes at the last election will be able to put forward candidates. This would, of course, decrease the number of political parties actually represented in parliament.

To counter-balance the lack of regional representation, there is a non-elected Regional Group which doesn't have clearly defined powers.

## THE PRESENT

With the publication of this edition of *CultureShock! Jakarta*, Indonesia has its sixth president, but the first chosen in a direct election. Sukarno assumed power by acclamation, Suharto through cunning, Habibie through Suharto's misplaced trust, Gus Dur because no-one really wanted Sukarno's daughter, Megawati, whose political party PDI-P had gained the most votes, so she was made Vice President only to become the fifth president because no-one trusted Gus Dur any more to look after the interests of the still entrenched élite.

And that brings us to Susilo Bambang Yudhoyono (SBY), who had been Megawati's chief security minister, a post he was uniquely qualified for with his army background. This of course also qualifies him to be Commander-in-Chief, which is important as the military reverts to civilian rule. SBY's vice-president is Josef Kalla, a businessman from South Sulawesi, with a deserved reputation for resolving civil strife in Aceh, Maluku and, hopefully, Sulawesi.

At present, every governor and regent is directly elected. Each has a running mate to serve as his or her deputy for a maximum of two five-year terms. Often, they are from different political parties, thus assuring themselves that there is broad enough support for them to be elected. There are moves afoot to have every politician directly elected, thus being answerable to the electorate rather than a particular grouping. They would continue to be backed by political parties, as in other countries, but having local representatives for constituencies is increasingly seen as a way to give the political process a public viability. There are even a few politicians who agree with this.

## THE FUTURE

The future of Jakarta could go several ways. Following the massive floods of February 2007, there have been calls to move the capital city to, say, Bogor. No one knows why. Anyway, within ten years or so, the entire floodplain will be one massive sprawl. Jakarta is not going to get any smaller or any less crowded. It could implode and come to a complete standstill, or the traffic situation might improve. As there's a limit to how many times a fly-over can actually fly over, there may yet be a good public transport system in place. Maybe each administrative area will deal with its own rubbish

And the rich will seemingly inevitably get richer, and the poor will continue to flood into the city in hope of work. The middle classes will swell the suburbs so that relatively rural areas like Bekasi and Tangerang will continue to become part of the bigger Jakarta. Whatever it becomes—it will be big.

The next governor may well have the interests of the people as his priority. Perhaps he will devolve some responsibilities, such as rubbish disposal, to the mayoralties, devise a programme of integrated public transport and will encourage the building of bicycle lanes and footpaths and parks and sports facilities and....the list goes on.

Perhaps the next best thing to considering the problem of Jakarta is simply being there. Living in Jakarta means being submerged in an entire planet of its own where nothing else matters, where the country can do no wrong, where the rainforests are not deforested, where life is better than it has ever been and where life could be worse. To be there is to find a place that knows no different.

# JAKARTANS

## CHAPTER 3

'The Javanese don't talk, they vibrate.'
—Blanche d'Alpuget, *Monkeys In The Dark*

## BETAWI

As the Cockneys are to London, so the *orang Betawi* are to Jakarta—a minority group. The Betawi are Jakarta's true originals—an authentic concoction of varied cultures and chance encounters. They are fiercely proud of their identity and have an attitude, dialect and culture different to other Indonesians. Perhaps that's why they're so 'upfront'.

Historically, Jakarta's role as first a minor, and then major centre for business, allowed all manner of influence to creep into old Batavia, as it was then. Traders from Holland, Arabia and Portugal; slaves from Bali, Sulawesi, Java and China; and mystics from India are just some of the people to have left their fingerprints on the city. Whatever it was that brought them to Batavia, it kept enough of them here long enough to set up their own 'camps' in the town. These original settlers to Batavia initially remained loyal to their origins, living in clearly defined *kampung* areas and trying their best to carry on as normal. By the end of the 19th century, however, their habits, food, music, religions and dress-sense had merged into one. The children born and bred under these conditions were known as the *orang Betawi*.

But with Dutch colonial rule at its fiercest, the Betawi, who were merely considered the offspring of visiting traders to Batavia, were rather low-down on the honours list. Being born 'Betawi' certainly wasn't anything to be proud of in the beginning as the majority of them were slaves, servants or labourers.

Betawi are not to be confused with *orang Jakarta*. These are the second and third generations born here. Their parents and grandparents came to Jakarta looking for work or an education and have stayed. Nearly all Jakarta residents can tell you their ethnic background, although there are many of mixed ancestry. These folks will say that their hometown is Jakarta. In fact, some 70 per cent of the population could well fit in this category as this is the percentage which does not now perform the annual *mudik*, the *pulang kampung* (return to hometown), for the celebration of Idul Fitri at the end of Ramadan. But scratch beneath the surface as it were, and you'll find that they'll generally feel a kinship with somewhere else in the archipelago. As the city swells, the emerging numbers of these *orang Jakarta* are set to eclipse the remaining strongholds of actual Betawi.

Stereotypically, *orang Betawi* are frank, down to earth folks. They are good joke-tellers, good Muslims and good at discussing the current price of land per square metre. They have a unique way of looking at the world. Unlike almost everyone else in Jakarta, who has an attachment to somewhere else, Betawi don't see themselves in a larger context. *orang Betawi* are always at home—the capital city is their *kampung*.

But they do have something of a bad reputation; they are not renowned as the city's hardest workers. The *orang Jakarta*, for example, think that *orang Betawi* are *malas* (lazy). Whereas everyone else has to slave for a living, Betawi work ethics are by contrast rumoured to be geared more towards sitting about than, say, hawking the street. *Orang Betawi* know they shouldn't have to go anywhere— after all, they come from Jakarta. Although in truth, Betawi have done the real hard work, historically speaking, when a foreign power ran the city and employed them all as slaves. *Orang Betawi* are, therefore, different to other Indonesians. Nowhere is this

A typical Betawi way of earning a living is to buy a second-hand car between them and renting it out—anything that lets the business come to them.

more perfectly illustrated than in the food they eat and the music they play.

*Tanjidor* is one such music and a truly bizarre sound it is too. Imagine a brass band gone wrong. It combines trombones, clarinets and various bits of a *gamelan* set with a hint of *jaipong*. (*Jaipong* is dance-music; just one of the many indigenous sounds of Sunda, West Java). For a challenging listening experience, try listening to any recordings by the mighty Grup Tanjidor Kembang Ros. If you feel like dancing to it, do the *yapong*. For other types of Betawi music such as *kroncong*, *dendang* and *gambang kromong* (a Chinese-style of music with Betawi lyrics on top), try dancing the *cokek* or the *ronggeng*. Betawi have a strong tradition of rapping, the most well-known exponent of which was the late great Betawi actor, Benyamin Sueb.

The food Betawi people like to eat, in addition to the obligatory *nasi* (rice) and *cabe* (chili), is heavy in *kunyit* (turmeric), *lengkuas* (ginger), *kayu manis* (cinnamon) and *pala* (nutmeg). Try ordering a bowl of *nasi uduk*, *kerak telor*, *sayur asem* or *pacri nanas*. But be careful where you order them. Ciputat, Kalibata, Pejaten, Condet and Tanah Abang may be some of today's remaining Betawi strongholds, but with each area excelling in a particular variation of the Betawi menu, you may never taste quite the same version of *nasi uduk* twice. Buy a book of Betawi recipes to be on the safe side, because even across Jakarta, the Betawi identity is fragmented; each sub-district offering a subtly different attitude, dialect and food to the next—such is the Betawi allegiance to their square plot.

The struggle to keep the Betawi identity alive today is an uphill one. Successive governors have declared various *kampung*, such as Condet, as Betawi cultural zones. However, as land prices increase in central areas, the Betawi sell up and move to the further outskirts of the city. The latest Betawi zone is Situ Babakan in South Jakarta, where you can see

For entertainment on special occasions, a Betawi household is likely to hire *ondel-ondel* puppets. These 2-m (6.6-ft) tall characters are wrapped in curtains and have huge papier-mâché heads with multi-coloured spikes glued all over. Young children find them most worrying.

renovated houses with decorative exterior woodwork and spacious terraces.

Traditional dances such as the vigorous *ronggeng* and the masked dance *topeng* are performed here, and if you're particularly energetic, you can join the workshops held throughout the week. Another area of interest is *Lenong*, which is a traditional form of Betawi street theatre, which regularly crops up on TV. *Lenong* is brash, comic and improvised and deals with the trials and tribulations of day-to-day living in Jakarta and shows not an ounce of mercy for authority.

While the bulk of Jakarta's population today probably originates from Sunda or Java, there are sizable representations of every other type of Indonesian. Some residential areas are predominantly Chinese, in the north and west of the city, or Indian, also in the north, but their trading areas are different. Chinese traders are predominantly to be found near Kota, as they have always been, whereas the Indian tailors and textile shops can be found in Pasar Baru. Elsewhere, apart from the numerical advantage of the Javanese, every area is relatively homogenous.

## CHILDREN

Indonesians revere children. Children are top priority in any situation in Indonesia, and always the ones to get that extra scoop of *nasi* (rice). The adoration parents have for their *anak-anak* (kids) is reflected in the names they give: Dewi (Goddess), Intan (Diamond), Suci (Purity), Ayu (Beautiful), Putri (Princess), Mentari (Sun), Wulan (Moon), Ratna (Diamond), Dian (Candlelight), Kurnia (Gift of God) and Mutiara (Pearl).

During their first year or so in the world, Indonesian babies are in near-permanent physical contact with their mother or *pembantu*, travelling everywhere by means of a *selendang* (sling). Never are they left alone. Yet traditionally, men are not expected to lend a hand in any way. In Indonesian families, the father is the seat of discipline; the mother is provider of love, as well as resident accountant. The children's obligations, particularly of the firstborn, are always towards the good of the family. And to support the parents in old age.

Indonesians spoil their children and seemingly let them get away with murder. Discipline does exist however—in the form of pinching. Whereas spanking would horrify the average Indonesian onlooker, disciplining a child through pinching is perfectly acceptable. Another way to guarantee children's good behaviour is to tell them ghost stories. The heads of Indonesian children are swimming with umpteen variations of child-snatching ghouls—partly the reason Indonesians are such vivaciously superstitious people, and partly why so many of them have to sleep with the light on. One of the worst beings to fear is the *kuntilanak*: the spirit of a Javanese woman who died in childbirth and appears (to children who don't behave themselves) as a beautiful woman with a gaping hole in her back.

Western children are equally as adored, if not more so. The display of affection for a cute Western baby is, however, sometimes overwhelming. A small crowd of cooing admirers will readily congregate upon the sighting of a white child—stroking hair, pinching cheeks and loving the kid to death. Obviously, this kind of attention isn't easy for a child to accept, and it's better (if possible) to explain to the child beforehand what to expect and how to react. If being touched does worry a child or parent, then simply say as much. Just say that he or she doesn't like it: "*Ma'af, dia tidak suka.*" Overall, however, the Indonesian adoration of children makes it a good place to live and travel with them.

For longer-term expatriate children, added difficulties may arise. Since Indonesia is the land of service, with a lot of expatriate families employing several members of household staff, it's all too possible for youngsters to become spoilt. Children who grow up accustomed to Indonesians running errands for them, driving them around, and generally serving their everyday needs, may develop a distorted view of Indonesians. They are certainly in for a shock when they do eventually go home. Other negative effects that living in another country can have on children include a sense of rootlessness, of alienation and of 'not fitting in'. The child may be confused as to where 'home' really is. Having spent a proportion of his or her developing years in a very foreign country, the youngster may have little in common with his or her peers at home—at first anyway. Of course, this very much depends on how much the family interacts with the local community.

Officially, the average family in Indonesia has 2.4 children, which is perhaps a somewhat surprising statistic. Suharto's government was praised for its population control, and in 1983 received a United Nations prize for its 'support of family planning'. Following the crash of Asian economies in 1996/1997, family planning has not been a government priority and it is only now, some ten years later, that it is beginning to feature on bureaucrats' agendas.

'*Dua anak cukup*' ('two children enough') was the well-worn phrase painted on school roofs and other prominent places in the 1970s through to the 1990s. Many *kampungs* throughout Indonesia still have a 2-m (6.6-ft) high sculpture of the two-finger salute to family planning. Certain religious attitudes had to be overcome in the implementation of the government's fervent family-planning programme— many Muslims holding the belief that Allah will always provide for them, no matter what difficulties occur and no matter how large a family becomes. The promotion of contraceptives then was in stark contrast to the Indonesian's inherent desire to surround themselves with offspring. In doing this, they assure themselves at least some sort of future insurance. Having children therefore means having a certain security.

However, Indonesian women are generally better educated and talk unashamedly about their own particular method of contraception. Having grown up with the idea, many are surprisingly un-*malu* (unabashed) about the whole affair and the population growth has, percentage-wise, been minimal.

Giving birth in Jakarta is not a problem; there are enough Western-standard hospitals and clinics with pre-natal and post-natal expertise to make birthing in Jakarta no more of a worry than it need be. Maternity clinics are called *Rumah Sakit Bersalin* in Indonesian. Certain aspects of pregnancy and birth will be strange for foreigners, but, as always, perfectly normal for Indonesians.

When the *bayi* (baby) is actually born, the *ari-ari*, or afterbirth, receives special attention. Again, it's the Javanese (without doubt, the most superstitious people in the land) who know best what to do. An elaborate ceremony is performed whereby the placenta is given a 'funeral'. The Javanese believe the afterbirth is the 'shadow' of the newly-born child—the twin that didn't make it. Throwing it away would therefore be quite wrong. Instead, it's carefully washed and placed in a clay pot along with any gifts the family might want to give. This is a time to make wishes for the newborn baby, a time to influence the future of the *bayi*. If you want it

At seven months into her pregnancy, a ceremony is held for the woman to wish her and her child good fortune. During the ceremony, depending how orthodox the family are, she is bathed in the flower-waters of seven different flowers, changes clothes seven times and eats seven kinds of food. The Javanese especially adhere to this ceremony, believing seven months a critical time in the *kehamilan* (pregnancy). They believe, quite rightly, that the unborn child is fully formed at seven months, and that it just needs to 'cook' for a while more. It's imperative, therefore, that a fuss is made. And for the mother-to-be, traditions aside, it's a welcome show of emotional support.

to be rich, put some money in. If you think it will become an artist, put some crayons in, and so on. The whole package is wrapped in white cloth before being buried, and a candle burned for 40 days.

In its first few years of life, an Indonesian baby wears various amulets and charms to promote a prosperous future. It may be 'tested' in various ways. A pencil, some money, a spanner and other objects will be placed in front of the youngster—the child's future may be determined by whichever one is chosen.

## BEGGARS

Without doubt, you will come across a colourful variety of beggars in and around Jakarta. But nowhere near as many as might be expected for a so-called developing country. The reasons are many. They may lie in the regular round-ups offered by police or in the considerable amount of social work done by the *Departemen Sosial*. Or they may lie in the Indonesian's inherent sense of dignity; that they would rather try their utmost to eke out some kind of living, no matter how small the returns. Maybe.

Jakarta regularly attracts numbers of *orang desa* (country folks) as beggars. They travel from nearby villages and, whether or not they really intend to, end up begging for money in the big city. The busiest times of the year are during redundancies in the rice-growing calendar, and in the month of Ramadhan when everyone is obliged to be acting more generously and courteously than usual.

But there are enough beggars and truly appalling sights around Jakarta for the average visitor to be justifiably horrified. Sufferers of leprosy are placed at traffic lights for the day; people with gaping holes for noses grab at your legs as you cross a bridge; immorally young children wander about in traffic banging tambourines. And of course, there's the old 'standard' mother-and-child variety: women who are rumoured to hire their babies by the hour as part of their garb. These are, by all accounts, 'professional' beggars. Rumours like these persist that many beggars are simply putting it on.

**Professional Beggar**
One such story has a 'beggar' grunting and shuffling his way onto a bus with absolute difficulty. The unfortunate man appeared to be lacking in legs and forced therefore to walk everywhere on his hands. Once onboard, the man continued grimacing and making dreadful guttural sounds, and was given as much space as is possible on a packed metromini. One passenger, however, became suspicious and decided to follow the beggar to wherever he was going. Sure enough, when the man had made his pained and pathetic exit from the bus, and believed he was comparatively 'alone', he quickly unbuckled his legs, leapt up and walked away— small change jangling in his pocket.

But the children are the most worrying aspect. Street kids are all over daytime Jakarta, busking on the trains and buses, in groups at certain traffic junctions, or stretched out on station platforms and huddled below underpasses.

## AMATEUR POLICE

Jakarta's amateur police are a law unto themselves. The police who direct traffic on the big roads are either in too short a supply or are too busy ensuring the safe passage of dignitaries to control the flow on lesser roads. You will recognise these because they stand vacantly by the roadside, one hand perpetually waving traffic on, sometimes with a red wand. They also wear a brown uniform and may have a gun in a white holster on their hip

However, there does exist a corps of unofficial cops who attempt to sort out the mess. Some call themselves *tukang parkir* (parking specialist) and actually do have a quasi-legal status. You'll recognise them because they have 'official' uniforms (light green or blue with a badge showing the city logo on the short sleeves). If you can determine where the official parking places are, you'll know to pay the official fee, some of which is destined, maybe, for the city coffers. Elsewhere, parking spaces in front of shops and offices are leased to the neighbourhood gangs. The *tukang parkir*, who may or may not wear a uniform purchased from their local market, jealously guard their few spaces. If they have to leave their spot, they will 'rent' it out until they return.

After a while, you'll instinctively recognise who is what and may even develop a familiarity, a relationship, with whoever you pay to protect your wheels from the loss of a wing mirror, dents and gouges in the paintwork. Yes, they can turn nasty. They are known to menace drivers and pedestrians into complying with payment. They let the tyres down on a car if it's parked in one space for too long without prior arrangement. Stake your place with a few thousand rupiah. These guys make money as they go and if someone doesn't play the game, then *ma'af* (sorry), you'll have to pay a lot more at a *benkel* (garage) to fix the damage. But don't take this apparent vengefulness to heart; they are merely protecting their interests. Although it's never much—Rp 500–1,000 usually—to a *tukang parkir* it's everything. Think of a parking fee as an unconditional and possibly unofficial road tax.

They are expert at cramming an almost impossible number of mobiles into a minute space on a footpath, and stopping the traffic when you need to back out later. Their directing methods are quite ludicrous; "*kiri* (left), *kiri*, *kiri*, *kiri*, *kiri*, *terus* (straight on), *terus*, *terus*, *terus*, *terus*, *kanan* (right), *kanan*, *kanan*, *kanan*, *kiri*, *kiri*, *terus*, *terus*", and so on. Do they really have to do this? Can motorists in Jakarta really not cope with the pressures of unassisted car-parking? Or is it more a case of the common man finding something to do, of finding another way of making a few rupiah, of free-enterprise? Of course it is.

Why some people won't pay up however is clear. Many people see the amateur police as nothing more than an irritation—unbound *preman*, villains, thugs, herberts, yobs, wasters and kackers—the very cause of traffic jams if truth be told. It's unfair to lump the 'professional' *tukang pakir* in with the many masquerading scallywags.

These can be found often at the head of a very long line of traffic. They are supposedly there to help you ease your way into a bigger line of traffic. The best ones blow a whistle non-stop, shout the familiar street cries of *kiri*, *kanan*, *terus* (left, right, straight) as you enter or leave your allotted space and, like the worst ones, claim absolutely no responsibility if you get hit by or hit another vehicle.

That their mere presence could well be the cause of the traffic jams is neither here nor there, although where and why a particular jam occurs is always open to conjecture. If they are not wearing a 'uniform', they would run a mile at the sight of the real *polisi*. But ultimately, they do a worthwhile job. Imagine you want to go straight over an impossibly *macet* (jammed) crossroads. For a thousand rupiah, the amateur police will make a hole in the traffic for you. Off you can go to the next jam.

## REAL POLICE

Real *polisi* are plentiful in Jakarta. They wear brown uniforms, brown peaked hats and black leather boots. And on a white belt slung low around the potbellied waist, they carry a gun. The extreme tightness of Jakarta policemen's trousers has been the subject of much speculation among the city's populace. What goes on in there? Are they wearing protective underwear? Have they all been routinely 'pulled back and tucked in'? The debate rages. There are some women police

in the city, but not in the profusion that the tight-trousered male police are. They are usually limited to a bit of traffic directing and office work here and there.

Clearly, since all *polisi* are armed, you don't want to upset one, even if they don't look too threatening. The public at large seem to display a genuine fear of them. *Polisi* have the reputation, you see, for stopping people at random and making demands on them. Identification of some sorts is the usual request, and they have very definite ideas about which form of identification (ID) they want to see. For an Indonesian, only the KTP (*Kartu Tanda Penduduk*) is accepted. The KTP is an identity card every Indonesian is obliged to carry; it states name, age, address, religion, marital status and a fingerprint. ID cards are confiscated if the individual isn't carrying enough bribe money. For a foreigner, strictly speaking, it's the passport and KITAS (temporary residence permit) they want to see. Yet since most people do not habitually carry their passport, and since the police themselves are not totally sure what ID a foreigner should be carrying, they either dismiss you immediately or dither around for hours debating what to do you for.

*Polisi* are known to set-up 'routine' road blocks and to stop those cars whose drivers have probably broken some traffic regulation on that road sign hidden by an overgrown tree. A BMW or Kijang, there's really no difference. If you can afford four wheels, then you can afford a little *uang rokok* (cigarette money) to avoid a day wasted at a court in order to pay a fine in order to get your confiscated driving licence back. Assuming you have nothing to hide, there's no need to be unduly worried about being stopped. It happens from time to time, that's all. Just keep a largish banknote folded with your vehicle documents, which must be carried at all times.

There's a saying in Jakarta that the laws and regulations here are some of the best in the world, that every sector of society receives its fair and just protection. But with the big boys continuously ignoring these rules, the rest of the country is forced to play the game by example and bend every rule in the book. But then this free-for-all rule-bending might even be government policy. With so many seemingly contradicting rules to adhere to, it has become impossible for the individual to not do something 'illegal'. Therefore, the state has complete control over everyone, can legally arrest anyone at any time, and the police can legally shake-down anyone they want. That at least is how it might be seen.

Police are paid peanuts in Indonesia; just don't call them by the epithet *monyet* (monkey). It's in their interests then to supplement their income in order to survive. Bribes are a way of life for traffic police. Minor driving mishaps are quietly and efficiently cleared up with the acquisition of a small unofficial fee. Basically, the more serious the crime, the bigger the bribe. Corruption has eaten its way through the entire judicial system, from the police on the streets to Supreme Court judges. But never assume you can get away with anything. There are just as many judges and police with morals intact, particularly the younger members of the force who, educated and well aware of their country's reputation for legal jiggery-pokery, are keen to dispel this unsavoury image. Some don't accept bribes; some want promotion and are out to fight crime—nothing more.

## An Unwise Move

There is the example of a Westerner living in Jakarta who, one evening when drunk, ran down and killed a *sate* seller. Quite rightfully, the victim's family wanted the individual locked up for murder, or at the very least for manslaughter. They were prepared to drop the matter however, if he could pay a lump sum in compensation. Unwisely, the accused tried to bargain the price down with the family. This merely served to anger the family further, who went straight to the high court where the man was given three years, even though he'd paid the judge.

Another example, although on a lesser scale, concerns another foreigner who, in the early hours, was stopped and questioned as he stood waiting, or rather swaying, for a taxi. When the individual couldn't produce any satisfactory ID, the police (there were two) demanded the man show them where he lived. Very suspicious of this, the man elected to say absolutely nothing, and, aware of the reputation the police had, decided under no circumstance to make any payouts. When they arrived at his home, they began to get frustrated that the man still hadn't said anything, nor attempted to give them any money. They questioned the *bule* again; he said nothing. They shouted; still nothing. In the end they looked nonchalantly around the house, and began picking up various things which took their fancy; some tapes, magazines, cutlery. Then they left. So, if you happen to get lost in Jakarta, you know who, or who not to ask for directions.

## UMBRELLA BOYS

When it rains, out come the umbrella boys, who may well be street kids making the best from a wet opportunity. Demand is high for these young entrepreneurs, particularly at bus stations and outside the few shopping malls without attached multi-level parking. In a good hour or so, the generally maximum length of a tropical downpour, a pleasing wage is earned. Standard fees for the use of the *payung* vary depending how far you need to walk. However, you may be tempted to pay greater sums when you see how utterly soaked and pathetic the children look running along behind you. Some have quite impressive umbrellas; accommodating enough for a couple of people.

But this personalised service is not affordable for everyone, and most people take refuge under a tree or shop doorway while the *hujan* (rain) lasts. And don't be at all surprised to see street-sellers carrying on apparently unaffected by the rain, albeit with plastic bags on their heads.

## HAVING THINGS DONE

For the *orang kaya* (rich folk), the rising middle classes and the foreigners residing here, Indonesia is the land of service. Try as you might, you can't do things yourself—you have them done for you. Telephones are answered; washing is laundered; bread buttered. Taxis are *dipanggil* (flagged down); rats trapped; visitors dealt with; guests watered and errands run. About the only things you can't have done for you are the basic bodily functions of human existence—everything else you can have done by someone else. A life of doing things by proxy can have its drawbacks however; the things you have done are rarely done as exactly as they might if you had done them yourself. And when something is being done for you, quite often it wasn't really a job worth doing in the first place, and therefore not often a job done particularly well. *Bingung*? (confused?) You should be. Having a *pembantu* (servant) or two around your home simply increases the temptation to send them off doing things, while you sit back and try hard to do nothing. It's not difficult but highly questionable.

Since there are more rich people in Jakarta than any other place in the archipelago, so there are noticeably more people running errands and living on the edge of other people's lives. The Indonesian wing of the American's Women Association recommends you employ the following staff: a *pembantu perempuan* (housemaid). She will do your housework—cleaning, scrubbing, sweeping, rubbing, fetching, receiving, shopping, bill-paying and a million other little things. In fact, she will do so much that she has the next section to herself.

For heavier household tasks like painting and decorating, minor repairs and general household maintenance, a *pembantu laki-laki* (houseboy) should be employed. A *juru masak* cooks your meals, lays your tables and keeps the kitchen in order. Outside should stand a *penjaga* to guard your house day and night. A *tukang cuci* (laundress) takes care of the household washing and ironing. A *tukang kebun* (gardener) weeds the garden, maintains the pool and keeps the banana trees in shape. To drive you around, a reliable *sopir* (driver) should be hired. If you are impressed by a particular taxi driver, then you could try hiring him. If you have children, the services of a *pengasuh anak* (nanny) will be needed. They are sometimes known as 'Baby Sisters', but that's just a spelling mistake.

You might also consider employing, perhaps on a part-time basis, a bartender, a masseur, a nurse, a hairdresser and a personal tailor to make your life as totally passive as possible. In addition to an army of household staff with which to surround yourself with, the passing services of Jakarta's million other *tukang jualan* (street sellers) are more than glad to do business and assist in the passive process by parading varieties of everything imaginable past your front door.

When you do do things yourself, people regard you with a hint of suspicion. They might think you are being somewhat *pelit* (tight) with your *duit* (cash). The social pressures to conform to this passive style of existence are, therefore, enormous. And after all, it's only fair to share— doing something yourself deprives someone somewhere along the line of the prospect of a few extra rupiah. This is how the distribution of wealth works for the urban poor of Indonesia. Riches are filtered off left, right and centre in Indonesia. Some of it goes abroad, some of it is 'forgotten about' and never mentioned again, while some of it gets re-invested, and some of it doesn't. A bit, however, trickles its way down into the pockets of the masses. The small change of Indonesia's booming economy is Joe Public's bread and butter.

## PEMBANTU

For the Indonesian middle classes, *pembantu* are quite normal. For Western people, they take some getting

## Can't Live Without Them!

*Pembantu* are an unavoidable aspect of Jakartan life. Love them or hate them, try and hide from them, but there's no escaping them. Some might say 'servant' or 'maid', or even 'domestic manager', but these are misleading titles, and serve only to make the speaker sound more important than they probably are. *Pembantu* are literally 'helpers'. And 'help' they do—'help' being the very point of the job. They are there to do things for you. To run errands, to tidy houses, to cook, to pay bills and to do countless other little tasks you will forget how to do yourself. And all on the promise of an agreed amount of rupiah, and possibly board and lodging too. Shocking really.

used to. Many first-time visitors are highly uncomfortable at first with the idea of having their underwear scrubbed so cheaply, and so often. For the average *orang asing* (foreigner) it can be a profoundly confusing situation. To compensate, they might be reluctant to give their newly-appointed *pembantu* any task at all. Yet with the gentle coaxing and encouragement of an Indonesian friend, not to mention a little practice, they soon get the hang of telling people what to do. And so it goes from one extreme to another. The foreigner, now confident with the idea of a *pembantu*, begins to apply this same one-way confidence to other situations: in the taxi, at the shops, in restaurants, at work, in the street, in fact, everywhere in Indonesia. That the majority of Indonesians are such apparently uncomplaining folk only encourages some Westerners to treat everyone like a *pembantu*. And this is far more shocking.

Yet, there are two sides to every coin. From the *pembantu's* point of view, it isn't bad work. There are a lot dirtier jobs to be doing and besides, everyone has got to do something. As long as you are in work, you are making *uang* (money). And *uang* means security, not only for yourself but for the 20 or so extended tentacles of one's *kampung*. In a country with very little in the way of welfare, people are left to find work in any way they can. And work they do—even the servants have servants.

Get a good *pembantu* and you need never lift a finger again. Complacency comes dangerously easily in Jakarta. Indeed, once used to the idea of *pembantu,* it's hard to imagine life without them. They will absolutely run your life for you—if you want. Of course not all are good, certain

Jakarta families may change *pembantu* every other day, while others who hit it off with their employers will stay for years and years.

For the cunning *pembantu*, a foreign person staying in Jakarta makes an attractive employment prospect. Since a lot of Westerners are so bashful about giving someone instructions, the chances of having to do real *kerja keras* (hard work) are considerably less. And even then, the Western employer's guilt invariably pushes them to overpay their *pembantu*. It begins to make you wonder exactly who is being taken advantage of.

Should you ever find yourself in the position of having to hire a *pembantu*, it's worth making it clear exactly what you expect from them. The time they should start cooking, what exactly they should clean, which clothes you want or don't want washed, and how etc. If you don't, all manner of confusion can arise. They will invariably be living in with you and expecting a room and *mandi* (bathroom) in with the deal. It's quite possible to have a *pembantu* visit you every day or so but they usually demand higher wages.

Painful though it may be, it's better to spell out a *pembantu's* duties from the word go than have to cope with blushes and side-long glances later on. Your *pembantu* may simply be too *malu* (shy) to approach you for a job description. Your *pembantu* may be just simple. The best way of locating a reliable *pembantu* is probably by word of mouth. There are agencies which contract them out, yet the price is inevitably higher. Details can be found in *The Jakarta Post* or the Indonesian broadsheet *Kompas*.

The perfect *pembantu* is almost invisible, like air. You might just see her out of the corner of your eye. Dirty plates disappear, books jump back on shelves and guests get refreshed on arrival. The perfect *pembantu*

*Pembantu* are actually part of the problem in Jakarta. Every year, they return to their *kampung* for Idul Fitri at the end of Ramadhan. They turn up at the homes of family and friends dolled up in lipstick and fancy new clothes, gushing colourful tales from the Mother City. To their *teman-teman* (mates), Jakarta, and the subsequent promise of work, becomes such an appealing idea that half the *kampung* follow her back. Most happily accept any work they can get—good or bad. And if particularly bad, they just don't tell anyone.

is immaculately clean, an excellent cook, a proficient bargainer, a natural first-aider, a witch-doctor and resident game show host. On the other hand, you might end up thinking they are just a pain in the *pantat*, for after the initial stage of acceptance come feelings of wrath. The unceasing regime of picking everything up after you may quickly drive you nuts. So might their cooking and the way they always buy exactly the same things. And then there are her friends who come to visit and stare.

What eats away most at your soul, apart from the obvious lack of privacy, is the nagging feeling that somebody you don't really know is living in close-quarters with you. You suddenly realise you have been paying someone to do things for you, only they haven't been doing them exactly how you would have done them. And anyway, you wouldn't have minded doing things yourself; you were just being culturally sensitive. This is a bizarre situation. Remember the old story about the king being ruled by his own servants? And the other one about doing things yourself if you want them done properly?

A *pembantu* might be male or female, young or old, Javanese or Sundanese. She might be shy or she might be downright *cerewet* (talkative). She might watch telly with you, although she would prefer one of her own, so she can keep her distance. It would be dangerously unfair to paint a picture of the average *pembantu,* although the following account by a long-term expat is a familiar one.

"She's the first one up every morning. By the time you wake up, your house will have been tidied and your yard swept out. This is probably what woke you up—the scraping sound of her broom. Your breakfast will be underway and the subject of any shopping that needs doing that day will have been mentioned. Routines are important to a *pembantu*, to the point in fact of terrifying monotony. Tell her you like *tempeh* and you'll get *tempeh* every meal.

"Syam, who was Javanese and short, was a very hard-working woman, 24 years old, illiterate and apparently, after three years of saying nothing of the sort, married. It seems in order to get out of her marital obligations, she'd left her *kampung* years earlier and joined a *pembantu* agency in Jakarta. Every evening in her room she would dress up in her prayer-kit and start going over her prayer book until she wobbled herself to a peak. She was strong: when the banana trees blew over one night in a storm, Syam was the first one up and lugging the trunks out front for the rubbish collector.

"When the family moved to a more strategic, albeit noisier, area of town, Syam lasted a mere three weeks before the firecrackers and passing traffic drove her out. She left suddenly one weekend, appearing in the front room and blocking the TV with her suitcase, asking only that the lady of the house would inspect the contents of her luggage to confirm she wasn't lifting anything. She was free to go.

"Her departure was a shock and the house was thrown into turmoil. Requests for a replacement were put out and after much fretting, one was eventually promised for the following week. What a long way away that seemed; what a lot of food to be cooked; what a lot of dusting, scrubbing and washing that would mean.

"The result was a relative of a friend's *pembantu*, a woman from East Java called Sum, who was incredibly short, very friendly yet possibly a sandwich short of a picnic. At one time in the backyard, there stood a fine papaya tree with two almost-ripe fruit on board. One day, some workers in the house next door, had leaned over and swiped the two fruit. In her fury at this discovery, she hacked both trees to the ground to make sure no one would ever do it again.

"Sum meant well, that's for sure, but sometimes her dog-like approach to life got the better of her. On the day of her departure I gave her a lift to the bus station. I asked her when and why she'd ever come to Jakarta in the first place. 'To make some money' she replied. 'Well, have you?' I asked. 'No!' she laughed, 'but it doesn't matter.'"

## EVERYONE ELSE
Wherever you live, hotel, apartment, *kost* (boarding house) or rented house, you will develop relationships with your local

community. This is, of course, no different from elsewhere, but expect a whole range of different occupations.

Living at street level, you will come to recognise the many passing by, often by their distinctive cries. In rough chronological order, starting in the morning, there's the *koran* (newspaper) boy followed by the sellers of *bubur ayam* (chicken porridge), *sayur* (vegetable) and *roti* (bread). Through the day, you might get to meet the postman, the electricity meter reader, the pedal-powered children's ride, vacuum cleaner demonstrators and others selling stuff that ranges from plastic furniture and bedding, to brooms and brushes. Not forgetting the shoe repairer, knife sharpener, disposable lighter refiller, the potted plant hawkers and scavengers.

Daytime food ranges from *gorengan* (fried *pisang*— bananas, *ubi*—sweet potato, *tempeh* and *tahu*—soya bean cake and curd) to *bakso* (meatballs) and regional foods too numerous to list here. Then, there are whichever fruits which are in season.

The evening is the domain of other food sellers starting with the return of the morning's bread sellers on their converted *becaks* (pedicabs). Then there is *sate* (grilled skewered meat, chicken or goat), *nasi goreng* (fried rice) and *martabak* (filled pancake).

Drinks could be milk, *yakult* (a yoghurt drink), *bandrek* (a hot ginger drink with bits of bread and other stuff in), *es cendol* (bits of jelly made from rice gelatin in coconut milk with Javanese brown palm sugar syrup), or *es cincau* (a slime-like jelly made from herb grass, sweet, mixed with syrup and shaved ice).

And if you 'book' her, there's the *jamu* lady offering her medicinal drinks for all your aches and pains, including *masuk angin* (wind coming in) and *panas dalam* (hot insides).

In fact, if you can run your business from home, there's really no need to leave it, except for those annoying visa runs. Everybody will come to you. However, if you live in an apartment, you won't meet many people so you probably don't need this book.

# WHAT MAKES A JAKARTAN A JAKARTAN
## Mosques

With Islam the dominant religion in Indonesia, you will find that mosques are not in short supply. If you don't see a mosque—or *mesjid*—you are sure to hear one. Size need not be a drawback in the construction of a *mesjid*, since it is popular to equip one with powerful and outstanding loudspeakers to help distinguish it from the neighbouring *kampung's*.

A small *mesjid* is known as a *musholla*. This could be either part of a larger building, a room set aside in an office or a building in its own right. Uproar will follow if it becomes known that a newly constructed building is *musholla*-less. This might be hard for Westerners to get their heads round—people in uproar because there is nowhere to pray. In the West, there's significantly less pressure on people to be so outwardly religious. In Indonesia, it is in the national constitution.

Every respectable neighbourhood is incomplete without its own *mesjid* and its importance to a local community is reflected in the hundreds of streets and alleys named Jalan Mesjid (Mosque Street) or Gang Mesjid (Mosque Alley). Its the centre of the community: a focal point, a common ground—the centre of life for Muslims in Jakarta. You meet your neighbours there, make friends there, spread rumours there, and you can sleep there if you need to. Friday prayers between 12:00 and 2:00 pm are exclusively male and one session which shouldn't be missed if you are a male Muslim. Expect to find the streets outside blocked for half an hour or so on these occasions because a *musholla* will not suffice on a Friday.

In the heart of the *kampung*, away from the big, mad roads but never too far from the traffic, Islam is practised by the people. Aside from the five daily prayers and the special prayers on the many of Islam-respecting public holidays, there are amplified speeches and sermons by 'special guests' from the world of Indonesian Islam.

To the expert eye, Indonesia's mosques are uniquely different to those in the rest of the world. They reflect its various

Islam came to Indonesia through the Muslim traders from Gujarat, India, who disseminated the teachings actively through trading and intermarriage with local women. In Java, for instance, they disseminated their teachings through *wayang kulit* (shadow puppet) shows which had its origins in Hindu culture.

cultures and the historical, social and even political conditions of the period in which they were built. Invariably tower-less, they depend in the cities on the afore-mentioned speakers to summon the faithful to prayer and, in the remoter parts of the country, on drums.

Early mosques blended Islam, Hindu and Chinese architectural styles. The roofs, for example, varied from flat tiers to tiered domes to flat domes. The main gates were decorated richly with Chinese or Hindu architectural elements. Architecture was also adjusted to the environment. In the 17th and 18th centuries, mosques in Jakarta were built beside rivers, areas which functioned as the city's business centres. They functioned as places of worship and for *ulamas* (leaders), traders and local people to meet.

The city administration has taken steps to preserve some old mosques which have witnessed the social, political and economic life of an earlier period, but many others are having to make way for new projects.

The Luar Batang Mosque was built in 1739 near Sunda Kelapa Harbour in North Jakarta. This two-storey mosque blends traditional Javanese and Hindu architecture. The main gate is decorated with reliefs similar to carvings on Javanese Hindu temples.

Tubagus Angke Mosque, now called Alanwar Mosque, is in Jalan Pangeran Tubagus Angke, to the west of Glodok and Kota railway station. The area was known originally as Kampung Bali and was established in 1687. The street is named after Prince Tubagus Angke, who came from the Banten Sultanate in West Java and was the ruler of Jayakarta (old Jakarta) in the 16th century.

The mosque was built in 1761 by a Chinese architect. It has been renovated several times, but its original structure remains unchanged. Its front steps, double-winged door, carved fanlight and door frame and the stone vase on top of the roof are typical Dutch elements.

The Annawir Mosque—the name means 'light'—is in Jalan Pekojan, West Jakarta, and was commissioned by a Sayid, a descendant of Prophet Muhammad through his daughter Fatimah. It was built by Abdullah bin Hussein Alaydrus in 1760.

Kebon Jeruk Mosque, in Jalan Hayam Wuruk in the downtown area, is a sacred place for the Chinese Muslims living in old Jakarta. Its architecture is a rich mixture of Indonesian, Arabic and Chinese elements.

One of the largest mosques in Southeast Asia, Mesjid Istiqlal, in Lapangan Banteng near Gambir station, can accommodate more than 10,000 people and 800 vehicles. It comprises five levels, and its walls, walkways and floors are almost entirely covered with marble from Tulungagung, East Java. This extravagantly beautiful mosque sits on nine and a half hectares of land. Ironically, President Sukarno chose a Christian architect, Frederick Silaban, to design it. Construction lasted from 1961–1967, but its official opening did not occur until 1978.

Another architecturally appealing mosque is Mesjid Al-Azhar. Set back from the main road just outside Blok M, it sports an uncharacteristic central calling tower—or

The Al-Azhar mosque in Kebayoran Baru. The mosque is an important fixture in the lives of most Muslims in Indonesia.

*menara*—only slightly less impressive than the tower of the five-tier roofed mosque at Banten.

One radical departure from traditional mosque designs is the futuristic Mesjid Pondok Indah, just left of the mall. It features a large flat blue-tiled roof over an open-plan bungalow-style building.

Ask first if you want to enter a mosque, wear trousers and remove your shoes. Ladies, cover your arms and legs, wear a headscarf and don't enter at all if you are menstruating.

## Rubber Time

You will learn the meaning of *kesabaran* (patience) in Indonesia. You certainly won't last very long if you don't. Indonesians have a view of time and space that is quite different to, say, that of the manufacturers of Rolex watches. They call it *jam karet*, or rubber time. It's a useful concept to learn. It has to do with shrugging off impossible delays, foul-ups and ceaseless corruption and it means never expecting too much. It means giving an extra few days leeway on every appointment made. Business meetings can seem directionless, even futile. The widespread practice of one-to-one dealings, with the all-encompassing method of face-saving etiquette, will test the very limits of those who want their results NOW! Things just don't happen this way—things are never late in Indonesia because everything is always late. Indonesians are people of almost infinite patience. But wear it out and watch out.

## Humour

Fear not, Indonesians have an excellent sense of humour. Indeed, to cope with living in a place like Jakarta, they would need to. But what exactly makes them laugh? Bananas? Not particularly. At least not the eternal one about slipping over on the skin of one. People might make jokes about its similarity to a *titit* (willy), so be careful eating one in public. And while an Indonesian man may be easily impressed by a woman's papaya, and the Betawi are fond of eating a cake they know affectionately as *kue tetek* (tit-cake), food is not generally something to laugh about.

Because sex is something which can't be talked about in an open and frank way, its only outlet is as something to be sniggered about. There is an overall sense of lacking and

Rude (or *jorok*) jokes are the most popular in Jakarta, the focus of the punchline being usually a not-so-subtle swipe at a man's trouser-facilities or a woman's personal hygiene.

insecurity running through many of the rude jokes heard around Indonesia. They invariably concern a local woman's 'difficulty' at coping sexually with a man of Arabic origin, for example, or of local men being somehow required to get out and compare themselves. Those old chestnuts.

The self-conscious theme of inadequacy is continued in the startling lack of *lelucon bodoh*, or jokes about stupidity. People are all too aware that their country is still somewhat behind in the international stakes. True, not as behind as some countries (and it has certainly done a lot of catching up), yet a sentiment of inadequacy persists which, quite clearly, is no laughing matter. But examples do crop up: a reluctant young woman asks her insistent boyfriend: "Tell me why you think I can't possibly marry you?" "I can't think," says the young man. "That's exactly why," says the girl. Ho ho.

There's limited political humour in Indonesia, hardly any ripping satire and no teasing ridicule of the authorities—not on primetime TV anyway. But some social comment is tolerated. In the newspaper *Kompas* is the long-suffering character Om Pak Si Kom. A cartoon of the 'average' Indonesian, he is uncomplicated and perpetually *bingung* (perplexed) at the rapid changes his country is undergoing. He represents the common man and speaks as only the common man can. In Om Pak Si Kom, we are given a rare glimpse of the Indonesian sense of irony. But then this is to be probably expected from this most 'intellectual' of publications in a country where the average man is still a semi-literate rice farmer or *bajaj* driver. On a more 'custard-pie' level of humour is the daily tabloid *Pos Kota,* which is composed almost entirely of cartoon strips, jokes, second-hand car adverts and sensational news stories.

Indonesians are frankly amazed when they see Westerners taking the mickey so mercilessly out of their leaders and 'respected' persons. Yet rarely do they question their own forbidden fruit, that is, the chance to speak their own mind for once. Instead, Indonesians make fun of themselves. They make fun of the regional stereotypes of Indonesia: that Batak people always manage to lift your wallet, and that the Javanese can't stop smiling, no matter how depressed they feel. This is depicted in immensely popular TV shows when entire households gather round the box and roar at the one who bears the closest resemblance to themselves. Everyday Jakartan life is oversimplified to the point of ridicule on these shows. *Tukang parkir* (free-form parking assistants) are the stereotype, slow-smiling Javanese: "*terus, terus, terus*" (straight on) he says ever so slowly as the car backs onto his foot, "*setop, setop, setop*" (stop) is his slow-smiling response.

Acronyms are an area where wordplay becomes the joke. For some reason, Indonesians love to make shorter versions of their language. Real *singkatan* (acronyms) are a standard part of the language, particularly with official titles and names. *Jabotabek*, for example, is the name given to greater Jakarta, the areas comprising central Jakarta, Bogor, Tangerang and Bekasi. *Polri* is another 'real' acronym, the one for the police force, and taken from the longer title, *Polisi Republik Indonesia*. Sometimes, however, a real word is made into a comedy acronym: *semampai* is a word meaning tall and elegant, but say it like an acronym and it means *semeter nggak sampai* (not even a metre tall). The word for pretty, *cantik*, becomes *cabo antik* (aging prostitute). Two words for difficult are *sukar* which becomes *susu mekar* (big breasts) and *sulit* which becomes *susu alit* (small breasts). *Kondom* becomes *konsultan domestik*, which you'll have to work out for yourselves. The joke may well be on you if an Indonesian asks "*Kamu orang penting*?" (Are you an important person?) They might just be using the comedy acronym of *penting—pendek dan keriting* (short and curly). Ha ha.

## Group Thinking

In an expatriate's dissatisfaction with life in Jakarta, the apparent 'incompetence' and lack of initiative of their local counterparts seem to be common factors. On a bad day, there'll be no limit to the number of times a seemingly straight-forward request will remain unfulfilled with no explanation beyond '*tidak bisa*' (can't) or '*nggak tahu*' (don't know). It's all too easy for someone coming to Indonesia from a developed country to use the word 'stupid'. All too easy and all too wrong.

With a population of over 210 million, there's bound to be more of everything—and that includes people without much in the way of formal education. The state ideology, *Pancasila,* remains, though with a generally more liberal interpretation. The official line is still that every God-fearing individual has the right to an education. The reality is that most cannot afford to continue studying to any level higher than primary and junior high, and that is because the government subsidises the education up to the age of 15. The only children who have the chance of a well-paid career are those of the well-off who graduate from senior high and then fit in three or four years of a university education. And since most people in Indonesia can't afford this, the nation's streets are filling up with scores of semi-educated people— too good for rice-farming but not quite good enough for office work. Besides, there aren't enough jobs for university graduates either.

Children in Indonesian schools do not ask why. All that's required is the ability to accept everything and question nothing. After all, there are exams to pass and anyway, for the average child of a middle-class, outwardly religious family, there's simply no time to be an individual. The days are swallowed up in a tightly-woven network of social, sports and religious activities.

Until recently, this unquestioning mode of acceptance was a feature of the three decades of relative stability that defined Suharto's presidency. Today's parents and teachers were 'brainwashed' to accept their 'guided democracy' so most are not yet adept at challenging pre-conceptions or being creative

> "The failure was that we succeeded gloriously to gain freedom for this country, but we have failed to free the Indonesian men and women as individuals."
> —Mochtar Lubis, writer

thinkers. Mochtar Lubis, for example, was one of those thinker-writers who were jailed by the Suharto regime.

Freedom of speech is therefore still an alien concept for a lot of people. Any decisions that need to be made are reached on the basis of mutual consensus, or *gotong-royong*. Rarely do people volunteer an individual opinion, much preferring to go with the flow than redirect it. Being in a group equals safety and freedom, i.e. no one is responsible if everyone is responsible, as any individual actions are as part of the group action.

Or inaction. At a social occasion, nobody wants to be the first to start: 'After you. No, after you.' This is island thinking: democratic, in its loosest definition, and collective. For the most part, Indonesians find it easier to share-alike than fight for what they want, or what they think they want.

Yet if you are not in their social group, do not expect them to respect anyone else's personal space. They push their way into elevators before others have stepped out. They will amble along the few sidewalks three abreast thus denying anyone the freedom to get by. They will stand talking on their handphones at the top and bottom of escalators. They will jump to the head of a queue, if there is one. If there isn't one, say in a bank, then expect them to stand beside you, as you deposit or withdraw your life's savings.

This isn't to say that Indonesia doesn't produce its own thinkers, philosophers and artists—of course it does, but there are so few who get the chance, let alone are prepared to relish it. Everything is against someone exercising their free will in Indonesia. The dominant religions in the land teach that beyond God's, and His preachers, there is no other will. All is pre-ordained.

## Superstitions

It's almost an understatement to say that Indonesians are superstitious. In almost any situation, the immediate reaction is a superstitious one. When Westerners fall ill, they are treated to the logical facts of the matter. When an Indonesian falls prey to bad health, it's a curse, a punishment for something done wrong somewhere along the line. This is why a visit to the doctor is so unsatisfying for many Indonesians, and why, as back up, more traditional forms of diagnosis are preserved. People need to know why they are sick and what it means. Far greater peace of mind is had by a visit to a *dukun*—the local witch-doctor, clever-feller and resident medicine man—than is had by a visit to a prescription-happy doctor.

Few aspects of Indonesian life are untouched by superstition. Even in Jakarta, modern as it is, superstitions prevail. Prayers and sacrifices, for example, are routinely made before any construction work begins on a building site. In Jakarta, you can even get your car fixed with the help of the spirit world. *Ketok* magic is a fine example of superstition being taken advantage of commercially. This is a network of workshops wherein your dented car can be returned to its near pristine condition by the laying on of hands, a motor massage as it were. You bring your damaged car along to the garage, where it remains locked up overnight safeguarded from prying eyes by a corrugated iron fence. Once the appropriate prayers have been said and the magic sounds of '*ketok, ketok*' been made, come morning, assuming no one has peeked in and broken the spell, the car will have been 'cured'.

Certain animals are to be avoided by the superstitious of Indonesia. One particularly ominous symbol of impending death is the body of a crow on your doorstep. Such a grim discovery would be ominous anywhere, and in Indonesia it means someone nearby is going to die very soon. If, upon arrival at some long-weekend destination, someone is greeted by a crow's corpse, they are advised to drive home very carefully and go straight back to bed.

The conflict in the lives of Indonesians is that they want to believe that it really is just cold, hard logic that gets the car fixed—they just can't help themselves. Once their superstitions have been aroused, they give in every time. Part of the problem of demanding an overall reformation of the Indonesian system is that politics are so tied up in superstition. The former President Suharto was said to have presided over the country like a mystical Javanese king, impervious and imperial and beyond the grasp of ordinary people. To have questioned his position or his decision-making was, for most people, too much like tempting fate. That was until a distinctly less superstitious younger generation clubbed together to demand his resignation.

## Ghostly Encounter

Take extra caution on Thursday nights—the Javanese believe it's the night in the week when all the ghosts are out and about.

Hitting and running over a cat is not something to be shrugged off either; the vehicle should be properly washed and blessed before continuing, and the cat's body laid aside. But the vehicle's karma will have been seriously tainted by this catastrophe and people have been known to sell a car purely on these grounds.

Fatal mishaps aside, more bad luck, but not that bad, is had when a tormented *cicak* (lizard) jumps on you: all the more reason not to tease them.

A single butterfly floating into your house, however, merely signals a guest's imminent arrival.

Black cats are symbolic the world over, but here the myth is that a dead person can be brought back to life if jumped over by a black cat. But don't die on a Monday, you will only be obliged to take someone else down with you.

When sleeping, try not to dream about losing your teeth—it means you are going to lose someone close to you. Upper teeth indicate an older relative, lower, a younger one.

If single people dream about snakes, marriage may soon be on the cards. Only bad luck, however, follows the woman who dreams she's wearing her wedding clothes. The apparently unwholesome dream of *e'ek* (poo-poo) is an indication of forthcoming wealth; the more poo-poo, the more *uang* (money) there'll be. And don't suddenly wake someone from their sleep, give their soul time to return to its body first.

When taking a photo, try to avoid framing three subjects in your picture; the middle one is doomed to die soon after. Take precautions if wearing red and green together. Take extra care wearing green in the water, especially along Java's south coast—it is rumoured to bring untold misfortune.

Be careful around the house. Spend too long in your doorway after dark and you'll unwittingly invite the neighbourhood ghouls to come in and mess with your well-being. Houses shouldn't be moved into until someone *yang bisa lihat hantu* (who can 'see' ghosts) has first checked the place over for troublemakers. In Bali, they wait for the *cicak* (lizards) and other *binatang kecil* (little creatures) to move in before humans take up residence. Once settled, you can take preventative measure against rain by chucking a pair of black trousers up on the roof.

Single women sweeping the floor are advised to make a decent job of it, or else they are destined to end up with a scruffy husband. And the giving of handkerchiefs between lovers is a no-no, spelling a swift end to the relationship.

If you hear dogs or *burung hantu* (owls) after dark, they have probably been startled by something you can't see, something from another world. Perhaps they can see the *kuntilanak*, a grim-looking character in black who snatches newborn babies away.

Oh, and ladies, don't eat a pair of bananas unless you want to have twins.

# FITTING INTO SOCIETY

## CHAPTER 4

'It is a mistake to expect good work from
expatriates for it is not what they do
that matters but what they are not doing.'
—Cyril Connolly

## FAUX PAS AND HOW TO ALMOST
## AVOID THEM

Indonesians are extremely tolerant people and are happy to forgive almost any blunder on the part of the foreigner. In the most polite circles, people strive their utmost to maintain a harmonious atmosphere, whatever calamity may occur. A sign of properly maintained self-control is that an Indonesian is adept at not upsetting others. The greatest importance is placed on preserving a delicate social decorum in which no one is in any way made to feel *malu* (embarrassed), even if this means individual opinions going unsaid.

Contradicting someone, for example, is bad form in Indonesia. When challenged, many people may automatically agree with you when, in truth, they may actually disagree. Confusing? The emphasis is placed on being wary of your own impulses, retaining self-control and doing your best to fit into the 'whole'—as opposed to living life as a 'loose unit' and actually speaking your mind. Even in the thinking Indonesian's Jakarta, this is still true although less so. Western-style concerns get more priority these days as the consumer mentality spreads and age-old traditions of mutual respect are traded for more blunt, outspoken manners.

This said, there are still certain things guaranteed to annoy an Indonesian person. One of them is moaning about Indonesia. They'll wonder why you bothered coming in the first place if all you can do is complain. Why are you here if it's so much better where you come from?

You must be careful what you do with your hands in Indonesia as mistakes are easily made. The left hand is the biggest no-no. Giving and receiving with the left hand makes the average person very uncomfortable, as this particular appendage is reserved predominantly for bum-cleaning. If you get your lefts and rights mixed up, you should give and receive with both hands to be on the safe side. In rural areas and some of the more humble households in Jakarta, the use of knives and forks has yet to be perfected; direct hand-to-mouth methods are still much in preference, with the right hand of course.

Be prepared to shake hands a lot in Indonesia. When you are first introduced to someone, you might notice them touching their heart after shaking your hand. Arrive at a social affair and you should shake hands with everyone there, not just the people you know, although exactly where you draw the line is unclear. Go to a wedding if you want to practise hand-shaking. Beware, however, of the rude-finger handshake. This mainly occurs upon the introduction of pretty females to excited young males, and involves the shaker's middle finger giving the palm of the other a little tickle.

Putting hands on hips superman-style, which could be considered by some a rather camp pose to strike, is a sure sign that you are *angkuh* (arrogant), if not a bit *marah* (angry). Sticking your thumb out from between your first two fingers is arguably the rudest thing you can do with your hands in Indonesia, as symbolic, perhaps, as the now worldwide misuse of the raised middle finger or the British two-finger salute. A fine example of this suggestive fist, for those who want to practise it (or indeed enhance their own fertility, as the superstition has it), is found on the bottom end of a huge bronze cannon known as Si Jagur (which translates as something like 'Old Sturdy') in Taman Fatahillah, north Jakarta.

Pointing is also considered rude, although acceptable if done with the thumb or the whole hand. Beckoning people with a crooked finger or upturned hand is another shock to etiquette. If possible, beckon people and oncoming traffic with a downward movement of the hand. Finally, since the head is considered the very 'seat of the soul' and therefore special, children-patting is something to be avoided. You get used to it.

One of the problems for an unsuspecting Westerner coming to Indonesia is that such apparently unassuming body language routinely goes unmentioned by those offended. That is to say, Indonesians don't tell you when you make a social error. They probably just smile and say "*tidak apa apa*" (it doesn't matter).

And remember that a smile is not necessarily just a smile in Indonesia. Smiling is used by Indonesians to mask all manner of social embarrassment and confusion. Smiles mean other things. If someone doesn't understand you, they will probably just smile. If someone feels uncomfortable with something you are doing or saying, they will also probably just smile. For the Indonesian, negative and aggressive emotions are dispelled by the wearing of a smile. Inform someone of bad news, or go to a shop to complain and expect the immediate reaction to be a smile. Smiling is a way of softening the blow.

Another way to mask the unpleasant truth is with a highly improbable story or excuse. The reason, for example, why someone lost their job might have been because he didn't eat enough rice—things like that. No one really expects to believe these stories but they do serve their purpose and take the edge off. When an unpleasant truth must be told, it's imparted on a one-to-one basis, preferably behind a closed door.

Perhaps the single most confusing aspect of Indonesian etiquette is the reluctance to say no. Rather than displease you with what might be the unpleasant truth, Indonesians go to scrupulous lengths to maintain the harmony. If one person is offended, everyone is offended. Instead, people say what they think the other person wants to hear, without necessarily being considered a liar. This is a real drawback when asking for directions somewhere. The closest many get to saying no is '*mungkin*' (maybe). The sentiment is sincere enough, but since many Westerners' frustration levels are not equipped for such widespread indirectness, the result can sometimes be nothing less than pure frustration.

In any group, the one person who mustn't be upset is the eldest male present—everything will be done to keep him happy. In *bahasa Indonesia*, there is an expression for it: '*asal bapak senang*' (whatever keeps the boss happy, or something similar). This idea runs the gauntlet of life in Indonesia, from the *kampung* to the skyscraper. For a visiting businessman who just wants to know a company's turnover, it's a real headache. Is this the truth he's hearing or is it what his younger Indonesian partner hopes he would like to hear?

There are a number of things Indonesians do that foreigners might find offensive. Belching after your food, for example, is perfectly okay—proof indeed that you are in healthy, functioning condition. Breaking wind remains, as ever, a universal no-no. Spitting, on the other hand, seems at times to be almost a national pastime. Blowing your nose into a handkerchief is socially offensive, and should be done in private. People will spend the day sniffing if need be rather than blow their nose in public. Regardless of this, it is still alarming common to see people clearing their sinuses by putting a finger over a nostril and blowing hard. Nose-picking is generally an accepted habit. People are offended if it's done too vigorously, but the odd nasal-rummage is nothing to be ashamed of. Tongues are not to be shown:

when affixing postage stamps to a letter, use glue. Most Indonesians would be horrified at having to lick something like that—like a dog.

During a conversation, it's okay to ask seemingly personal questions and make apparently personal comments. Asking if you have washed yet is a standard question, as is asking a complete stranger why, for instance, she has only got one child. When you haven't seen someone in a while, it's acceptable to comment on their physical appearance: "you look fat" or "you look old", without being considered especially rude. Amongst themselves, in the safety of the group, Indonesians are free to make cruel and teasing remarks about one another. This isn't meant to upset anyone, but anyone who is weak enough to bite the bait is clearly lacking in self-control.

When engrossed in the conversation of a crowd on the move, a lot of Indonesians seem to not look where they are walking. People are consequently forever bumping into one another, crossing streets without apparent care, and blocking stairs and escalators. To test this theory, stand in the middle of a Jakarta pavement and see how many people shuffle up to you in a snail's pace, heads turned to one side, only to jump out of their skin upon impact. And don't get angry when a door gets shut in your face, as holding them open for the person behind you is not standard etiquette either.

When you get invited to someone's home, there are all sorts of social blunders to avoid. Ideally, you should remove your shoes upon entering a home, and although many Jakartans are quite prepared to forego this tradition, you should still go through the motions until told otherwise. If you do get to keep your shoes on, try your best not to let anyone see the soles of your shoes. Your host will invariably show you to a room before promptly disappearing for what seems like ages. More than likely you will be given a drink in the interim: hot water, an intensely sweet syrup drink or tea. Indonesians always wait for their host to say "*silakan*" (please, go ahead) before drinking. It's quite acceptable, mind you, to not even touch your drink, whereas finishing it all off in one go indicates a need for more. The compromise is to leave the glass half-full. In polite circles and formal meetings, hot coffee will be served to indicate the conclusion of the meeting. By the time it's cool enough to drink, it's time to go. If you do get to eat, then be sure not to leave your spoon face down on the *piring* (plate), not unless you hope to get some more, for this is what will happen.

To add to the overall awkwardness of being a *bule* (a white person but literally 'albino') in Indonesia, you might find people you thought you didn't know very well giving you little gifts for no apparent reason. Presents are not restricted only to birthdays and the like and are given out with far greater frivolity than you may be used to. Return from a weekend away and you are expected to produce an *oleh-oleh* (knick knack) of some sort, just something small: an extra mango or two, a little snack perhaps. It's all part of Indonesia's complex system of sharing-alike, and it is, after all, the thought that counts. When given a present, it should be opened in private, as it's impolite to expect people to open them in front of you. The Indonesian way is invariably to just smile and nod when they want to say thank you for something, so don't think them rude because you blinked and missed it.

Indonesians are polite people—let it be said. Everyone counts and no one is made to feel left out.

### Indonesian Friendliness

One expatriate in Jakarta recalls how he'd tried to make a discreet exit from a meeting he'd been invited to. He decided to whisper a fabricated excuse in the secretary's ear about it being his birthday and him having an appointment to keep. The woman passed a note to the chairman of the meeting who, upon reading it, stopped the meeting in mid-flow and made everyone there sing 'Happy Birthday' to him three times. After shaking hands with all 50 people, the man was free to leave. And he had only been attending out of politeness.

But it's not all good. Sometimes the 'sharing-alike' turns to pure selfishness, such is the Indonesian's expectation that 'it's only fair to share'. The stories to back this suggestion are limitless.

In Indonesian society, a single working person living at home is expected to make their bank account details public. Their salary is not necessarily theirs alone to keep. Put a communal dish of food out with the proviso 'help yourself' and see everyone's inherent refinement disappear in a flash as they fight to fill their pockets.

## Taking For Granted

One such story has a semi-permanent foreigner in Jakarta expecting a package from home, which was to include a packet of her favourite cigarettes. The package arrived eventually but when she opened it, she was surprised to find only three of the original 20 cigarettes had made it through the post. It seems the remaining three had been sent on as a goodwill gesture; the rest meanwhile had been fairly and squarely shared out.

The system of titles is an aspect of Indonesian etiquette which foreigners easily get wrong. Depending on who is talking to whom, how old the person is and where he or she comes from, different words, titles and expressions must be employed. A younger person forced to cross the path of an elder is supposed to 'dip' one shoulder. In Jakarta, only the *pembantu* (servants) do this; the average Jakartan is far too hip for such behaviour.

## TITLES OF RESPECT

In Indonesia, age is widely respected. Theoretically, the older a person, the more respect they command. This is revealed in the different forms of address reserved for different folks.

There are, for example, at least three ways of saying 'you', depending on whom you are addressing. *Anda* is the most polite form, used between polite strangers as well as in formal writing, advertising and poetry, and the form to use if you are confused as to which form is appropriate. *Kamu* is a more casual term, used between familiar friends and family. Then there is *kau*, reserved by parents for *anak-anak* (children) and used between gushing young lovers. In Jakarta, they say *loe* (pronounced as 'loo'), but only between good *teman-teman* (friends). A middle-aged man you don't know very well should be called *bapak*, or more commonly, *pak*. Mature women are *ibu*, often shortened to '*bu*, and younger ladies *mbak*. Younger men can be referred to as *mas*, although strictly speaking it's a term used in Javanese. These will be the titles that are tagged at the beginning or end of every statement, in much the same way that schoolkids tag a 'sir' on the end of everything. But don't get muddled: it's respect for age, not authority.

---

**Importance of Address**

As Jakarta adopts more and more Western attitudes with every passing year, this system of titles is wavering slightly. But still it remains the definite way to address people in Indonesia. It may take some getting used to, but for the sake of gaining the respect of those around you, as well as for your own self-respect, it's an approach worth mastering. In general, Indonesian conversation begins in a highly formal way and gradually becomes more informal as the talk progresses. Nicely nicely, politely does it.

---

Within the family, *ibu* and *bapak* are how children say 'mum' and 'dad', but the regional diversity of Jakarta's populace means a million other varieties exist. Modern Jakartan families might just as easily use mummy and daddy, as opposed to more traditional forms like mama and papa, *ayah* and *ibunda* or *mami* and *papi*. Betawi children (those native to Jakarta), however, might say *enyak* and *babe*.

In Javanese families, of which an awful lot of Jakartans are somewhere linked to in origin, Grandma is *nenek* and her man *kakek*. Their grandchildren will be *cucu*. Younger brothers and sisters are *adik* while older ones are *kakak*. Their cousins, meanwhile, are *sepupu* and their nephews and nieces *keponakan*. The Dutch introduced *om* to the language, which means 'uncle' and is widely used by children for all men, family and non-family alike. *Tante* (aunt) is of similar origin.

Another way of maintaining *kehormatan* (respect) is by speaking to people as if they were not there. Speaking in the third person is an affectionately polite, almost cloying, way of talking. It gets confusing: (speaking to you) "Would Derek like a drink?", "Does Derek like rice?" Your immediate reaction is to look about the room to see if there's someone else there called Derek. Or Terry.

But at the end of the day, all white people are known as 'mister'—women too—and this too can become annoying.

## MARRIAGE

Marriage is still a high ideal in Indonesia. It used to be that if a woman wasn't married by the time she was 30 years old, something was assumed to be wrong with her, although this sentiment is fading as more Indonesian women become financially independent. However, perhaps because of religious ideals, or perhaps because there are more women than men in Indonesia, there's still considerable pressure on single women to get married. And anyway, everyone expects to get married at some point.

In Jakarta, even if you only mix with a few people and don't stay very long, you are bound to be invited to a wedding sooner or later. There always seems to be one about to happen although, as in many countries, there are 'seasons'. For Indonesian Muslims, it's in the six weeks following Idul Fitri and before the Day of Sacrifice, Idul Adha.

Indonesian weddings are generally not as extravagant as in the last days of the Suharto era. In fact, since he 'abdicated', the most ostentatious and commented on was the wedding of one of his grandchildren. However, parents will still get into debt in order to give their children a good send off, even if the happy couple stay in the parental home. Low-key weddings don't really happen, not unless the bride is eight months gone.

Depending on the religion and ethnic background of the couple, there will be three or four parts to the ceremony spread, quite feasibly over two days or even a week, depending on finances. Only close family are invited to the initial ceremony; the reception is where everyone else gathers. The family is an all important part of any wedding. It's said that when you get married in Indonesia, you don't marry an individual—you marry an entire family. The size and splendour of the reception are a direct reflection of the bride's father's intentions. It's a chance for him to impress his long-standing colleagues once and for all, and invite people he would normally be reluctant to approach. The newlyweds themselves are almost dispensable.

The importance of attending weddings in Indonesia is immense. Just as some businessmen establish feelings of mutual trust over a round of golf or a session in the sauna, so relations are improved 100 per cent by attending a wedding, no matter how brief the appearance.

The bride's family is expected to foot the bill. This may involve hiring a *gamelan* orchestra, hiring costumes for several dozen people, hiring a reception hall, transport, a maitre d' to give a running commentary of events, and two large ice-sculptures of the couple's initials, which by the end will have melted into one. And of course, tons of food.

If it's a Muslim wedding, the groom should attempt to prove to his bride's family that he can provide financially for his wife-to-be. This he achieves by presenting *emas* (gold), aside from a ring (which is worn on the right hand in Indonesia), and numerous other gifts during the ceremony.

At more or less the appointed hour, the couple walk in, followed by their immediate families. They make their way slowly to the stage, where they will remain for the duration. When the initial entrance procession is complete, a receiving line is formed so guests can begin shaking hands with the couple. Throughout the reception, the bride and groom are on stage, all tucked-in and painted, as the guests file past to *kasih salam* (congratulate) and say either "*selamat menempuh hidup baru*" (all the best for your new life together) or "*selamat bahagia*" (wishing you happiness). Expect lengthy electronically amplified speeches from various family members which may well go on for hours.

As a guest, you are expected to give a gift of some sort. The usual 'bottom drawer' a just-married couple requires is welcome, although increasingly money is the preferred gift. Guests are given a small souvenir of the wedding such as a pair of ceramic miniature shoes inscribed with the couple's names.

Don't be too surprised if you wake up on a Saturday morning to find the traffic being held up by a wedding procession moving from *mesjid* to reception. Don't be too surprised either to find you can't drive down your street because the neighbours have built a stage in the middle and filled the road with chairs. Quite often, a mini-marquee is erected, stretched from one house to another, blocking

The typical Indonesian wedding where the couple sit on the *dais,* primed and ready to received blessings from their guests.

the street completely. To add to the frenzy, a *dangdut* group might be hired for the entertainment of the guests and the deafening of the neighbours. True to the group-throng mentality so typical of Indonesia, even the smallest *kampung* wedding will have swollen to festival proportions by evening. *Sate* sellers and others will have set up shop on the outskirts of the gathering, hovering like expectant fathers-to-be. In this environment, new friendships are made, rumours are spread, nervous *cewek-cowok* (girl-boy) glances exchanged and a cumulus cloud of *kretek* smoked.

A foreign person walking home through this could not be a more conspicuous sight. Should your Jakarta neighbours happen to be having a wedding reception, and you have no option but to walk through the middle of it, you may as well make the best of it. Get fed, get watered, get introduced, and make more friends.

You will know when a wedding is imminent because to highlight the fact, a number of giant yellow *janur* will have been set up near the reception. *Janur* are decorations, 5-m tall and constructed of *daun kelapa muda* (woven palm-leaves), which bend over at the top like triffids. Whereas *orang Jawa* (the Javanese) in Jakarta erect these, *orang Betawi* put up *umbul-umbul,* which—although of multicoloured bamboo—ultimately serve the same purpose.

The youngest people can legally get married in Indonesia is 19 for men and 16 for women. Written parental consent is required for both parties until the age of 21. Under the marriage law of 1974, ten working days' notice must be given to the Registrar of Marriages in the district where the marriage is to be performed and two witnesses must be present. If a Muslim woman is remarrying, there should be a waiting period of 100 days before the proposed marriage can be contracted.

## SEX

Sex is not a common topic of conversation in Indonesia. Any mention of it is in an embarrassed, jocular form, with a nervous laugh and hand-over-mouth snigger. It's not that people are necessarily repressed, but it's such an unmentionable subject that it remains something to be ashamed of. Basically, it's so unmentionable that everyone is dying to know more.

There's no sex on television, in the press or at the cinema. Most things sexy are censored to an almost ridiculous degree, sometimes after publication when a small offshoot of some fundamentalist group reckons it's time for them to act as Indonesia's moral arbiters. When the local edition of the *Playboy* magazine was first published in 2006, its pictures were no more titillating or revealing than those in locally produced glossy magazines. However, such was the furore surrounding the mere thought of the name that the editorial offices were moved from Jakarta to Bali, and the editor and lead model faced criminal charges. As the judges were not aroused, all cases were subsequently dismissed in March 2007 and *Playboy* remains inoffensive.

On the black market, there exists a proliferation of blue movies on pirated DVDs, most of them from China. New technologies such as mobile phones with video cameras and the Internet have enabled the circulation of short videos, often of prominent politicians and celebrities who've been caught *in flagrante delicto*. These are then talked about endlessly on the TV gossip shows. At the time of the *Playboy* editor's trial, supposedly devout Muslim leaders who had taken younger second wives were roundly condemned.

As a negative consequence of Westernisation as viewed on pirated DVDs, many Indonesians generally presume that 'free-sex' is the norm among Westerners, that AIDS comes from the West, and that Westerners are its chief spreaders. However, one report claims that AIDS hit Irian Jaya, before Jakarta, brought in by trespassing Thai fishermen. Bali, with its well-established tourist and expat scene, was next to have the scaremonger's finger pointed at it.

AIDS awareness campaigns on TV and in the press have been surprisingly blunt in their messages, but there are other obstacles to overcome. Condoms are widely available, but their promotion has been reluctant to say the least, even as a way of checking the spread of AIDS. Religious leaders frown upon the notion of what they consider to be tantamount to condoning promiscuity. The notion of 'safe-sex' is an alien one to the Indonesian way of being, since the only acceptable sex is that within marriage.

The Indonesian Council of Ulama (a Muslim Advisory Council) states that they 'neither accept nor reject the use of condoms either in the national family planning programme or in the prevention of AIDS but would support the use in certain cases; i.e. a man infected with HIV would be obliged to wear a condom when having sex with his wife.'

Yet sex is for sale all over Jakarta. It's not as obvious as, say, in Bangkok or Amsterdam, but it's not hard to miss either. North Jakarta used to have a red light district, but this was pulled down to make way for an Islamic study complex. It's a screaming contradiction that presumptions of Western promiscuity are condemned on one hand while an abundance of brothels are allowed to operate on the other. Your authors cannot tell you where the greatest concentration of 'massage' services now are, but expats are known to congregate in Jl. Felatehan in Blok M, South Jakarta. Is this how real-life goes in Jakarta? The answer is simple—people have to pay the rent somehow. One thing is certain: there wouldn't be any business of this kind at all if there weren't a market for it.

In 2006, the United Nations Development Programme estimated (http://www.youandaids.org/Asia%20Pacific%20at%20a%20Glance/Indonesia/index.asp) that there were approximately 190,000–270,000 female sex workers, and clients of sex workers numbered approximately 7–10 million, with condom use estimated at less than 10 per cent. HIV transmission in Indonesia was initially related to sexual transmission, but transmission among injecting drug users has increased eight-fold since 1998. The majority of infections are concentrated in groups with high-risk behaviour, particularly sex workers and injecting drug users. Risk behaviour among injecting drug users is by far the most common. HIV prevalence as high as 48 per cent has been found in drug injectors at rehabilitation centres in Jakarta. The epidemic fuelled by drug injection is already spreading into remote parts of the archipelago.

Most of these drug users are young, relatively well-educated and live with their families. Experts warn that if risk behaviours among drug injectors, among male, female and transgender sex workers, and among clients of sex workers do not change from the levels observed in surveillance performed in 2003, Indonesia will be seeing a far worse epidemic. Surveys have found that although most injectors know where to get sterile needles, close to 9 in 10 (88 per cent) of them still use non-sterile injecting equipment. Many injectors are reluctant to carry sterile needles with them for fear that police would treat this as proof that they inject drugs (which is a criminal offence). The incarceration of drug injectors is a significant facet of Indonesia's epidemic. In Jakarta, between 1997 and 2001, HIV prevalence among drug injectors in Jakarta rose from zero to 47 per cent, for example. Subsequently, in the capital's overcrowded jails, HIV prevalence started to rise two years later, from zero in 1999 to 25 per cent in 2002.

## BULE

If you are white and you are in Indonesia, you are a *bule*. A honky, a white-boy, a snowflake, a *gaijin*, a *hindung-ee*, a gringo, a farang, a paleface, a howie, a white, a big nose, a miser. You are worldly, educated and probably important. You represent a world of wealth, power, peace, free speech, easy living, free sex, drink, drugs, freedom and fun. You also represent some three centuries of colonial rule.

The word *bule* is widely used by Indonesians when referring to Caucasians—*orang bule*. There are alternatives: *orang Barat* (Westerner), *orang asing* (foreigner), *orang Spanyol* (Spaniard), and to some in Jawa Tengah (Central Java), Westerners are still *wong Londo* (Dutch) and still smell of cheese and onion. Yet from the *kampung* (village) to the *kantor* (office), *bule* remains the common term for the white-skinned. It shouldn't be misconstrued as a racist term. Rarely is *bule* used in a derogatory way, although in theory that's quite possible. But still it continues to offend the sensibility of Westerners—long-term expats and short-term visitors alike—mainly because Westerners lead much less open lives than Asians. This one small word highlights the sometimes enormous world of difference in attitude and outlook between life in Indonesia and life in the West.

*Bule* simply describes something pale. A pair of old jeans could be describe as *bule* for example. Many dictionaries define the word as slang for 'albino'. Besides, in Indonesia and especially Jakarta, people are very aware of their origins and have a strong sense of regional identity. They like to stereotype the people of different regions, perhaps merely to reinforce their own identity. The fact that someone is *orang Jawa* (Javanese) or *orang Sunda* (Sundanese) is a justifiable reason for all kinds of behaviour. The same is true for *bule*.

It seems no one is happy with the way they were born. To be white in Indonesia is considered an asset, to be dark means you have spent too long outside labouring for your living. In short: the darker you are, the poorer you are. Skin-bleaching products are big sellers among the fashion-conscious of Indonesia, as is heavy white foundation. In its most rudimentary form, a whack of talcum powder over the face and shoulders does the trick. Unfortunately, smothering the natural dark of Indonesian skin means it takes on an unglamorous grey complexion. Conversely, many white people's sole priority when visiting a hot country like Indonesia is to get a suntan, go brown and do everything not to look white.

For the most part, life as a foreigner in Jakarta is in your favour, even for the hippiest *bule miskin* (slang: cheapskate, backpacking traveller). For the most part, you represent money, and you have a big nose.

## MAKING FRIENDS

You won't find it hard to make friends in Indonesia. It's as easy as showing your face; as easy as going out your door. You will find most people are more than happy to make conversation with you. The average person in the street should therefore be considered a friend, not an enemy. They'll look out for you if you look out for them. But being so visibly 'different', i.e., taller, whiter, uglier and hairier, you are nothing but a prime target for attention. You might decide that today is not the day for making friends, but no one has told your potential new 'friend' this.

Although generally friendships are made in a somewhat instant manner in Indonesia, many Jakartans these days are totally indifferent to the presence of a *bule*. To a degree anyway. The very fact that many trendy young Indonesians choose to ignore foreigners is a reaction in itself. And this is not necessarily a sign of the times: Jakarta has never been easily impressed, having seen it all before.

You might wonder how deep these friendships run; how sincere they really are. Is it simply because you are different? Is that why they are talking to you? Not really. On what is the world's most densely packed island, you

## Collective Security

*Maling* (burglars) don't stand a chance once someone has alerted the neighbourhood to the fact and hollered "maling!" What happens next, however, once the misfit has been confronted, is a lot less friendly.

don't have much choice in the matter, other than to try and get on with one another. The system is self-supporting; any problems or disputes are settled fairly and squarely through general consensus. It's a case of the more, the merrier. The more people there are with you, the easier it is to merge into a single collective *orang* (person). Indonesians like to lose themselves in a crowd; it's the finest living example of ego-loss there is. Neighbours look out for one another in Jakarta.

Jakarta is a good place for paranoids to overcome their fears. With everyone—many of them total strangers you will never, ever see again—looking at you, talking to you and quizzing you about your life almost every time you are outside your home, you will soon be cured.

As real as friendships are in Indonesia, there may be times when you feel the friendship is going nowhere; that you never seem to talk about anything; that it all seems superficial. It may seem like your friend is pampering to you or is over-keen to please you. This is just the way of the people; to keep everything smooth and everyone unoffended. Once everyone agrees upon this basic principle, life is a lot smoother.

Whereas the English, whenever stuck in a lift with someone they don't know, talk about the weather, Indonesians try to talk about nothing. They might ask about the other person; whether they have eaten yet, prayed yet or bathed yet. Alternatively, they might talk about traffic jams, or about some good rice that's going around. But, like the rest of the world, they are more than likely these days to talk about what was on television last night.

Indonesians practice what they call *basa-basi* or rather 'nothing talk', in which they strive their hardest not to offend anyone by speaking about absolutely nothing. In these conversations, special care is taken that no direct reference is made to another person. The subject matter is kept, at best, vague. Very often in Indonesia, no one is really sure who is talking to who and what indeed they mean, if anything at all.

And this makes the predominance of gossip shows on seemingly every TV channel a puzzle. And why do the same old, or young, celebrities keep appearing?

## HASSLE

A lot of visitors and expatriates complain of hassle in Indonesia. Why is this? Do they mean that everyone stares at you or at least does a double take? Do they mean that everyone wants to talk to you and ask you the same questions over and over? Do they mean that people are always trying to sell you something and then overcharging you because you are Western and supposedly wealthy? Do they mean that Western women, especially blonde-haired, blue-eyed ones, are in for a hard time? Do they mean that a couple which is one part Western and one part Indonesian is open to an unfair amount of verbal abuse and suspicion? Well, probably.

It's important to consider each of these problems in context, that is, from the Indonesian point of view. From here we may be able to understand better why such complaints arise.

As for the issue of being stared at, it's certainly true that while you are in Indonesia, you are unlikely to be able to move around unnoticed. It's not such a problem in Jakarta, especially in the places where a *bule* is expected to go. That is the well-to-do residential areas like Pondok Indah and Bintaro Jaya, the offices stretching along Thamrin to Sudirman, major shopping areas like Plaza Indonesia and Sarinah, the bars and pubs in Jl Faletahan, Blok M, and of course, the big hotels. In these places, you are guaranteed relative anonymity, especially if you are walking alone and look as if you know where you are going. However, you can still expect a 'hello mister' every few minutes.

The 'hello mister' factor increases tenfold when you stray from the above places or enter a *kampung*. It increases a hundred-fold when you leave Jakarta. For many Indonesians, 'hello' and 'mister' are probably the only words of English they know. They are keen to say hello and make a connection with you. They are being bold, nothing more. Take the example of Jakarta's school kids who like to hang about in intimidatingly large groups when school lets out. True to the group mentality that is so peculiar to South-east Asia, Jakarta school kids, particularly the teenage boys, love to shout obscenities at a passing Westerner. Hanging out in a group, they are free from all responsibility (and, some would say, a brain) and any individual actions are diffused within the group. In any other situation and on an individual basis, the story is different.

Often, the only Westerners Indonesian people see are those in trashy American TV shows where everyone shoots each other and women jump into bed with the hero at the end. This limited media portrayal of *bule* is commonly the only association an Indonesian can make with a white person. Dress modestly and you shouldn't gain so much attention. A revealing dress is just asking for hassle. Let's be honest, being a *bule* means not only being a target but a walking bull's-eye. While *bule* are conspicuous by definition, some Indonesians say that foreigners invite a lot of the attention on

TRIGG

themselves—that they dress inappropriately, talk too loudly and often make an unknowing display of their wealth.

As for staring, Indonesians stare at all sorts of things all the time. It's quite a normal thing to do and not considered especially rude. In fact, so aware are young Jakartans of this that they go out on a Saturday simply hoping to be stared at. It's all part of the course; all part of life's great television. A popular pastime in Indonesia is an afternoon spent *cuci mata*—staring (literally 'washing the eyes').

*Bule* are generally considered an attractive breed despite certain bad reputations they might have. In a country where almost 200 million people have black hair and few men can grow a decent beard, to see a woman with long blonde hair and a man with a bushy beard is something worth getting an eyeball of, especially when they are a head taller than everyone else around.

As for being talked to by complete strangers, this is certainly true but not something to worry about. Again people are simply being bold. They might want to practise their English, which is why you get asked the same questions again and again: "Where are you going?", "Are you married?", "Where do you come from?", "What do you think of Indonesian people?", "How many children have you got?", "Do you eat rice?" That kind of thing. Even if you can speak *bahasa Indonesia*, there won't be much variation in the interrogation. Many Indonesians are keen to have a foreign 'friend' and, thereby, hopefully distinguish themselves from the crowd.

At the same time, an Indonesian is supposed to know their limits when mixing with Westerners. An Indonesian girl seen accompanying a Western male is open to suspicion: she might be considered a girl of low moral standards. She might well be called *perek*, the acronym for *perempuan eksperimen* ('experimental' woman)—perhaps the worst thing an Indonesian woman can be called. This goes to highlight the negative reputation that *bule* have, that they are promiscuous and unfaithful. The girl might also be considered to be 'only in

Being, perhaps, the only *bule* at a wedding is normal; your mere presence has raised someone's self-esteem.

it for the money', that she would do anything for *uang*. The fact that Jakarta has more brothels than the average European capital is apparently not taken into consideration.

Indonesia is a country with limited access to world affairs for the average citizen, not much money per capita, a large and religious population, and where independence from colonial rule is something your grandparents still remember. Try and take these factors into account next time you feel hassled. Rarely are people out to deliberately upset or offend you—rarely.

## PRIVACY
Contrary to popular expatriate belief, words for privacy do exist in Indonesian. The words are *kebebasan pribadi*. Admittedly, they aren't the most overused words in the language, the meaning (rather than the spelling) escaping the average citizen. Western notions of 'respect my space, please' fly clean out the window in Indonesia, and foreigners need to be aware of this fact—otherwise they are likely to lose their minds. One example might be if, on a rare occasion, you manage to find a relatively empty bus with empty seats. You can guarantee that the next two people on the bus will shoehorn themselves in next to you, even when other seats are available and your seat itself is only a two-seater. Strange for some; normal for others.

Indonesia holds all kinds of world records. It's a country of superlatives: the world's largest Muslim country, the largest archipelago, and Java the most densely populated island on the planet. If everyone in Java stood at an equal distance from each other, each square mile would have a couple of thousand people in it. Privacy is not therefore the most accessible commodity in Java. Walking down a Jakarta side street in the late evening, you may think you are walking alone in the darkness. But when your eyes get accustomed to the dark, you soon become aware of the very many people *lagi jongkok* (crouching) in the dark. Sometimes it's only the glow of their *kretek* cigarette that gives them away. People are everywhere in Jakarta. The only way to guarantee privacy is to close the door behind you.

You would assume that home is the only place where you could relax without comparative strangers around you. You would be wrong. More than likely your every step is tracked by a shadowy *pembantu* (housemaid), cleaning up after you, emptying ashtrays after a single cigarette-end, answering the phone before you can get to it and waiting for you to finish in the bathroom so they can mop up after you. Just as you instructed them to do. The irony of the routine that you instigated is that you find yourself avoiding the *pembantu* because you want privacy. You don't want to see anyone. You want to relax at home. You want to put your feet up, sit with your legs apart, pick your nose, leave the toilet door open and do the million other things you can only do with family and close friends, or on your own. It's imperative you make it clear to your *pembantu* when you do and when you don't want privacy. If you don't like seeing people when you have just woken up, make this clear also. Any kind of rule can be made, there are no fixed job descriptions for the *pembantu*. It's your home, you pay the wages, you make the rules—it's your sanity after all. But then if your sanity is hinged so precariously around maintaining your privacy, you are probably better off having nothing at all to do with the *pembantu* world.

### Touch Me Not

Between people of the same sex, touching is standard practice. When another man rests his hands on your leg during a conversation, the immediate Western response is to recoil in horror. It doesn't seem natural. Conversely, physical contact between men and women is rarely seen in public. This leads to the bizarre situation where two men hold hands on one side of the street, quite obviously good friends, while on the other side, a married couple strive to keep a distance from each other. The space that it seems Westerners need around them to maintain mental stability is virtually nonexistent to an Indonesian. Look at any passing bus and wonder at the packed conditions inside.

If you are seen doing things alone in Indonesia, people will assume something is wrong with you. People hardly ever do things alone: even on the most mundane task, Indonesians prefer to have a friend come along. Everyone knows everything about everyone else in this country, and no more so than in the *kampung* (itself only a extensive outgrowth of two or three families). Here, even a girl's first *lampu merah* (menstrual period) is celebrated by the preparation and giving out to neighbours of *nasi kuning* (yellow rice)—the all-purpose Indonesian party-stuff. Food appears mysteriously in doorways: the leftovers of a nearby rice-rave. Neighbours know who works where, who fancies who, what goes on with who, where, what time and how often. Everything.

## OTHER WESTERNERS IN INDONESIA

Westerners come to Jakarta for all sorts of reasons. A few opt to live here indefinitely, while some give up after six months. Some come as tourists, almost always passing through Jakarta on their way to better places, and some are 'sent', perhaps as part of a multinational aid package. Other people come looking for work, recommended to the place by a friend. Others decide after a holiday that they like Indonesia and decide to extend their visas. Some return time and again to Jakarta, keeping one foot in the door, as

it were. Some come looking for love or rather the guarantee of cheap sex. Some are tax evaders, some are gay, some die here. Some don't know why they came in the first place, some just can't remember. Some probably don't want to remember. For some, it's like dropping out, throwing in the towel, giving up—too sad to face life in their own world. To each his own.

Some have more specific reasons for living in Jakarta: that they want to climb every volcano in the country, or they need a base from which they can venture forth to catalogue frogs, lizards and snakes. The opportunity to spend time exploring the virtually inexhaustible amount of jungle, mountains, coastlines, hot springs and wildlife that make up Indonesia is presented to you on a plate. While travel in Indonesia may not be as hassle-free as it could be, you stand a greater chance of seeing elephants in the wild by being based in Jakarta than you would by living in London.

Jakarta offers the widest range of work opportunities in Indonesia for everyone, be they Javanese, Sundanese, Batak, Betawi, Ambonese, Irianese, Sasak, Diak, Korean, Japanese, Australian, American, Irish or English, all of whom over the years have found a niche in Jakarta and, in their own ways, left their mark. Oil workers comprise a large percentage of Jakarta's expat population, although a great many are in managerial positions, having been transferred to Jakarta by their company. They are invariably male and have wives and children with them. Expat wives in Jakarta have a vibrant social scene going. There's the well established American Women's Association in Cilandak and similar scenes organised by British and Australian women alike. Work as an English language teacher is probably the most viable option for those who come looking for a job on spec.

For people who choose to live and work in Jakarta (as opposed to those who get sent), a variety of lifestyles are embraced. Some live well and spend well, eating in the five-star hotels every night and regularly jetting off to more obvious holiday locations. Some remain exclusively expat in their socialising, choosing to mix only with other foreigners, while others marry Indonesians and live a thoroughly

Jakartan lifestyle. Some become fluent in *bahasa Indonesia* and regional languages, then spend their time discussing the price of rice with the RT, while others progress no further than *bahasa bir* (*satu lagi*—one more) or *bahasa taksi* (stop *disini*—stop here).

---

**Making Your Money Go Further**

The reasons that keep people staying in Jakarta or returning are many. The chance of having a comparatively affluent standard of living, the likes of which might not be attainable elsewhere, is certainly high on everyone's list. Although some things like cars or glasses of beer, for example, are disproportionately expensive, it can be safely said that money can be made to go much further. Take for example Rp 50,000, which, even at its weakest in 1998 when it was worth only about US$ 5, could still buy you 25 kg (55 pounds) of rice or 50 meals from a street vendor or hire a maid for a month or a car for a day or pay for ten haircuts. Ten years later, Rp 50,000 is worth US$ 5.50 and will buy you 'only' five meals or four big bottles of Bintang in Jalan Jaksa or two glasses during the Happy Hours in a five-star bar.

---

Some Westerners let the attention, standard of living and relative prosperity go to their heads. They become 'virtually famous'. People who are totally anonymous in their own country become celebrated individuals in no time at all in a place like Jakarta. You see, you are always guaranteed a second look in the city. Boys and girls alike are instant superstars: free to re-invent themselves as something far more interesting than they really are. There are make-believe sugar-daddies, would-be white-boy gigolos, pretend gangsters and desperadoes. Some even delude themselves into believing they are Indonesian, speaking a caricature of the language with all the well-studied mannerisms of a local. Some live a life of overindulgence, imagining they are living like a king, surrounded by faithful servants pampering to their every need. Very sad. There's nothing essentially wrong in becoming 'famous' in Jakarta, but you may be in for a let-down when (if) you move on.

It's important therefore to keep your head in Jakarta. Very generally speaking, Asian people consider the white skin and round eyes of Westerners attractive. Likewise, very generally speaking, white people consider the dark Asian beauty a natural asset. These factors, in combination with the fact that much of the country's people are poor, mean that propositions—often outrageous propositions which belie the apparent *kesopanan* (politeness) of the Indonesian character—can come fast and furious. On occasion then, it can be hard to establish whether people are reacting to you as the person you are, with all the character traits you are convinced make you unique from the next person, or simply as a foreigner who represents a distant, strange and unquestionably more affluent world.

The lure of the East-Asian sex scene lingers on in Jakarta, and while it's by no means as obvious as certain parts of Bangkok may be, sex is readily available for those who want to buy it. The bars of Blok M and a number of hotel bars are populated with all sorts of 'nice' girls who wouldn't normally be in a bar; it's just that they arrived in Jakarta to meet their friend who was supposed to be putting them up and it looks like they haven't shown up yet and...

The common sight in Jakarta of overweight, middle-aged Australians with young Indonesian women on their arms has resulted in an unfair reputation that unfortunately accommodates all foreigners. Genuine friendships and relationships happen every day in Jakarta, yet there continues to be an element of suspicion in the minds of a lot of Indonesians when confronted with a mixed couple. You have been warned.

And only an idiot would assume Jakarta was an AIDS-free zone. Take precautions, for everyone's sake

What exactly might a foreigner complain about? Well, they might complain that life is just too 'different' for them; that it's so hard to form genuine friendships with Indonesians; that they never have anything in common. For some, this is the challenge: to be plunged in the deep-end of a culture so completely *lain* (different) to the West; to attempt to see inside the Indonesian mind with its attitudes to life which, for the foreigner, can be either fascinating or exasperating; to witness a thousand-year culture coping with the increasing intrusion of Western ideals.

They might complain that there's nothing to do in Jakarta. They might complain that the other expats in the city are diabolical. They complain about the heat, that it's too hot to do anything, that the humidity, mosquitoes and racket make life too hard. They might complain that all they get is hassle on the streets. And, rather dramatically, that they want to experience 'real' Indonesian life, not merely the trivialities of a small circle of expat misfits. In time, any person choosing to live in Jakarta will find a lifestyle that is *cocok* (suitable) for them. Of course if they really can't get to grips with the Jakartan way of living, then they probably shouldn't prolong the agony.

## CORRUPTION

The culture of corruption is going to take a generation or two to wipe out. It's also going to need a thriving economy and a focus on long-term goals rather than short-term immediate profits. Trying to live a morally clean life may make you feel virtuous but it can also leave you feeling very frustrated. This doesn't mean that people need to bribe their maids in order to have their homes cleaned or need to bribe hairdressers into cutting their hair. But bigger things such as the isssuance of any kind of official paperwork or documentation is most definitely speeded up by the simple introduction of a 'brown envelope'.

The giving and taking of bribes is not necessarily a sordid affair. They can generally be made in a very casual, unspoken manner, and with a certain dignity. The reference isn't to a 'bribe' itself but to something like *uang rokok* (cigarette money) or *uang kopi* (coffee money) to take the edge off. Think of your day-to-day bribes as an unofficial tax on living in Indonesia and that it's not so much greasing the

'If you have knowledge of good and bad, then logically you know that corruption is bad. But in Indonesia sometimes corruption is considered a good thing.'
—Emha Ainun Najid, poet

wheels as, in the case of lower echelon officials, ensuring that their wives have cooking oil for the month.

When driving through town, keep a largish banknote—Rp 20,000 or Rp 50,000—among the vehicle documents which you are supposed to keep with you at all times when driving. If your time is worth money, then you'll make immense savings if you don't surrender your license to the traffic policeman who pulls you over for you-don't-know-what infringement of the traffic laws and opt to appear in court.

And if you find yourself in a position of someone not accepting your offering, don't automatically assume that they want more. It may mean, hallelujah, that you've met an official who is financially or morally secure, so don't embarass yourself or him/her.

Many companies employ a 'Mr. Fixit' whose main job is to keep the wheels of business turning. They may have social or political connections, and this is important because however much society officially decries KKN (*korrupsi*, *kollusi* and *nepotisme*), another K, *kronyisme*, is still rampant.

## VIGILANTES

While there are a great many fear-evoking police in the city, the 'eye for an eye' approach is still much preferred in settling minor cases of burglary and other domestic crime. Should a *maling* (thief) be caught red-handed, he will be dragged screaming to the local security man's office and systematically beaten up by everyone in the neighbourhood. Naturally, the first to join in is the thief's victims. Only then is the thief taken to the police station for further questioning.

Sometimes, however, this free-for-all system of revenge goes too far.

### Be Careful of What You Say

There is the story of a woman in Jakarta who bought a TV on hire-purchase. One day, after she had forgotten to keep up with the repayments, a man arrived to repossess it. Infuriated as she was, she decided to shout "*maling!*" as he was on his way out. Hearing this alarm call, the local *kampung* boys (and there is never a shortage) appeared in force and set about putting to right what they believed was a serious misdeed. The man died later that day from his injuries.

After a while in Jakarta, you start to get the feeling that you ought to be careful what you say to people; careful that you don't upset anyone because if you do, there is every chance a couple of their relatives will come and get you one night while you sleep.

## GETTING INTO TROUBLE

Ideally, you do not want to get into trouble when in Jakarta, for a number of good reasons. First is the fact that you are foreign. While much of the time this is to your advantage, imagine how much more attention you draw to yourself by getting somehow involved in a fight, for example. Second is the ever-present mob tendency in Indonesia. Actions are very rarely undertaken on an individual basis in this country, and you should be prepared to be amazed at just how quickly a crowd, in the case of a road accident or other dispute, can appear nowhere. Should you be unfortunate enough to be involved in a minor accident, it's recommended you remain calm, polite, apologetic and get ready to make an on-the-spot payment. If necessary, you should locate a policeman—but don't try to run away.

## TRANSVESTITES

Transvestites seem to hold a special place in the world of Indonesia. Indeed, cross-dressing is a far more acceptable pastime in South-east Asia than it seems to be in the West. This may (or may not) be because Asian men, when 'done-up', make such convincing women that they can participate in beauty contests such as Miss Waria Indonesia. *Waria* is a combination of the Indonesian words for woman (*wanita*) and man (*pria*).

Known locally as *banci* (pronounced 'banshee') or *bencong*, transvestites are the brunt of many a joke; nearly every TV comedy show has its token *banci* somewhere in the line-up. They tend to reinforce the stereotype of the Indonesian *banci* in Jakarta, exaggerated features and long fuzzy hair pulled back to look like a giant coconut atop his/her shoulders. But constant ridicule is not a good thing. The fact that they generally only play low-life characters such as servants and street workers reflects the generally low opinion people have of *banci*. They are tolerated, made fun of, but never totally accepted. Never are they seen in positions of authority. There are no *banci* RT patrolling the streets; no *banci polisi* directing traffic—at least not in Jakarta.

This is in sharp contrast to the time when *banci* were held in higher esteem. In certain parts of Sulawesi, *bisus*, as they are known in that part of Indonesia, were believed to be something special; a living halfway house between heaven and earth, a communicator between the real and spirit world. Until they were outlawed that is.

On a day to day basis, you are most likely to encounter *banci* at Jakarta's traffic lights where they can be seen 'performing'

### Bad Influence?

In 2005, the notorious Islamic Defenders' Front (FPI) barged into a club where the Miss Waria contest was taking place. "Transvestites should not be made into a role model," they said. "We are worried it could influence our children."

with tambourines. They seem to take particular delight in targeting Westerners, going on to serenade the individual until he or she pays up. It's a very effective method; hardly anyone can ignore a man they have never seen before dressed as a woman singing a *dangdut* song, as you sit in the back of a taxi waiting for the lights to change. Try not to make eye-contact—fatal. *Banci* have no qualms, they will interrupt you in the middle of a meal in order to sing at you if they have to.

The *banci* of Jakarta have their own club going—they are an entire subculture of their own. Jl Kendal, round the corner from the night-time fun area of Belora, is one nocturnal hangout for Jakarta's transvestites, and nothing less than a walk on the wild side. The annual Jakarta Fair often features talent competitions with the city's performing *banci*. They hardly need a platform to perform on however, their talents being always rather more spontaneously recognised.

If you get the chance, watch *Dunia kami, Duniaku, Dunia mereka* ('Our World, My World, Their World') by noted independent film-maker, Adi Nugroho, which narrates the life of a transvestite in Yogyakarta.

## HOMOSEXUALITY

Homosexuality is considered a bad way of life, but there is no bashing here. People see it like prostitution. But historically, homosexuality was more accepted until the protestant Dutch arrived and stigmatised it.

Today, there are no specific laws against homosexuality. There is no age of consent because homosexuals do not have any legal existence, in religious law nor in civil law. As if to conform to such invalidating standards, gay life here is generally subdued and shrouded from public view. Much of gay social life takes place under the cloak of darkness, in certain places on certain nights.

Being gay is felt to be a curse by young gays first coming out. As they age, they hide their friendships and underground affairs, going off to meet and cruise anonymously at malls or parks. If they can afford it, many go to the increasing number of bars, clubs and discos on designated nights to socialise with other gay friends in the safety of the dimly lit bar area or the flashing strobes of the dance floor.

As for lesbians in Indonesia, the scene is very closeted. Most lesbians are married to Muslim husbands and their lives highly confined. In the bigger cities, they have more freedom to form discreet friendships and some organisations have been formed.

Yayasan Mitra Indonesia is an HIV prevention and educational resource centre that has grown to become an important contact centre for the lesbigay community in Jakarta. Their services include anonymous HIV testing, counselling and referral services for medical, social and legal aid.

# SETTLING IN

## CHAPTER 5

'Because of the city's outdated sewerage and drainage system, two-thirds of Jakarta is inundated each rainy season when all municipal and central government offices close down, there are traffic snarls and stranded vehicles, and up to 250,000 people in need of shelter.'
—Bill Dalton, *Indonesian Handbook*, 1980

## VISAS AND IMMIGRATION

There are a number of visas pertaining to coming to Indonesia. You are strongly advised to check with the Indonesian embassy in your country regarding current regulations as they are subject to change. As the website of the Indonesian embassy in Japan says, 'It is most desirous that any traveller to Indonesia understands and duly respects the Indonesian Immigration's regulations.'

This is very true. Unfortunately, the Immigration Department is the most secretive of any bureaucracy anywhere which it has been our displeasure to deal with. As one senior official at Soekarno-Hatta Airport replied when asked how the public could find out the regulations, "It's for me to know and you to find out. And no, I won't tell you."

To the best of our knowledge, the information given below was correct at the time of going to print. However, if you relied on this information and get deported and blacklisted from further visits, please do not cite *CultureShock! Jakarta*.

In the absence of easily accessible official information, we are indebted to the good folk at *Living In Indonesia* (http://www.expat.or.id) and in particular Gary Dean of http://www.okusi.net for most of the information given below in brief. Please don't blame them either if things change before they have had a chance to update their web pages.

It is your responsibility to ensure that all is A-OK, an assuredly Orwellian task.

## Passports

Passports for your family members are issued by a passport office from your own country. While your government may allow children to follow on their mother's passports, just in case separate travel is required, it is better to have separate passports for every family member.

In order to apply for any visa to Indonesia, your passport must be valid for at least six months. Bring a passport with a good many blank pages left; after only a short time in Indonesia, you accumulate lots of stamps, each one filling a whole page. Also, if your passport is nearing expiration, we recommend you renew it to the maximum time allowable before you begin procedures to apply for an Indonesian visa and/or work permit.

## Tourist Visa

- The Free Visa Facility (length of stay: max. 30 days) is issued to citizens of the following countries: Brunei, Malaysia, Philippines, Singapore, Thailand, Vietnam, Hong Kong, Macau, Morocco, Chile and Peru.
- The Visa-on-Arrival Facility (length of stay: max. 30 days) is issued on a reciprocal basis to citizens of the following countries: Argentina, Australia, Austria, Bahrain, Belgium, Brazil, Bulgaria, Cambodia, Canada, the People's

Republic of China, Cyprus, Denmark, Egypt, Estonia, Finland, France, Germany, Great Britain, Greece, Holland, Hungary, India, Iran, Ireland, Italy, Japan, Kuwait, Laos, Liechtenstein, Luxemburg, Maldives, Malta, Mexico, Monaco, New Zealand, Norway, Oman, Poland, Portugal, Qatar, Russia, Saudi Arabia, South Africa, South Korea, Spain, Suriname, Sweden, Switzerland, Taiwan, the United Arab Emirates, the United Kingdom and the United States of America. This list is liable to change at any time.

The current (2006) cost is US$ 25 for a 30-day stay. If you ask nicely when you arrive, you may be able to get a seven-day visa for US$ 10; and if you only want to stay for three days, it's free. Supposedly. But if all goes to the plan announced just as we finished writing this section, by the time you get here, you may be able to take advantage of a 120-day tourist visa which will presumably cost US$ 100. This will be a very good deal for students on a gap year and other backpackers intent on packing in as many sights and experiences as they can during their stay. Onward or return tickets are compulsory.

- Citizens of countries not stated above are required to apply for a visa at the Indonesian embassy/consulate in their country of domicile.

To stay longer than 30 days necessitates leaving the country and returning. For all practical purposes, short stay visas are not extendable. There are exceptions, however, as the Ministry of Tourism outlines: A short stay visa may be extended under the permission of Indonesia is conditions as follows, the natural disaster happens in the place that is visiting by the tourist. And if, the tourist is sick or got into an accident during the visit.

Got that?

You cannot work on a tourist visa, and it's notoriously difficult to change to another visa without first leaving the country. This usually entails a trip to Singapore if you are in Jakarta.

All other non-tourist visas have to be approved within Indonesia and picked up at an overseas Indonesian embassy or consulate.

---

**A List of Useful Acronyms**

- **BKPM** (Badan Koordinasi Penanaman Modal)
  Investment Coordinating Board
- **Depnaker** (Departemen Tenaga Kerja)
  Department of Manpower
- **DPKK** (Dana Pengembangan Keahlian dan Ketrampilan)
  Skill & Development Fund fee
- **EPO**
  Exit Permit Only
- **IMTA** (Izin Memperkerjakan Tenaga Asing)
  A work permit
- **KITAS** (Kartu Izin Tinggal Sementara)
  A Temporary Residence Permit Card
- **MEBV**
  Multiple Entry Business Visa
- **PMA** (Penanaman Modal Asing)
  Foreign investment company
- **RPTKA** (Rencana Penempatan Tenaga Kerja Asing)
  Expatriate Placement Plan
- **TA01**
  Depnaker approval for a work permit and by extension a residence visa
- **VITAS** or **VBS** (Visa Tinggal Terbatas)
  Temporary Residence Visa

---

## Social Cultural Visa (Sosial Budaya or SosBud)

A stay up to six months for social and/or cultural purposes such as visiting relatives/friends or social organisations, exchange visits between educational institutions, or undertaking research and attending training programmes is possible, but sponsorship must be obtained within Indonesia.

Initial permission is given for a two-month stay; this can be extended four times on a monthly basis to give a total stay of six months. Visas are extended at the immigration office in the area of residence of the visa sponsor.

## Temporary Residence Visa (KITAS)

KITAS are issued to work permit holders, students, dependents of Indonesian citizens or foreigners already holding a work permit, whose purpose of visit is to stay in Indonesia for a limited period. It is valid for up to 12 months and needs authorisation from the Immigration Office in Indonesia.

## Business Visas

There are two types of business visas which are for those visiting Indonesia for normal business activities, including attending a conference or seminar, which do not involve taking up employment or receiving any payments whilst in Indonesia.

A Single Entry Business Visa is valid for a maximum stay of 60 days but can be extended up to four times on a monthly basis by the Immigration Department to give a total maximum stay of six months. This visa is useful for buying trips, negotiations and consultations and is easier to obtain, as well as being cheaper than, say, a working visa which you may not require if you are paid or are funded overseas. This visa does not entitle you to work in any manner whatsoever whilst you are in Indonesia. It is the immigration office that defines what is and is not work—not the holder of the visa.

A Multiple Entry Business Visa (MEBV) is issued by your local Indonesian embassy upon authorisation of the Immigration Office in Indonesia. The applicant's counterpart/business sponsor in Indonesia has to apply locally on his/her behalf. If you need to come into and out of Indonesia on business frequently, then a MEBV is much more convenient than the standard single entry business visa. The MEBV is valid for 12 months and you may enter and leave Indonesia at will.

On entry to Indonesia, you are given a stay permit for two months. This visa is valid for up to 12 months but holders are required to leave the country every two months.

## Work Permits

The processes of obtaining proper documentation to live and work in Indonesia can seem like an endless maze of bureaucracy. The lack of posted regulations, the irregular application of existing regulations, vested interests and other matters complicate what one would think should be a relatively smooth processing of paperwork.

Company sponsorship is required as the first step in order for a foreigner who wants to work in Indonesia to be issued with a work permit/visa. The Indonesian government has strict guidelines on what foreign expertise is required for the development of the country and these guidelines determine who can be issued with work permits. The intention is to 'transfer technology', i.e. skills, to Indonesian nationals.

National, multinational or joint venture firms must submit a manpower plan to the Department of Manpower (Depnaker) detailing their annual foreign labour requirements. Before employing foreigners, a company must submit an Expatriate Placement Plan (RPTKA, *Rencana Penempatan Tenaga Kerja Asing*) to the Manpower Department if the prospective employer is a domestic company.

Work permits for senior positions held by foreigners are up to three years and can be renewed just before expiration. (NB: Foreigners can only hold director positions in PMA companies). Based on the approval of the RPTKA, a TA-01 is issued, and then a work permit, Izin Memperkerjakan Tenaga Asing (IMTA), is issued by Depnaker to the employer after your arrival and the issuance of the KITAS card and the payment of your annual Skill & Development Fund fee (DPKK).

Got that so far? Good.

---

**Call a Spade a Spade**

Deportations of foreigners for 'abusing' their work permits are not uncommon. The usual offence is that the person is working in a position other than what is allowed by the work permit. If your work permit says you are the production manager and your business card says you are the director—these are grounds for deportation. BEWARE and be cautious about what you put on your business card—make sure it agrees with your work permit!

---

Now, companies employing foreigners are charged DPKK, currently US$ 100 per month per expatriate employee, supposedly to offset the costs of training Indonesian nationals. (The fact that this is charged for expatriates in locally managed education institutions is a major anomaly.) This tax is administered through Depnaker. Before a Work Permit is approved, proof is needed of payment to Bank BNI of the DPKK fee for one year in advance.

After the RPTKA has been approved, the TA01 recommendation has to be applied for at Depnaker in order to get a temporary residence visa. The original approval letter on the TA01 recommendation will be needed to apply for the VITAS or VBS (Visa Tinggal Terbatas).

The RPTKA & TA01 recommendation are only necessary for foreigners working in Indonesia. Dependent family members—accompanying spouse and children up to 17 years old—will be under the sponsorship of the working spouse. Dependent family members are only entitled to stay with the working spouse/parent.

If a spouse is also working in Indonesia, their sponsoring company will have to apply for a separate Work Permit and Residence Visa.

We expect that by now you are as confused as we were in compiling the above, but DON'T PANIC.

Although the immigration department is notoriously 'difficult' to deal with, there are many Mr. and Mrs. Fixits who can ensure that things go relatively smoothly. If you're lucky in your company's choice of agent, then apart from losing sight of your passport for a while (and always ask for an official receipt from your employers when they take it), your only involvement in the process could be to go to the local immigration office and be fingerprinted. Whilst there, observe how bureaucrats work, in premises that resemble a cross between a dole office, a street market, a railway terminal and a Turkish bath, and be grateful that your office is (probably) air-conditioned.

It is possible your prints are sent to Interpol, but given the number of times we've given ours, we suspect it's unlikely. We think it's all part of a job creation scheme.

Eventually you'll receive your KITAS, the one-year, temporary stay identity card with your photo on it. This offers the best security for foreigners in Indonesia and is a must if you want your children to be admitted to international schools. In theory, it should be carried with you everywhere, but most expats carry a photocopy or one scanned on a computer which is so lifelike that it fools even fellow expats.

---

**A Word of Caution**

For your peace of mind, never trust your sponsor! Always keep the KITAS, police card, *Buku Mutasi* ('blue book'), passport and IMTA (work permit) safely stored away, out of sight of bureaucrats and Indonesian sponsors, unless you have your own PMA company and thus are the sponsor!

---

And that's all there is to it. Now you can live in Jakarta for a year knowing that you are unlikely to be kicked out. You may find it difficult to leave, however, because your employer is responsible for seeking an exit permit for you, which is why you should keep your original documents yourself!

The second liability is the *fiskal* needed to get out of the country. This is an 'exit tax' imposed on all Indonesian residents—both local and foreign. It is not imposed on foreigners on tourist, social or business visas as it is considered as income tax which can be credited to the sponsor company's corporate tax. Currently, Rp 1 million from Jakarta and Rp 500,000 from other exit ports such as Batam, *fiskal* cannot be paid, however, without first obtaining an Exit Visa Permit from Immigration.

Inevitably, all this is a nightmare should you attempt to do it yourself. Best have a word with your 'fixit' man. Jakarta's immigration offices, resembling a cross between a benefit office and a Turkish bath, are not the best places to spend the afternoon.

Immigration officials at Soekarno-Hatta are known on occasion to be rather awkward concerning the particulars of a foreigner's passport. If you are taken to a room for 'a closer look' at your passport, and assuming you are not a smuggler, there's no reason why you should have to make any payoffs, unless it becomes clear you really have no other option. Try asking for an official receipt; this should determine if their charges are legitimate or not. While you can, just say no.

## Income Tax

Employers are responsible for the calculation, payment and annual income tax return of all employees for the year in question. However, individual taxpayers are legally responsible for ensuring that they've registered with the tax office and comply with the regulations and payment of the tax due.

All expatriates resident in Indonesia are required to register with the tax office and obtain their own separate tax number (NPWP) and pay monthly taxes and file annual tax returns, and pay tax on their income earned outside Indonesia, less tax paid in other jurisdictions on the additional overseas income.

According to the law, those who must pay Indonesian income taxes are those who have been in Indonesia 183 days in a calendar year, including those expats here on KITAS, KITAP, business visa or social/visit visas. If you stay less than 183 days in a year, then you are not obligated to pay income tax, but you must prove it by showing your visa stamp and fill out FORM 1770 Individual and Monthly SSP (Surat Setoran Pajak). Of course, you must have an income tax number first to complete this form.

Dependent spouses are included in the husband's tax number and do not have to have a separate number and nor do children.

Indonesia's financial year is the calendar year, so if you are salaried and your employer has agreed—as stated in your contract—to pay personal income tax, you should ask early in the New Year for receipts showing that taxes have been paid for you on a monthly basis. The form required is 1721-A1, which is the actual annual return, and an S.S.P., which is the actual proof of payment.

Of special concern to expatriates whose salaries are quoted and paid net is that although your employer may have agreed in your contract to pay your taxes, you are still personally liable for their payment. If you work for a local PT company (rather than a multinational firm), you may find that your employer 'negotiates' with the tax officials. This could come back to haunt you in the future. If your salary is quoted net and you feel your local employer has paid your taxes according to your agreement, you may find in fact that the taxes have not been paid and you are now liable for back taxes.

## ACCOMMODATION

Like most things in Jakarta, accommodation comes in varying extremes. Take your pick. Some are palatial palaces with swimming pools, umpteen rooms and an army of staff, while others are more humble *kampung* abodes where the families of the staff are more likely to live. Accommodation in Jakarta is amazingly varied. Some of the strangest shapes exist depending on the owner's requirements or whims.

Generally speaking, the cheaper the house, the more connecting walls there are, and thus the higher the risk of noise pollution. At the cheapest end, houses have only thin wooden partitions with neighbours mere inches away. You may feel comfortable like this, more 'at one' with the people. Maybe. But living too humbly in Jakarta only serves to arouse the suspicions of your neighbours. If you can afford to travel

Middle-class housing in Ragunan.

away from your country, surely you can afford to live in a decent house? Why choose to live like a poor person? Perhaps you're just *pelit* (mean). If you are prepared to muck in, contribute to local *kampung* causes, pass the time of day with everyone, and basically not upset anyone by complaining too much or running a brothel, you will be just fine in a *kampung*. But do remember that what's yours is everybody's; you won't have any privacy, as every house is open to all and neighbours like to drop in, and drop in, and drop in.

For the largest houses, areas like Pondok Indah, Kemang (the original expat zone) and Menteng offer colossal, Spanish-villa style houses where a great many diplomats and expatriates—here at the behest of a head office 'back home'—choose to live. For details of these and other properties where rents are quoted in US dollars, try the classified ads in the English language daily, *Jakarta Post*. These homes come decked out with swimming pools, grounds, AC, jacuzzi and other modern trappings. Permata Hijau, Simpruk, between Pondok Indah and the business district, and the still-being-developed Jl. Casablanca are also areas such houses can also be found as well as high rent apartments.

Places in the medium price-range are widely spread. The north is dominated by industrial activity because of the port at Tanjuk Priok and the extensive recreational area of Ancol. If this is your residential area of choice, explore Pluit, Sunter and Kemayaron.

The areas of Kebon Jeruk and Puri Indah in West Jakarta and Kelapa Gading in the north-east are similar in that they are recent developments with vast areas of new houses. A two-storey house appears to be a Palladian palace with its Ionic pillars reaching to the roof. Inside, rooms echo thanks to the extensive use of faux marble imported from China. You should not forget that these areas were originally designated in the City's Master Plan as water catchment areas. If you do choose to live there and you are re-reading this during the rainy season, don't blame us for your predicament. There are some horrific tales of extortion in circulation from victims of the February 2007 floods in those nouveaux riche housing complexes.

Pejompongan, Cinere and Tebet are well-established communities with facilities such as markets and public transport. They are good areas to look for houses in a reasonable condition, although prices are rising as the original houses are being pulled down with more 'modern' houses being erected in their place. Unfortunately, 'modern' does not mean better.

Older houses are generally better ventilated. In a polluted city such as Jakarta, this does mean a higher dust level in the dry season, but it also means that you aren't dependent on air conditioners to keep cool, air conditioners that don't work during power cuts and contribute to global warming when they do.

There are several advantages to living in an apartment instead of a house, primarily concerned with maintenance and security. Apartment buildings also allow you to live above the street level, which can help reduce noise, bugs and rodents. And people. Living in an apartment can help you replicate the life you are used to 'back home', although claustrophobics need read no further. Large apartments are for those with large incomes who can afford a larger staff and greater privacy and large mansions.

Jakarta apartments have generally been built for the recently emerged middle class, youngish business professionals, although there are some apartment complexes which cater for young families. These have playgrounds and kindergardens *in situ*.

Apartments can be rented from the complex management company or private owners who have bought long leases. Apartment living is relatively new in Jakarta, so your main concern must be the condition of the building. Is there graffiti? Are there any light fittings missing? Talk to tenants: ask about electricity backup in the case of a power cut; check the following: electrical capacity and overall wiring condition, water supply, telephone, air conditioners, woodwork and structure. Living in an apartment leaves you dependent on a hopefully good management.

Single rooms are also available to rent and good value they can be too. Boarding houses are known as *kost* and are a good way for single foreigners to become familiar with the Indonesian way of life. *Kost* are generally either for *pria* (men) or *wanita* (women). Some, such as those in the *kampungs* which still exist on the fringes of the central business area such as Setiabudi, advertise themselves as for *karyawan* (workers). Elsewhere near university campuses, they will be for *siswa* (students). Expect to share the kitchen, bathroom and, if there is one, the TV room. Before renting a room in one, however, you should remember that Indonesians are generally very early risers, rendering a 'lie-in' a distant memory. *Kosts* are advertised regularly in the daily paper, *Kompas*.

Wherever you choose to live, remember one thing. You are going to have to commute to your office, your children's schools, the mall, the market or your favourite bar and wherever you go, the traffic is hell. If your office can provide you with a car and driver, borrow him for a day or two and do some trial runs, explore different routes, in and out of the morning and evening rush hours.

## What to Expect and Look For

One of the major drawbacks with renting any accommodation is that landlords and ladies often demand two years' rent up front. Sometimes it's only a year, sometimes it's five. You may be able to negotiate a deal where you pay half first, half later, but you are still looking at paying a lump sum to move in. Apartments, serviced or otherwise, can be rented monthly, but expect to pay extra for short-term deals.

When you consider that the rent paid on one of these Jakarta apartments is more than many workers earn in an entire year, it may put things in perspective. In many respects, Jakarta is as cosmopolitan as any other big city in the world, and consequently has the prices to prove it. Quality accommodation commands a fair price. Yet, ignoring the very few penthouses developed for Bill Gates, accommodation is still cheaper than the equivalent in Western cities and most Asian metropolises.

Whatever you rent, you should sign a mutually agreed contract specifying the period of rental, the price and, if furnished, the inventory. The cost of this is a mere Rp 6,000 for the *meterai* (stamp) you sign across.

Before settling on the home of your dreams you'll first need to consider its location. How close do you want to be to work, schools, shopping malls and other amenities? Try and assess the traffic situation when getting to and from the house. Since there very few, if any, areas of the city that don't experience *macet total* (gridlock) during the rush hours, it's an idea to view the house before or after rush hours to see how well the traffic flows the rest of the time. Are taxis prepared to go there?

It's probably best to ask your new colleagues and their spouses for advice. Better still if you have a bilingual friend with time to spare because she/he will assuredly be pleased to help you seek something suitable.

When you have chosen a suitable area, enquire about properties for rent—*"Ada rumah dikontrakken dekat disini?"*— at the street corner shops. You can also ask that bunch of guys clustered around their motorcycles; they're probably *ojek* (motorbike taxi) drivers and should know the area well and who has houses to rent and even how to contact them.

If you are not a Muslim, you probably won't truly appreciate the delights of Islam, so check how close the house is to the nearest mosque. You are never going to be far from the sound of one in Jakarta, but if you see a loudspeaker

protruding into your potential home, you might think twice before committing yourself. The calls to prayer are made five times daily: at around 4:30 am (*subah*), 12:00 pm (*zhuhur*), 2:30 pm (*ashar*), 6:00 pm (*maghrib*) and 7:30 pm (*isya*). You might want to view a house at a time that coincides with one of these calls for the most accurate evaluation of the house's noise potential.

If you see a house being renovated, then it's acceptable to wander around, but do ask for permission from the workmen first. A newly renovated house should be better than one that isn't, but you will still need to consult your checklist.

The roof is important. This might be too obvious to mention but few are the houses which do not spring a leak in the rainy season. The roof tiles shrink in the intense heat of the dry season and may have been shifted by the feral cats which romp around aloft or by the snagged nylon strings of the kites flown by the local *kampung* kids. If you can't get access to the roof, or are scared of heights, then look at the walls and ceiling tiles. If there are damp patches or brown stains, then you have evidence of potential leaks.

Check the lower walls for tidemarks and other signs of flooding. Ask the neighbours if this place is *sering kebanjiran* (prone to flooding); you wouldn't want to wake up to a foot of sewage water in your house. You'll also need to check the water supply to the house. Would you be dependent on one of the two inefficient foreign-owned water supply companies or is there a well as a backup? And what is the colour of the water?

Check for signs of termites by tapping the window and door frames. If you can poke holes in them, then they will have to be replaced.

You should check that there's enough electricity coming in to your household appliances. It runs at 220 volts of 50 cycles AC and utilises round two-pin plugs. If coming from the UK, all you need do is change the plug, and everything electrical you care to bring should function normally (and vice versa). 2,200 volts is probably enough unless you want AC in every room and want to use an electric oven, a spin dryer and a deep freeze, in which case consult a qualified electrician—if you can find one—and make sure you have a 12,000-volt fuse box installed. This will hopefully reduce the number of times your fuses give out on you. Be warned, however, that wiring is not always adequate or earthed, and in some places outside Jakarta, 110 volts are still used. A great many electrical items in Indonesia are dual voltage, 110/220 volts.

Another essential electrical pre-check is for signs of tampering. It's all too possible to find yourself being poached of electricity by means of coupled of extra wires twisted onto your connection box. You don't want to find, to your horror, one day that you have been supplying half the neighbourhood with *listrik* (electricity). To clarify matters, turn everything off in the house and see if the discs in the meter are still turning.

Commonly, rooms in Indonesian houses feature only a single electrical outlet, often at light-switch level, so invest in some good quality multi-plugs and extensions. If running sensitive equipment like a computer, you should invest in voltage stabilisers as precautions against the frequent power surges. Also, make sure the place is well grounded against lightning; inadequate grounding will serve the reverse effect and actually attract lightning. In a storm, you should switch off all electrical things or risk them exploding.

Once settled in your home, you might want to invest in a couple of battery-operated fluorescent lamps, the kind that come on automatically when the power goes off. You see, wherever you live, there's a good chance of a power cut. If you're in a hotel or apartment, generally there's a generator to keep your light bulbs lit, although your AC will be off. The blackouts themselves tend to occur in zones; some areas may be without *listrik* for hours while next door seems to be working normally. If it keeps up for more than six hours, you can try calling the local office of PLN, the state electricity board, but don't expect any miracles. Just remember where you keep your supply of candles, batteries and torches. And go to bed early.

Worried about security? Although there is a city ordinance limiting the height of perimeter walls to 2 m (6.6 ft), this is not strictly adhered to. Broken glass, barbed wire and razor-spikes can be embedded in these walls as a deterrent. Indoors, bars can be fitted over windows. There are security firms which install sophisticated alarm systems, but find out if the neighbourhood employs *hansips* (night security guards). This is the cheaper option as you will only have to pay a small monthly contribution to their salaries. Get to know them and if you give them some *uang rokok* (cigarette money) before you go out of town, they'll keep a watchful eye open for you.

If you are in any way perturbed about becoming part of the local community, then rent a rather cramped and expensive apartment. Alternatively, consider living in one of the housing complexes which can almost totally insulate you from the world 'out there'. Here life goes on unabashed as it would in any middle-class, American suburban trash-pad: lawns, sidewalks, satellite dishes and garden sprinklers with a country club for committee meetings, coffee mornings, slide shows and optional wife swapping. All this fake happiness is surrounded by an insurmountable wall and round-the-clock security. Not just anyone can walk in; you have to be invited.

Of course, if you need to go to such extremes for your home comforts, you ought to reconsider, if possible, your decision to read this book and live in a place like Jakarta.

## Satellite Towns

The concept of a green belt surrounding Jakarta has yet to be adopted, and when it is, it will be too late because all fields will have been built on. And Jabotabek—Jakarta, Bogor, Tangerang and Bekasi—will be the new name of what is already the third largest urban area in the world, following Tokyo-Yokohama and New York. If other satellite towns such as Depok, Serpong, Lippo Karawaci and Lippo Karawang are added, there would be a combined population of about 25 million and an even more cumbersome name. But at least you'll have more places to search for a suitable residence.

## LOCAL GOVERNMENT

Once you have chosen your home for the next year or so, you'll need to register your presence. There is a system of local government which, at its best, is possibly the most democratic you'll ever encounter. Away from the auspicious heavy hand of Big Brother, the people of Jakarta's backstreets and *kampung* turn a blind eye to the actions of the 'real' government. The average person, it seems, prefers relating to something more down-to-earth.

At the most fundamental, domestic level of government is the *Rukun Tetangga*. Literally, the 'peace keeper', he is known more commonly to the local residents, his neighbours, as Pak RT (pronounced Pak 'Air-tay'). Pak RT is the reason people sleep well at night in Indonesia because he is the Domestic President, the Man In The Know, the Trusted One.

The RT is aware of exactly who is living on his allotted patch, who is visiting, who is dying, who is getting born, and who is getting married. Apart from organising rubbish disposal for some 30 houses, he provides neighbourhood security in the form of night patrols, known as *hansip*. They make their presence known by whacking a stick against your gate every hour, on the hour. This sort of defeats the object of a good night's sleep, but for the average Indonesian, this racket-making is a subconscious message that all is well, thus they sleep even better.

The RT is elected by the people of the neighbourhood and is unpaid—most RT have day jobs. If the neighbours are happy with a particular RT, he will be voted back into 'office' time and time. The importance of his job is immense. He's a vital means of communication between the government and the common people. The RT is a focal point for the neighbourhood: people know there's always someone to go to if there's a problem. Neighbourhood protection of this kind was introduced during the Japanese occupation of the country, and is something lacking in most Western countries. Indonesians have greater peace of mind knowing their area is protected.

It is possible to run into trouble with your RT, depending on how liberal your lifestyle is. He might read you the riot-act: no friends of the opposite gender after 10:00 pm and no more than four guests at once. Expect all overnight guests to get his clearance first, unless you know him well and you've lived in your house a fair while. Strictly speaking, if you choose to sleep at an address which is different to that stated on your identity card, you must report to the police, as well as to your RT. You may then want to break a minor law and sweeten your RT's disgust at your Western ways by plying him with small but regular gifts, particularly if you live in an area which gets shut off at night with a security barrier.

Put eight RT together and you have an RW (*Rukun Warga*). Twenty RW (pronounced 'air-way') are a *kelurahan* and 20 of these, a *kecamatan*. And there is more: put a few *kecamatan* together and you have one of the five municipalities that make up Jakarta. Each of these is headed by a *walikota*, or mayor, who is in turn responsible to the Governor of Jakarta. The rest is Big Boys' stuff and best left that way.

## FLOORS AND FURNITURE

Given the choice, Indonesians would rather relax on the floor than in chairs. The furniture in Indonesian homes is mainly reserved as a place for newly-arrived guests to be sat bolt upright in. But there's still a fine variety of furniture with which to fill a house with.

Carpets are not normal household necessities in Indonesia. Tiles are the standard floor cover, possibly with a few small rugs for decoration, and make for a much cooler and cleaner house. Shoes are out, bare feet are in.

When setting up home, finances are usually tight so you might like to consider having some large scatter cushions made. Buy some 'ethnic' fabrics, have them made into covers by a local tailor and then have them stuffed with *kapuk* (cotton fibre) by the guy passing your house crying "*kasur*" (mattress) and carrying striped mattress cover material over his shoulder.

Some of the cheapest and most hardwearing furniture available is made from bamboo, which grows thick and fast in Indonesia. Its natural hollow-block form lends itself perfectly to furniture construction, besides being excellent value for money. The major drawback with bamboo, however, is its noise potential. Bamboo chairs continue to creak and crack disturbingly, hours after the sitter has upped and gone

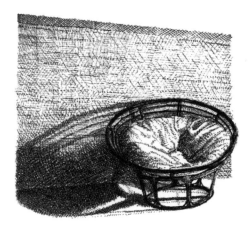

The ubiquitous egg-cup chair, comfy and affordable.

elsewhere. Sex on a bamboo bed is out of the question, unless you feel the need to draw attention to yourself. Being the bottom end of the market, you don't have to look hard to find this kind of furniture, as it's just as likely to come to you. Street sellers regularly make the rounds of neighbourhoods carrying three-piece suites.

Rattan furniture is a common sight in Jakarta homes and can be inexpensively custom-made to your designs. Jl. Duren Tiga in Mampang and the streets of Kemang have reputable rattan furniture shops. Ciputat Raya and Jl. Fatmawati are also good places in Jakarta to find furniture. An excellent idea in rattan furniture is a giant egg-cup chair which is a cushion-filled, semicircular dome, some 2 m (6.6 ft) in diameter, which can be swivelled about upon an eggcup-like base. You sit in rather than on it.

Traditional furniture is harder to find and much of what does exist is heavily Dutch, Chinese and Indian influenced. Indeed, it was the Dutch who introduced teak to Indonesia and were responsible for Java's teak plantations. Yet it doesn't look particularly foreign; like most things that comes to Indonesia, furniture has had to be distinctly 'Indonesianised' before being accepted at large.

When buying a bed, after making sure it's long enough, you need to decide whether to buy a wooden frame and equip it with a foam mattress or with a more traditional *kapuk* (cotton fibre) one. *Kapuk* is generally a much harder surface to sleep on, and mattresses and pillows need a daily beating to ensure they stay in shape. If not, a trough develops in the mattress after a few nights and you end up sleeping directly on hardboard. If you think you'll be here for the long haul, then a good investment is a spring bed. After all, we do spend as much as a third of our lives lying down, so the least we can do is to ensure our own comfort.

No matter how posh or cheap the furniture, no matter how springy the rattan, chairs, sofas and beds, they are routinely spoiled by the use of protective plastic. Presumably in an attempt to maintain the stain-free illusion of the piece being *masih baru* (still new), plastic is stretched over surfaces so unwitting foreign guests squirm and sweat on squeaky polyurethane. Eventually, the plastic is holed and the furniture collects a number of dark patches to show where the holes used to be. A similar anomaly occurs in a great many cars and taxis.

Nevertheless, furniture can still be a confusing concept for our country cousins. Have too much furniture and a visiting *orang kampung* will opt for the floor every time. Put them in a room with two single beds and the next morning find them sleeping on the floor between the two, or even under one. Entire families are accommodated in this way.

There is just one item of furniture which once used you'll wonder how you ever coped without. That is a bolster, the metre long sausage-shaped cushion known as a *bantal guling*. This is sometimes known here as a Dutch wife or, by gays, as a Dutch uncle. In bed, it is hugged with one leg cocked over and thus provides a cooling air space.

## HOTELS

Being a foreigner in a city like Jakarta, you find that even if you're not staying in an international hotel, you are at liberty to pop in unquestioned anytime to use the facilities of one. You'll also find that comparatively, prices for the use of a five-star hotel pool, fitness centre, restaurant and business facility are good. Thus, 'breakfast at the Sultan

Hilton' or 'lunch at the Hyatt' are benefits that can accompany 'being foreign' in Jakarta and the assumed affluence that this generally entails. The major international-style hotels are in the city centre, close to the main boulevards.

Many visitors comment that, rather than pre-booking, it's a lot cheaper to turn up and ask for a discount. Occupancy rates have yet to reach the heights of pre-krismon.

The Sultan—formerly the Jakarta Hilton International—on Jl. Gatot Subroto is well established and typically provides the five-star, albeit generic, treatment associated with the name 'Hilton'. Set in 32 acres of garden, the hotel is a fine place to find a bit of anonymity. At the end of 2006, a major trial was underway because it shouldn't have been built on such a scale. The original owner and developer was Ibnu Sutowo, who made his 'fortune'—possibly as much as US$ 4 billion—from ripping off Pertamina, the state oil company. The current trial concerns the illegal granting of land usage rights, presumably for generously-filled brown envelopes: the Senayan area is supposed to be for public rather than private facilities. And the hotel has been renamed, presumably in recognition that the new owner is the Sultan of Brunei, who is also obscenely wealthy thanks to his country's oil fields.

Not far from the Hilton and of similar five-star anonymity are the Crowne Plaza, Shangri-La, Sari Pan-Pacific, Sahid Jaya and Le Meridien.

The Welcome Statue roundabout on Jl Thamrin is host to a number of hotels and shopping areas, making it an obvious focal point for the first-time visitor. On the east corner of the roundabout, opposite the British Embassy, is the Mandarin Oriental, which has always been popular with business people and was the base for journalists during the riots of May 1998 which saw the abdication of Suharto. The Grand Hyatt, which had the backing of Bambang Suharto, the second son of former President Suharto, is built onto the end of Plaza Indonesia on the west of the roundabout. Both are widely considered to be among the city's 'poshest'.

To the south of this is the Hotel Indonesia. Designed by the first president, Sukarno, this was the original star-rated hotel of Jakarta and first high-rise building. It is where the city's foreigners took refuge when Sukarno's government fell to pieces in the mid-1960s, as featured in the movie of that very fraught period, *The Year of Living Dangerously,* starring Mel Gibson. It is currently being remodelled to incorporate yet another upmarket shopping mall, but it is expected to retain a certain sense of history, if only in its façade.

## AILMENTS

Although the city is such a hot, humid and polluted place, it offers fewer everyday health problems than might be expected. Commonly, people in Indonesia seem to suffer from four basic ailments: *masuk angina* and *panas dalam* (hot inside), which are peculiar to Indonesia, as well as *sakit flu* (*sakit* means 'ill'), and the inevitable *sakit perut* (sick stomach).

Indonesia has recognised that it has an AIDS problem. As elsewhere, you are advised to take precautions.

For general aches and pains, take the paracetamol-based Panadol or the Ibuprofen-based Ponstan. You'll find that many *apotik* (pharmacy) are very obliging and sell any number of medicines over the counter. If you know what you want, then you can ask for generic drugs, although, surprisingly, aspirin isn't one. It's possible to suffer more serious complaints like dysentery and gastroenteritis, but if you are careful with what you drink, you need not be over-concerned.

## Masuk Angin

If you stand in a draught too long or drive with the window down, you will notice people becoming very agitated. They are worried about getting the most common ailment of all: *masuk angin* (which literally means 'entered wind'). This is not to be taken lightly, although most of us believe that breathing is a normal and very healthy activity.

*Masuk angin* is the reason people take the day off work. It's the oldest one in the book and often dismissed outright by obstinate Westerners who think it doesn't exist. But it does. *Masuk angin* is an aching, rheumatic-type complaint and readily treated with the wearing of *koyok cabe* (Bandaids impregnated with chillies) on each temple. Alternatively you can get *kerokan*. This is a particularly intense form of massage whereby the afflicted individual has balsam rubbed slowly and repeatedly in long lines across the back with the edge of a coin. It's very effective, bringing heat to the surface of the skin and relieving muscular pain, although you do look like a red zebra afterwards. It's quite feasible to have *masuk angin* without having flu. Watch out.

## Panas Dalam

Being hot inside is generally one way of indicating that you're alive. However, the Indonesian penchant for drowning all food, including fruit, with sambal (chilli sauce) can lead to this condition, as will eating any food that disagrees with you.

If you can taste your bile after burping or have a few spots on your tongue, then you'll have to drink a bottle of *Adem Sari* or *Kaki Tiga* (Three Legs)

## Sakit Flu

What is known as the common cold in the West and rather inaccurately as the flu in Indonesia is a surprisingly common problem. Presumably, it's the unhealthy combination of heat, humidity, air-conditioning and electric fans that causes this. For after standing ten minutes in the midday sun, then

jumping into a taxi with an air-conditioning system that is only effective to about three square inches on the side of your neck, before stepping back into the blinding sun, it's easy to see the kind of temperature changes which contribute to cold-germ build up.

## Sakit Perut

At some inevitable point, you are going to get *sakit perut*— an upset stomach. If afflicted, it's best just to drink a lot of water and avoid fruit and fatty foods. Above all, avoid getting dehydrated. Charcoal tablets like Norit are good stomach medicines, and Entrostop is good for the more serious bouts. The Indonesian equivalent of indigestion, *sakit ma'ag*, is another common complaint, a result perhaps of the tons of *cabe* (chilli) people like to eat. Take Promag or the heavier duty Milanta if this is the case. Just ask at a *warung* near you.

## Pusing

Listen to loud music for too long, being nagged by your spouse or boss, concentrating on one thing for a long time (like reading *CultureShock! Jakarta*?), or being stuck in the traffic can all lead an individual to complain of feeling *pusing* (dizzy). The first symptom of *pusing* is to be *bingung* or *heran* (confused). If your Indonesian friend comes over all *pusing*, a head massage is the only solution.

## DOCTORS AND DENTISTS

When you first arrive, you will be amazed at the number of surgeries operated by *Dokter Gigi*, often in neighbourhood back streets. Wow, he must be really busy you think, until you are told that *gigi* means teeth.

As elsewhere, becoming a registered doctor is an expensive process taking many years. It also promises to make medical graduates relatively wealthy. During the Suharto era, as a contribution to the nation's development, new recruits to the medical profession were expected to work for a couple of years in the poorest regions of the country. Community health clinics, known as *Puskesmas*, were built to provide basic medical care, including pre-natal. Opportunities for enrichment are few. Similarly, working for a salary in a city hospital is not very lucrative.

Hence the proliferation of neighbourhood surgeries, perhaps in the spare front room or a converted garage. Hours are minimal and signposted, generally black lettering on a white background. If you can't work out for yourself what is wrong with you, then you'll need a general practitioner, a *doktor umum* (public doctor). He or she will then refer you to a *spesialis*: some are *spesialis* in *anak* (children) or body parts, such as *jantung* (heart), *mata* (eyes) and *kulit* (skin).

Eventually, you'll be given a *resep* (prescription) which you take to your local *apotik*. Hopefully, you will get well soon.

## HOSPITALS
There are a few *Rumah Sakit* (houses for the sick—hospitals) which meet expatriate expectations, and many more which have ER facilities. When you see, for example, RS Tebet on your travels, look for the 'Emergensi 24' signs. If you are registered with a local health insurance scheme, you should be given a list of 'approved' hospitals along with your membership card. However, you will only be given one of these if you have a work and residence permit. You may possibly register your spouse and children in the scheme by paying the necessary contributions.

If, however, you only intend to stay in Jakarta (and Indonesia) for a short while, you should consider a health insurance plan from your home country, possibly with repatriation cover.

## ALTERNATIVE MEDICINE
Western medicine is relatively modern. It is worth bearing in mind that what is termed 'alternative medicine' in the West has been readily available for centuries in the East. Treatments available range from acupuncture to reflexology to *pijit* (massage). And then there's the universal panacea—balsam. There are a number of brands which come in a variety of colours. Unfortunately, manufacturers haven't set an agreed colour-equals-strength code, so you'll have to

experiment in order to find which brand and colour suits you best.

All contain eucalyptus oil (*minyak kayu putih*) which is available in bottles, all that is except for a super-duper strength red liquid called *obat gosok* from Ambon, at the heart of the fabled Spice Islands, which contains oil from the root and bark of the lawang tree from star anise.

Of course, not getting sick in the first place is best, so a healthy diet and lots of exercise is important. For this, you could try living in Bali.

## JAMU

One of the biggest selling domestic products in Indonesia is the herbal remedy they call *jamu*. Spend any time in Jakarta and you soon see a woman in tight *sarung* carrying a wicker backpack of coloured bottles. She is a *tukang jamu*, a travelling medicine show, the local street herbalist. She patrols her allotted streets just in case someone nearby or a regular customer isn't feeling right. Most *jamu* ladies come from Central Java, although yours may be from East (rather than West) Java.

You never ask for a specific combination of *jamu*—describe your general symptoms and the appropriate concoction will be prepared thus. No ailment is beyond the scope of *jamu*. A lot of people still make their own, relying on plants grown nearby as well as a supplement of prepared ingredients to complete the recipe. Indonesians take *jamu* as well as conventional medicine—it's certainly no cheaper.

So what's in it, and does it really work? Well, it sells truckloads and because the concoction tastes so foul that a small glass of a sugar drink is given as a chaser. Lots of things in fact: mainly extracts of the leaves, roots and herbs which grow all over this fertile land, as well as loads of other things found only in the rainforest.

Indonesian women swear by their *jamu* and are by far its biggest users. Varieties are sold to them along the lines of 'essential feminine hygiene'. Following childbirth, for example, women are given a variety of heavy *jamu* preparations. An external *jamu* is rubbed over the stomach to help remove any

In Indonesia, the *jamu* is a cure-all for any illnesses, no one knows if it is merely placebo effect or if it really works. But Indonesians swear by it.

stretch marks, and gallons of internal *jamu* are drunk to help get the woman's insides settled again. She probably took a certain *jamu* to get pregnant in the first place and another during the course of her pregnancy. Some women change their minds the next day and seek out *jamu* for *terlambat bulan* (late period)—at least that's what it says on the packet.

But a lot of it is wishful thinking. Much of the over-the-counter *jamu* (as opposed to that sold by the *jamu* ladies in the street) is packaged with pictures of rippling musclemen and sweet-lipped, sultry women on the box.

### The Medicine That Cures Everything

One TV advert showed a woman chatting to a neighbour upon return from the market one morning. Something slips out of her basket. "What's that?" inquires the friend. "That?" says the women, all red-faced and *malu* (bashful), "Oh, that's just a little something I picked up for Bapak." In her hand is a packet of 'special' *jamu*, guaranteed to make her husband *kuat* (strong). Oo-er.

Whether or not it does enhance virility so vividly remains open to question. Mind over matter, perhaps. Besides, you'll spot many small *warungs* selling *Obat Pria* or *Obat Perkasa* (men's medicine), including Viagra. Be careful though, much of it is fake and may give you unexpected side effects (which we'll leave to the imagination). However, the fact that *jamu* is packaged like Western medicine and that there are an estimated 1,500 producers of *jamu*, mostly in Central Java, and that it is sold in pill, capsule, cream, liquid and powder form and that Indonesians enthusiastically *minum obat* (consume nostrums), is an indication that the *jamu* industry is guaranteed a rosy future.

## STRESS RELIEF

When you are in a bad mood in Jakarta, you are in the worst place in the world. You will wonder what made you ever come in the first place. The heat will make it difficult to breathe. Your head will get hot. You feel sweat running down every crevasse and cleavage. Your crotch rot reminds you to wear cotton boxer shorts and not nylon bikini knickers. Your taxi driver hasn't a clue how to get to the airport. The next one doesn't stop for you, and a passing bus drives through a puddle leaving you drenched in oily gunge. The passengers stare at you and laugh. Appalling things go on all around, and no one seems to mind. The Goat Leg Soup you had earlier starts repeating on you. Someone with a cheese-grater for a voice starts a conversation: "Why aren't you married? Do you get paid in rupiah or dollars?" Someone else refuses to acknowledge that you can speak a modicum of *bahasa Indonesia* and tries to con you. Yet another person asks you where you are going. Another shop overcharges you. Another group of children starts laughing and pointing. Then you realise the hairdresser you visited earlier has made a hilarious wedge (à la *kampung*) of your hair.

*Aduh…..pusing, pusing.*

Methods of stress relief vary from person to person. Some start eating. Some start drinking. Some have to lie down with the curtains drawn and all doors shut. You don't want to go to prison by doing something outrageous so it's best to try and contain any wilder inclinations.

So where do you go when it's all too much? What do you do when you can't take any more? What outlets are there for your frustrations in this blighted and hostile city? You start wishing you were in prison. (Although Westerners are reputed to make well-respected cellmates in Indonesia prisons, invariably ending up teaching the entire prison to speak English, it's probably not the best way to gain experience in the field of applied linguistics. And your stress level…?)

When this is your frame of mind, it's best to step back, keep calm, add the incident that disturbed you to your list of 'What-the-(insert-choice-of-expletive)?' moments which seem to happen every day and remember that living in Jakarta is far from boring.

## WATER

Jakarta sits on the northern coast of Java. Thirteen rivers flow from the surrounding hills and meet somewhere in the centre of the city before flowing into the sea.

To escape the heat of the city, Jakartans have, over the years, built themselves plush villas outside the city and more recently whole townships have mushroomed on the flood plain, inevitably at the expense of the fields and trees which absorbed much of the water heading towards the city.

This unabsorbed water is one of the major causes of the floods which are common every rainy season. When they occur, the city simply grinds to a halt and headlines appear in the next day's papers. A further cause is the commonly perceived notion that rivers and storm drains are good placers to dump rubbish. After all, it all gets carried away out of sight, doesn't it? That's as may be, but when the Dutch were here, they built a system of drainage canals with floodgates where the present day rubbish piles up and water backs up and overflows the riverbanks which are home to many squatter families.

In 2006, Jakarta had a water deficit of 36 million cu.m per annum from the total demand of 400 million cu.m. The city water company PT PAM Jaya, through its two privatised operators, one predominantly French and the other predominantly English, can only supply 40 per cent of the city's needs from reservoirs, not including the water which seeps away because of the inadequate infrastructure. Until recently, most of the city's raw water was taken from the Citarum river in West Java, via the Jatiluhur dam. The companies have had to look further afield for cleaner water, siphoning supplies from rivers in Tangerang, west of Jakarta. This has, of course, reduced the amount of water available for other purposes, such as irrigation of agricultural land.

The needs of other domestic and industrial users have been met by the drilling of artesian wells in the water table which supplies the rest of Jakarta's water needs. The inevitable consequence has been a sinking of the water table. Sea water has seeped in to the north, thus further diminishing potable supplies, and there are some factories and households which continue to dump their untreated waste into the rivers and storm drains, thus rendering more of the city's water unusable.

There are water purification systems on the market which claim to leave your tap water drinkable; whether they do or not is open to question, and boiling is really the only answer. If your water seems to have a high mineral content and is perhaps a brownish-red colour, it need not necessarily be a health risk, although for your guest's sake you may prefer to filter it to a recognisable colour. The Departemen Kesehatan (Health Dept) on Jl Kesehatan, Central Jakarta, will test the quality and contamination level of your water for a reasonable fee. All they need is a couple of litres in a sterile container and a couple of weeks.

Around the house, you are going to be using well or mains water for your cleaning and cooking. This is perfectly safe. Well, moderately safe anyway. You can get away with washing clothes and yourself in it and it's generally okay to brush your teeth with it. You just have to be careful not to swallow any. If you don't like this idea, then use your boiled or bottled water.

For customers of one of the water companies, there is a meter showing usage and a monthly bill to be paid. Well water, incidentally, is theoretically taxable, although we have yet to hear of a domestic well user paying anything.

Tap water in Jakarta is usually of a painfully low pressure. To combat this, many houses have pressure pumps installed and elevated water tanks to let gravity lend a hand, and allow at least a little water to be used in the event of a power cut.

If you live in South Jakarta, your water supply will probably be from a well. Depending on your location, this will be between 10 and 15 m (32.8–49.2 ft) deep. If you are lucky, you may hit 'clean' water at a lesser depth. Whether from a pipe or well, your water may be perfectly adequate for

washing purposes, but unless it has been thoroughly boiled for five minutes or so, it's best not to risk drinking it. The agony of a *sakit perut* (upset stomach) is simply not worth it. Many households boil up a large pot of water in the evening ready for the next day.

At times during the hot season, the well may run dry. This highlights the importance of getting on well with your neighbours because it is their supply you will have to borrow while you have your well dug deeper. Either that or spend a fortune filling your *mandi* with bottled water.

---

**Where You Get Your Drinking Water**

Your drinking water needs are met by a number of companies. The most common brands are Aqua, now owned by the multi-national Danone, Sosro and Oasis, the 19-litre (20 quarts) plastic bottles of which can usually be delivered from your neighbourhood *warung*. Other popular brands include Ades, which is a two-syllable word, and Wet, which naturally is. Every sensible office block and home uses water dispensing machines. These offer very hot and very cold water on tap(s), and once you have got into the habit, are quite impossible to live without. It's an idea to clean your dispenser out every now and then; *cicak* and cockroaches have been known to find their way through pipes at the back and up into the bottle with the next 'blub, blub, blung' of the machine.

---

Handy for travelling around the city are half litre bottles which can be refilled at the next available dispenser. Some people have been known to carry the same Sosro bottle for months, filling it up periodically. Check for drink seals that might have been tampered with. It would not be wise to pay for what turns out to be just bottled well water. You may also like to try the green and fruit teas which are sold in similar plastic bottles.

Upon arrival at someone's house, you may be given a glass of hot water. This may not seem appealing, but at least you know it has been boiled. If you want water in a restaurant, ask for *air putih* or *air matang* (boiled water), or *air minum* (bottled drinking water). If you want it cold, specify *yang dingin*.

You may wonder when you order a drink with ice whether the ice has been made from boiled water or not. This is a good question with a hard to determine answer. You will see huge blocks being transported through traffic jams on converted *becaks*, and dragged across streets and dropped on the ground a few times. Not to worry, as this ice is for cooling bottles of soft drinks on sale in the street kiosks. It's generally outside Jakarta that you have to be careful.

## MANDI

Get dirty in Indonesia and you'll need the *mandi*. A home is not a home without one, for this is the *kamar mandi* (bathroom), usually with the toilet. The *bak mandi* is a water tank, about the size of a tea chest; it's often a tiled affair, although there are shaped cement and fibreglass varieties. Indonesian bathrooms always have sloping floors and a hole somewhere for the water to drain. Sitting on the side is the

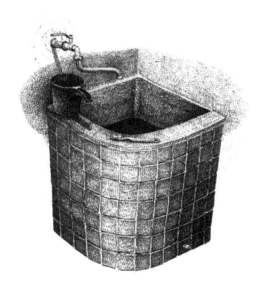

Not to be mistaken for an upright bathtub, the *bak mandi* is essential to Jakartans sweltering in the tropical heat and humidity.

*gayung*, a plastic scoop for pouring water over yourself with. Instructions for use are thus:

1) Strip naked.
2) Fill plastic saucepan with water.
3) Brace yourself.
4) Pour all over.
5) Repeat process to ensure total wetness.
6) Soap well all over.
7) Repeat steps 2 through 4. You get used to it.

*Mandi* is a verb. It means to shower; to wash; to soap and scrub. You *mandi* before you *tidur* (sleep); you *mandi* when you *bangun tidur* (wake up). If you don't *mandi*, you tend to *bau* (stink). *Mandi* is also a noun. You have a quick one. You spend too long in someone's house, they ask you if you would like one. An awful lot of modern houses feature shower units and Western-style baths, but it's the *mandi* that dominates.

The *mandi* is something worth talking about. A standard greeting in Indonesia is *"Sudah mandi?"* (Have you bathed yet?) You have to do it at least twice a day—less just wouldn't be Indonesian. The water is cold, the country is hot—it feels good to *mandi*. Exhausted? Hot? Hungover? You'll need a *mandi* to make you feel better. In the hot season, for those homes without AC, a frequent *mandi* is the only solution. It's real bathing after all; it's not showering and it isn't 'having a bath'. Having a *mandi* is really a continuation of the river washing tradition. They make the most reassuring of sounds, its 'splash-splosh' another of the defining sounds of Indonesia. Hear it early morning and late in the evening; hear it all day.

Change the water in the *mandi* regularly; otherwise it will quickly become a haven for insect life. Wriggling worm-things and mosquitoes are among the first to set up shop in your *mandi*, their eggs hatching soon after and you itching not long after that. On the other hand, you might consider keeping a few fish in your *mandi* to eat any passing mosquitoes and eggs. Works a treat but we all know what fish do in water.

New visitors to Indonesia may be tempted, in their confusion, to climb into the *bak mandi*. They think: 'What do I do? What is this? I'm not sure; maybe I should just climb in. Perhaps the host knew I was coming and filled the bath ready for me; perhaps people in Southeast Asia always have upright bathtubs.' Never do this;

never ever climb into the *mandi*. This is very bad form in Indonesia, a social error of massive proportions.

## TOILETS

There is a distinct lack of public toilets in Jakarta, but there is a National Movement for the Socialisation of Standard Public Toilets in Indonesia sponsored by, among others, Toto, the World's Largest Toilet Manufacturer which, we understand, has no connection with the rock group, and Domestos, the all-purpose toilet cleaner and smell remover. The campaign has yet to yield major results and with few expectations that it will, don't hold your breath. Unless, you get caught short.

Using one in a shop, a restaurant, a hotel or shopping mall without any other obligation is perfectly acceptable. The toilets in star-rated hotels, which employ toilet-staff to ensure that the time spent in their *kamar kecil* (little room) is satisfactory, are worth a visit. Toilets in public facilities, such as Soekarno-Hatta Airport, are generally well maintained. Be prepared for some appalling lavatorial experiences elsewhere, particularly in Padang restaurants. These could lead you to convert to stoicism in an effort to self-impose constipation.

Do not expect to find paper in Indonesia WC (pronounced *way-say*), as this is still not common practice. Keep some handy, as in a back pocket, if using it is your practice. Traditionally, the left hand is the preferred bottom-wipe in Indonesia: a bucket of water and a left hand is all that's needed. To add to the horror, there may be a sign asking you to place the soiled paper in a bin. This is a grim reminder that Jakarta does not have a fully integrated sewage system.

Although the Western-style 'sit-down' toilet is the upmarket choice in Jakarta, the traditional 'squatter' is still prevalent. Many Indonesians are *bingung* (perplexed) at the idea of actually sitting down on a toilet seat. There's nothing essentially wrong with 'squatters', but they can be taxing on the calf muscles. And great care must be taken that loose change, wallets and hand phones don't disappear down the hole; fishing them out is best left to the imagination.

Expect some toilets to be wet and some to be dry—there are no woolly bathmats around Indonesian amenities. True to the bucket-of-water-and-scoop concept of the *mandi*, not to mention the sloping tiled floor, you need to remember to take off your socks before entering. Many offices where Indonesians work alongside foreigners have installed both types of toilets in an attempt to keep everyone contented.

Unless you exclusively use five-star facilities, do not expect to find a hand towel for use after you have washed your hands. The knack is to know when you've shaken off enough moisture to complete the drying on your trousers or handkerchief. When you can do this and when the footmarks on the toilet seat are yours, you will know enough to give this book away.

If your child gets caught short in a residential area and there is no sign of where to go, you could, with discretion, knock on someone's door and, possibly through mime, ask to use the *way-say*. There is every likelihood that the sheer novelty of the situation will lead to success with smiles all round.

But, one word of warning: whereas some owners of 'public' facilities expect a payment of, say, Rp 500, do not insult your host by offering a tip.

## BANKING AND MONEY

Contrary to what you may have heard, Indonesian banks are safe. Those banks which were treated as personal fiefdoms before the Asian Economic Meltdown of 1996/1997 (krismon) have been closed down or amalgamated with others with less shaky foundations. Their directors either fled abroad, mainly to Singapore and China, or have faced criminal charges.

Throughout Jakarta, there are numerous foreign and local banks all offering a full range of banking services, such as both rupiah and foreign currency (usually US dollars) savings and checking accounts, term deposits, as well as credit and debit card accounts and foreign exchange services. There are very few that do not issue ATM/debit cards with the links to internationally recognised money clearing systems such as MasterCard, Visa and Alto. Most local banks also belong to the nationally networked ATM Bersama, thus allowing withdrawal of cash in most Indonesian towns. Foreign banks are also well represented, mainly in their part-ownership of local banks, but also, like HSBC, in having major branches here. Major branches offer safe deposit boxes.

Banks have several strict requirements for opening a personal bank account, including letters of reference from your employer or sponsor as well as copies of your passport and KITAS card. In order to open a personal account in US dollars, many banks also require a minimum deposit be maintained. For checking accounts, a reference from your previous bank, your company's Tax Registration Number and a letter from your company verifying that Indonesian income tax is paid by the company should also be submitted.

Because of the vast range of services and policies unique to each bank, it is advisable to call and make inquiries directly, then follow up by a personal visit. However, some companies prefer their staff to have accounts in a particular bank. Supposedly, this makes the transfer of salaries and other monies easier. It is not necessary, particular if you stay any length of time and change employers. You decide which bank you're comfortable with, perhaps because it has a branch near your home or because, like BCA, it offers Internet banking.

Many expatriates living in Indonesia choose the option of maintaining their normal account in their home country or of opening an account in Singapore. Their employer will then transfer their salary each month directly to this account. You may choose to receive part of your wages in Indonesia in rupiah to cover your cash expenditure in Jakarta.

When you travel outside Jakarta, first make sure that you have enough cash for your immediate needs. Not every town has an ATM.

---

### Money Transfers

Western Union facilities can be found in many banks—just look for the yellow and black sign. They are by far the quickest and most convenient way of receiving money transfers from abroad.

## Automatic Teller Machines

ATMs are conveniently located in shopping centres, malls and office buildings throughout the city and operate with widely accepted international credit and debit cards affiliated with: Alto, Maestro, Cirrus, Plus, Master Card and Visa. Indonesian banks are also connected to ATM Bersama, a countrywide network. Cash withdrawals in US dollars are available from Citibank ATMs.

## Credit Card Fraud

Credit card holders are advised to be extremely cautious using credit cards in Indonesia due to the danger of credit card fraud. Crimes related to credit card misuse are prevalent and include the use of stolen or counterfeit credit cards for Internet transactions. Such has been Indonesia's reputation that it was only in late 2006 that PayPal accepted online credit card payments emanating from Indonesia.

It is preferable to use cash for purchases and only take local currency from ATMs using your banking network. Do not use VISA or MasterCard debit cards tied to your current account when making purchases, since debit cards allow thieves to wipe out the total amount from the current account.

As a rule, no matter where you are, never lose sight of your credit or debit cards when using them to make any purchase.

## Money Changers

Money changers are conveniently located throughout the city as well as in most shopping malls, department stores and hotels. It is recommended to bring only brand new unmarked notes, as old, dirty or marked notes are often rejected by money changers.

By comparison, local banks (BII, BNI, BCA, etc) often give exchange rates that are at least as good as the money changers, and sometimes a bit better. Banks also have a lower risk of giving you fake Indonesian money, but they offer shorter opening hours and can take longer to change money.

## Currency

Once you understand the mysteries of Indonesia's money and banking system, you will soon feel comfortable with the local currency. For expatriates with foreign currency salaries to convert into rupiah, Indonesia offers many great bargains!

Apart from wandering round the malls gazing at those with money, nothing comes free in Jakarta, so you'll need money. This comes in various sizes and colours. The smallest bank note is Rp 1,000, followed by Rp 5,000, Rp 10,000, Rp 20.000, Rp 50.000 and Rp 100,000. The colours are changed regularly as counterfeiters, some even from the country's mint, learn how to make fairly reasonable copies on personal computers and photocopiers. The largest note is now heavily plasticised.

As we write, there are still a couple of 'real' coins in use. The yellowish Rp 500 and the Rp 1,000 which is silverish with a yellowish centre make a satisfying clink when you drop them. You may also come across some Rp 100 coins with the same propensity, but these are being withdrawn in favour of lightweight alloy discs. Other lightweight coins in circulation are valued, if value is what they have, at Rp 200 and Rp 500. None of them are suitable for making a choice of heads or tails as they are liable to be carried away in the slightest breeze. The boiled sweets which are substituted when such coins are scarce can't be used either.

## CLOTHES

For visitors from temperate climates, Jakarta's heat and humidity is a test of endurance, so for the most part, light cotton *pakai'an* (clothes) are best. Natural fibres are definitely the ones to wear, the climate leaving little choice as to what can be worn comfortably. If you travel in air-conditioned vehicles and work in an air-conditioned office all day, you have more flexibility in what you wear. Around the house, a *sarung* is certainly the next best thing to being naked, and certainly the coolest. Shorts and T-shirt come a close second. A single jumper is a good idea, for those times you spend in cooler climes like Puncak or Bandung, or if you really do get ill. Also, it's essential that you have an outfit for when you return home. There's nothing worse than going from tropical climes to the depths of winter in lightweight, short-sleeved cotton tops.

Around town, you are expected to dress a little formally. Kuta beach in Bali aside, Jakarta is the most easy-going place in Indonesia, where the latest fashions are slavishly followed and tailors work overtime to copy ideas from fashion magazines. However, a woman in a short skirt or a low cut top, for example, is automatically assumed to be of a lower moral standard than her counterparts in fuller, more modest attire. Indonesian men in singlets and shorts are generally of the very lowest social strata and most Indonesians, as well as resident expats, wonder why Western tourists should wander Jakarta's streets dressed as for a beach.

Modesty is the keyword. This doesn't mean that women need to start wearing a *jilbab* (the Muslim headscarf), but for a hassle-free passage, wear bikini tops and g-strings on the beach, not while shopping in Pasar Baru. Indonesians are generally *bingung* (baffled) at the idea of a woman not wearing a bra. You can prove this point by visiting any public swimming pool and seeing how many female bathers are still wearing their underwear beneath their costumes.

Indonesian white-collar workers either wear a uniform provided by management or are expected to dress formally. Expatriates generally do not have to wear the company's outfit, but there will be sartorial expectations. These may include long or short-sleeved shirts with or without a tie, well-creased long trousers and black or brown shoes. Some may prefer unflattering safari suits, as much favoured by civil servants. Shorts and sandals are definitely out.

On formal occasions, such as meeting the President or going to a wedding, long-sleeved *batik* shirts are the standard garb for men. The textiles themselves may be impressive enough, with ornate designs of floral *batik* outlined fastidiously in gold, or large geometric zigzags and stripes on the *tenunan* (fabric), yet the stiff collars and tight fit of formal *batik* shirts means they are fairly appalling outfits to be seen out in. They should be worn tie-less and over the trouser belt rather than tucked in.

Women generally wear a stiff blouse known as a *kebaya*. With a floor length skirt, hair tied up in a bun and seemingly starched, they look as uncomfortable as they probably feel, but being dressed properly does ensure that the protocols of the occasion are strictly followed.

Larger-sized ready-to-wear clothes can be hard to find, so if you have a favourite pair of trouser or a shirt or blouse you really like, bring it/them with you and let a local tailor put together a few clones for you. Other clothes should be brought with you, especially underwear and footwear, although a great many department stores these days have pricey imported selections. And they need to: the average young Indonesian is a clear foot taller than his or her parents. Clothes for babies and small children are, however, not a problem to find.

Young Jakartans are fiercely fashion-conscious and those from affluent families flaunt it by dressing accordingly. High-fashion with its accessories is an obvious outward sign of success in Indonesia. For the vast majority of youngsters, those born into more humble households prefer bright and colourful clothing. Perhaps as a way of compensating, the hardest-up in Jakarta are often the most striking dressers.

T-shirts are big business in Jakarta. So are slogans. The most obscene phrases imaginable jump out at you from young Jakartan chests in every shopping mall in the city. These often sexy or druggy slogans are clearly lost on the wearers—they certainly wouldn't wear them if they knew the actual meanings. But it's in English, so it must be cool.

When it comes to getting your clothes washed, you might want to avoid giving your *pembantu* the most prized possessions in your wardrobe. The traditional method of *cucian* (washing) is to scrub and pound the item to death on a washboard, as once used in skiffle groups, with several handfuls of the all-round detergent, Rinso.

Most middle-class homes have washing machines. These offer the full range of wash cycles with the added bonus of using cold water. The strength of the equatorial sun means you don't have to buy a special dryer, but be careful to ensure that your clothes are dried inside out. That same sun has a powerful bleaching effect.

If you don't like ironing—does anyone?—you will have to give very detailed instructions to your *pembantu*. It is common to find that your socks have a very nice crease, but the elastic has melted. The same goes for your underwear, and if you're not standard Indonesian size, then you're going to have problems replacing these items in a hurry.

## Sarung

*Sarung* are all-purpose lengths of material which every visitor to Asia will end up wearing at some point. Some *sarung*, particularly in Muslim households, are sewn up into cylinder shapes. Many more are the wrappable, cotton-sort which double as slings, curtains, sick-bags, blankets, pillowcases, shawls, tablecloths, laundry-bags, towels and wall-hangings.

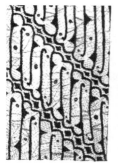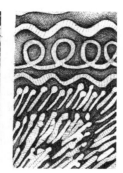

*Sarung* comes in many different designs, but the women are usually more partial to floral designs than men.

You don't need to undress to sleep in a *sarung*, just loosen it and pull it over your head. *Sarung* are worn formally and informally. They are worn formally to the mosque, when visiting the neighbours at Lebaran and at a *pengajian* (Islamic social function). They are worn informally around the house.

There are as many variations on the theme of *sarung* as there are bananas in Indonesia. For a cross-section of *sarung* across the archipelago, visit the textile floor of a Pasaraya department store. Here you will see traditional *batik* (wax resist) *sarung* from Java, heavier *ikat* (woven) *sarung* from Nusa Tenggara and psychedelic ones from Kuta, Bali. For cheaper ones, try Pasar Tanah Abang. About the only drawback with *sarung* is how plainly ridiculous they look with shoes on.

## Sandals

Sandals are worn by everyone, rich and poor alike, but not in the office. The sound of dragging flip-flops is a characteristic of Jakarta's background hum. They cost next to nothing and protect your feet from electric shocks, scorpions, the distinct chance of crushing a cockroach or rat underfoot, and slipping over in the *mandi*. But the generally perilous nature of Jakarta's streets means sandals are the wrong things to wear on long walks around town.

Be sure also not to wear your best pair to the mosque, as the risk of having them taken is apparently high.

## SHOPPING

Many Jakartan families spend their weekends at the one of the 80 or more air-conditioned shopping malls. Window shopping has replaced visits to outdoor recreational sites such as parks and gardens, because the malls have been built on areas designated as 'green spaces' or water catchment areas. Recent statistics show that just over 70 per cent of visitors to the malls don't actually buy anything, so mall managements have created 'play areas' with an entrance fee to detain the kids whilst Mum and Dad wander off and dream about what else they would like to purchase along with their windows.

You can spend as much or as little as you want in Jakarta. However, don't expect to get everything in one day because getting to different places is nigh on impossible. (For the reasons, see the Getting Around section a few pages on.) Serious shopaholics are more likely to pop over to Singapore or spend a week in Hong Kong. That said, you can get anything in Jakarta—literally anything at all. After all, trading is, always has been and, presumably, always will be Jakarta's raison d'être. It's the process of buying and selling, offering and accepting, that keeps the rupiah moving, and some 80 per cent of the country's rupiah supply is in Jakarta.

Before rushing off and exclaiming at the perceived cheapness of goods on the shelves and racks, it's always worth doing a little sightseeing first. Note that most if not all malls have a branch of Hero's, the supermarket chain. Gelael is the other supermarket chain. You may also find a branch of both Swenson's Ice Cream and KFC here as the Indonesian franchises are owned by the Gelael family. Many self-service convenience stores have opened up in recent years, including Indomaret, Alfamart and Circle K. For your major monthly shop, you may prefer to spend a few hours in a hypermarket such as Carrefour, the French concern. It isn't necessarily cheaper to shop here, nor can you always find their own brand Dijon moutarde or, surprisingly, decent cheese. If you really need a taste of home, then check out Kemchicks in Kemang or Sogo in Plazas Senayan and Indonesia.

Probably the best shop in Jakarta is the Sarinah department store above Indonesia's first MacDonalds in Jl. Thamrin. This multi-level store was named after the nurse of Sukarno and in 2007/2008 is due to be totally renovated and enlarged into the neighbouring office blocks so it can go even further upmarket. We don't know why its 'clones', the Pasaraya stores, are so named: there isn't much sentimental value in 'main market', although they are aptly named. Each has a catchy and distinguishing slogan to differentiate it: the one in Manggarai thinks it's Young and Trendy, but isn't. The best one, in Blok M, is Big and Beautiful, which it is if you like virtually everything under one roof. It's a bit like Harrods of London, though not quite as snobbish.

On your way in, get sprayed, rubbed and painted by the ever-present promotion girls and enjoy the air-conditioning. In the basement of Blok M's emporium is a food court, a whole floor array of cheap to moderate eating places. They offer the best and the rest of Indonesian dishes and is a popular place to find Jakarta's young hopefuls hanging out and staring at one another.

Two of the other six floors of Pasaraya are crammed with things from all over Indonesia. Every kind of *batik*, *ikat* and ethnic textile is on sale, along with handicrafts from all provinces of the country. This is where you buy presents for family and friends back home before you actually visit the provinces which supplied the artefacts.

Other floors have clothing, both imported and locally made for export, sports equipment, electrical goods, stationery and computer accessories, etc. All in all, Pasaraya is a perfect self-contained place in which to go shopping for an afternoon.

---

**Electronic Products**

For electronics at reasonable prices, try Glodok Plaza and Mangga Dua Mall in North Jakarta. The latter has a complete floor of computer shops, as does Ratu Plaza at the bottom end of Jl.Sudirman. Here and at Ambassador Mall in Jl Casablanca are good places to buy pirated DVDs when the police haven't confiscated the stock, but don't tell anyone we told you.

---

Local markets are at street level as in Blok M, or in multi-level buildings in need of renovation as at Pasar Tanah Abang, northeast of Plaza Indonesia, which is where you go for textiles and fabrics. The real bargains are had in the street markets. They probably offer everything that the air-conditioned Pasaraya does, only cheaper because they're possibly copies of branded goods. Ask for what you want or just browse.

And don't forget to bargain. Good prices can be had on everything from real gold to fake Gucci watches, if you know how to do it correctly. The point of bargaining is to come to a compromise.

---

**Tips for Bargaining**

Don't show an eager interest in anything at first; try to look as if you really couldn't care less and are merely curious. If you get quoted a price, you'll naturally offer something lower. As a foreigner, it's unlikely that that you'll 'win' in this battle of wits, and why should you? You won't be bargaining your life savings away but you might be taking away the price of a meal away from the stallholder. However, even if you don't feel confident bargaining, you should always ask for a discount on what you are buying. It's an accepted practice and you nearly always get one.

---

When you walk into a shop in Jakarta, it might look as if the place is deserted. Don't be fooled; a quick glance over the shop counter should end any doubts you have. For down there on the floor, hiding from general public, will be several noodle-eating shop assistants. On other occasions, you get swamped by a thousand uniformed shop assistants with nothing to do. Many shops in Jakarta are ridiculously overstaffed, and there are consequently an awful lot of bored shop staff dying for a customer to attend to. Although, given their low salaries and that they'd far rather chat with their friends than deal with someone who probably can't speak Indonesian, they may well ignore you.

Very often in Jakarta, you will simply end up shopping by accident. The shopping comes to you. The widest variety of produce imaginable is paraded past your front door on a daily basis by the city's million *kaki lima* and 'shoulder-pole' sellers. These characters are out there plying their trade in all weathers. An underground economy, they make up a high percentage of Jakarta's workforce. This is self-employment at the most minimum, yet it pays more than the average factory worker gets.

## Warungs

Jakarta wouldn't be the same without its *warung*, nor would much of Asia in fact. A *warung* is the generic word for a place which sells something, a place which isn't otherwise

A *warung* sells everything. Some are like mini provision shops, some sell Indonesian food at low, low prices.

labelled as a *toko* (shop), *pasar swalayam* (self-service shop or supermarket) or *rumah makan* (restaurant). *Warungs* exist happily in all shapes and sizes everywhere.

Some *warungs* are so small that there's barely room among the stock to stand up, let alone sit. They often have axles so wheels can be attached and the stock within, generally small items such as cigarettes, tissues and soft drinks, can be moved to another stretch of otherwise vacant pavement, such as a bus stop. Yet these mini lockup *warungs* are more often than not lived in by the owner and family. They are a good investment because a *warung* can be passed on down the family. To own a *warung* is to be self-sufficient, to have dropped out of the rat race, to be pampering to no-one's needs except your own. It simply means being there and staying there and letting everyone come to you, which they always do. Great.

Some expand over the years into something far sturdier than their humble bamboo and plastic origins. Some become large, tile-roofed numbers which are clearly fixed buildings, but they are still called *warungs* because they generally serve a fixed clientele. Every street has its *warung* for people to pop to when they need a couple of eggs, headache pills, a snack, a pack of cigarettes or mosquito repellent. It's where people meet, where the people who do nothing all day go to do nothing all day. Remember this: there's always a *warung* open somewhere near you no matter what the time is; there'll always be one to help you out of your crisis.

Open-air restaurants are *warungs*, an area of tarpaulin or plastic held up over a long table with benches. The front is a bedsheet hand-painted with an advertisement for whatever is always on the menu, everything from *nasi goreng* (fried rice) to seafood. That's all really; there's actually nothing much to a simple *warung*. No glamour, no refinements, just a basic service with something to keep the rain off. They occupy the same stretch of sidewalk every day or every night. Some occupy whole forecourts; check out Jl. Peconongan in Central Jakarta, which is a street of second-hand car dealers by day and seafood *warungs* at night.

## Tailors

Tailors are cheap and abundant in Jakarta. People use them is a very casual way, like going to the newsagent or popping out to buy an egg. Keep an eye out in your neighbourhood; you'll be surprised how many sewing machines you'll espy. Buy some cloth from an Indian run shop in Pasar Baru or from the second floor of Melawai Plaza in Blok M and have yourself measured up. Take in your favourite clothes to be copied, add an inch here or there, and you will soon be looking a treat.

And if you're buying clothes off-the-rack and they don't quite fit, ask if they have an in-store tailor or seamstress to have your 'must have' garment cut, altered and sewn and fitted before you and it leave the premises.

## Hairdressers and Beauty Salons

To promote a good head of hair, babies' heads are routinely shaved when they reach three months old. Hair in Indonesia, therefore, has significance beyond that of many cultures. Black is the predominant shade; it's surprising how common dyeing is, whether to jet black or to henna-ish shades is a personal choice.

A good head of hair can actually be an investment for some. It is not uncommon for some people to save their hair clippings and brush-deposits in the hope of selling them for use in a wig. There are well-established traditions of wig use among Indonesian women and many are still quite unashamed about wearing one. Naturally, the longer the hair, the greater the value of the potential hairpiece.

Many hairpieces, however, are kept in the family: a young girl with long hair might, for example, be persuaded by her elders into cutting off her flowing locks in order to make a nice *konde* for *nenek* (grandma).

Opening a salon in one's front room is one way of boosting a family's income. There are various vocational schemes available for school leavers who are unable to go to university; they learn how to wield a comb, scissors and the other tools of the trade including giving a cream bath and neck massage. There will be a dozen salons in your neighbourhood, many catering for both men and women, so the biggest problem facing an unkempt foreigner is finding someone unafraid to tinker with your tonsure or tresses.

The cheapest is a roadside barber who will give an excellent trim for an absolute pittance. Barbers like this are invariably situated below trees to allow for at least some shade, as well as a place to hang the mirror. A newspaper with a hole cut out for your head to collect the clippings is all part of the service. It's best to go before or after the rush hours to avoid the full force of the traffic pollution.

For the most part, Indonesians have very thick heads of hair, which lends itself perfectly to almost any haircut. But sometimes the individual strands are so thick that no amount of hairdressing can help, and all it can do is stand on end. Generally speaking, Indonesian men have little in the way of facial hair, so moustaches are grown to demonstrate seniority and masculinity; few young men have them.

Unless you really don't mind what happens to your crowning glory, it may well be advisable to go with an Indonesian friend the first few times you go to a salon. Alternatively, simply take along a photo you have cut out of a magazine of a hair style you like. Some salons will have their own in-house catalogue which you can leaf through until you find a style you think the hairdresser can copy. Remember though that some terrible things can happen to your hair in the hands of an enthusiastic hairdresser keen to experiment non-Indonesian hair. Fine fair hair is a rarity; Asian hair is thicker, which leaves fewer free-styling opportunities.

## MEDIA
### Radio
The Jakarta airwaves are packed with a seemingly overlapping abundance of radio stations. If you don't understand *bahasa Indonesia*, you'll be lost among the phone-in programmes, so keep turning that dial until you find something you think you can listen to. You may recognise much of the music, but then again you may not want to. On the FM dial, it can be hard to tell one pumping station from another. Ever popular with the hip young crowd, and happily utilising American jargon, is Kiss FM. For the classically-minded listeners, there is Klasik FM, which sponsors a number of events around the town. And for the classically rock-minded, there is 97.4 FM playing 'nonstop' classic rock. Fans of *dangdut* music are also well served.

The oldest radio station is the national station, RRI (Radio Republik Indonesia), which broadcasts across the entire nation, and which is essentially a news station for the country. For local news, especially where the nearest traffic hold up is, tune into Radio Sonora.

### TV
If you turn on a TV in Jakarta, you should be able to get (at the last count) 13 channels. TVRI (Televisi Republik Indonesia) is a government-run station, broadcast throughout Indonesia, and the oldest in operation. It's a far more sober affair than its counterparts, almost wooden in its presentation, mainly because its brief is to broadcast educational programmes such as *Fun With English*. TVRI also gives exposure to local culture, such as performances of music and dance, and puppet shows such as *jaipong*, *legong* and *wayang kulit*.

The majority of the TV channels are owned by members of the political élite, generally from the major political grouping of the past 30 years, Golkar, or with former links to the Suharto clan. There is a law which limits foreign ownership of the media; this is either a contributory factor or a protectionist manoeuvre. It cannot be argued, however, that TV exists as a tool of the government as it was in the Suharto era.

Bhakti Investama Group, headed by Hari Tanoe—a long-renowned banker—owns several stations including RCTI and SCTV, which he bought from Bimantara, controlled by Bambang, Suharto's second son.

Gramedia used to own TV7, but later sold a very large chunk to Chaerul Tanjung's Trans TV. Chaerul Tanjung owns Bank Mega group and while definitely well connected, he doesn't have a direct political affiliation.

ANTV is owned by Bakrie but with 20 per cent of the stock owned by the Star TV Network of the Murdoch empire. It is strongly believed that Star influence extends beyond that 20 per cent in the form of other securities and guarantees. The rule on foreign ownership of media companies doesn't extend to public companies. Thus, Star TV also has 'arrangements' with Bhakti Investama.

Metro News is owned by Surya Paloh, a Golkar official who also owns Media Indonesia, the third national paper. Metro is by far the best for its coverage of the news and was especially outstanding for its early coverage of the Aceh Tsunami in late December 2004.

MRA, which owns Cosmo magazine group, Hard Rock FM etc., has shares in JakTV and O, both local TV stations focussed on the happenings in Jakarta.

The rest are also strictly commercial stations struggling to garner profits from their slice of the advertising pie, and they therefore appeal to the lowest common denominator. They seem to offer the same diet of local soap operas (*sinetron*), Korean or Latin American soap operas (*telenovellas*), news bulletins about violent crimes, gossip shows, variety shows, pop videos and repeats of cartoons and not-very-good American shows. Of late, there have been a growing number of reality shows and quizzes, many of which are the local version of the internationally successful ones such as *Amazing Race* and *Who Wants To Be A Millionaire?* (The latter was interesting in that the title stayed the same but as a million rupiah is the monthly minimum wage, about US$ 100, the top prize was actually Rp 500,000,000.)

There may be an interesting documentary or two, but all programmes are constantly interrupted seemingly every five minutes with incredibly inane adverts which are endlessly, mind-numbingly repeated.

Sometimes a film you really want to see is shown, but it may be dubbed. If not, it will have sub-titles which will tell a completely different story to the one you are listening to. Martial arts films are made all the more switch-offable by having three sets of screen-obscuring subtitles scrolling across the screen, in Mandarin, English and Indonesian. Far better to watch a (pirated) DVD.

Sport is very popular, international sport that is: achieving the highest rating on any channels are the live broadcasts of the EPL, Champions League, F1 grand prix and NBA (play offs—finals only).

### Moment of Pride Gone Unseen

When Taufik Hidayat became the 2004 Olympic gold medallist as the men's badminton singles champion in Athens, he dedicated his victory to the folk back home who were supporting him all the way. Unfortunately, we weren't because, the TV stations claimed, the Olympics were too expensive to cover. Our TV diet that evening was 'a really crappy film on one channel, two fat female celebs on another two, a *dangdut* party on another and some boring talking heads yakking on about whatever armchair political pundits chunder on about'.

If you must watch TV, then you may be lucky and live in an area served by Kabelvision, which offers the same channels as the satellite provider Indovision which you can subscribe to if you can't get the cable service. There are three other 'broadband' providers, although we know of no one who's yet subscribed to them.

## Newspapers and Magazines

Among the print media, the *Jakarta Post* has long been considered the most 'reliable' English-language paper.

Published daily, it offers a fixed diet of local, national and world news. What makes it interesting is the fact that because it is in English, it can be quite candid in its criticism of state affairs, a situation only recently seen in other print publications. Thus, the *Jakarta Post* is held as a reliable source for the foreign media to base their reports on and gauge the day-to-day direction of Indonesia. Aside from its political implications, the occasionally ludicrous letters page. Do note that having your consumer complaint aired in this column can achieve results.

Other English-language papers do occasionally exist but they tend to go bankrupt quite quickly. In the past 20 years, we have lost the *Indonesian Times* and the *Indonesian Observer*. Now we can get *The Point*, which is owned by the Bakrie family, financial backers of President SBY and owners of Lapindo Brantas which has been held responsible for the Sidoarjo volcanic mudflow in East Java. It offers nothing new or original which naturally leads to the question, what's the point?

Of the local *bahasa Indonesia* press, *Kompas*, with Christian/Catholic leanings, is the best-regarded broadsheet. It is owned by the Gramedia group which also publishes the *Jakarta Post*. *Republika* is a similar paper to *Kompas*, although Islamic-oriented. For stories of *pembantu* who murder their employers, gossip about who has been seen holding hands with whom, and the generally garish sensationalism of the day, the tabloid *Pos Kota* is the one for you. It is also quite useful for its classified ads section.

There are a number of weekly news magazines published which are modelled on *Time* or *Newsweek*. In English, probably the best in terms of in-depth coverage is *Tempo*, which has an interesting history. Founded by Gunawan Mohammed, a respected intellectual writer and commentator with a social conscience, *Tempo* had its licence withdrawn by the Suharto regime in 1994. After Suharto's forced abdication in 1998, *Tempo* hit the newsstands again but still faced entrenched forces which didn't like having their business ethics, or lack of them, publicised. Intimidation by thugs and libel actions followed, with long drawn-out court cases. In many ways, *Tempo* serves as a barometer of how far *reformasi* has progressed.

## TELEPHONES

Since the first edition of this book, there has been a marginal improvement in Indonesia's telecommunications systems. You no longer have to wait years for a landline and the authors know of no one with a shared party line. That's in Jakarta, mind you. At the end of 2005, more than half of the country's population did not have access to a phone; that's 50,000 villages. Countrywide, for a population of 213 million, there were just 8,500,000 fixed phone lines. Those who could afford one (or two) bought mobile phones; there were 22,300,000 of them, representing a 610 per cent growth in five years.

There are peak and off-peak rates, but these seem to be variable. All calls are cheaper by about 25 per cent after 9:00 pm and at weekends and on most public holidays. Some international calls still have to be made via the operator but it's possible, if your local connection box can handle it, to get an IDD (International Direct Dialling) line installed. Landlines are provided by Telkom, which is the national state telecommunications company. Another national state

telecommunications company is PT Indosat. Both companies are quoted on foreign stock exchanges and shareholdings are variously controlled, although the government does retain equity. Both companies appear to offer similarly haphazard and inefficient services, albeit profitable ones. Wrong numbers are a regular nuisance in Jakarta; you could find that your number has mutated without Telkom informing you.

Hence, the popularity of cell phones in the metropolis. As to which phones are best or which phone cards are for what purpose, our resident Luddite, Terry, hasn't a clue. Work out your communication needs when you get here. You may have to have two phones: one for local and one for inter-local (outside Jakarta) and international calls. Following the terrorist bombings, mobile phone numbers have to be registered before they can be activated.

## Useful Telephone Language

There is telephone etiquette, although not one you would necessarily recognise as the initial greeting could be in Arabic.

**Receiving a call**

| | |
|---|---|
| You: | *"Assalam mualai'kum."* |
| Caller: | *"Alai'kum salam."* |
| | |
| Caller: | "May I speak to ____, please." |
| | (*Tolong, saya mau bicara sama ___.*) |
| You: | "Oh sorry, you've got the wrong number." |
| | (*Oh, ma'af, salah sambung, Pak/Ibu.*) |
| Or: | |
| You: | "Speaking" |
| | (*Saya sendiri*) |
| | |
| Converse: | Rabbit, rabbit, rhubarb, rhubarb … |

Either person ends the conversation with *"Sudah*?" (Finished?) then abruptly plonks the receiver down.

Note that it isn't usual to give your phone number at the start of a received call as you might in, say, the UK.

## INTERNET

You won't find anyone with a kind word to say about Internet provision in Indonesia. Broadband is largely confined to hotels and offices, some of which may even have wi-fi hot spots. If you subscribe to Kabelvision or Telkom Speedy, you can pay a lot for minimal service. The problem is that Telkom and Indosat are the only two main portals which link the country to the web. All other ISPs are, perforce, their sub-subscribers.

One of the biggest differences between ISPs is their bandwidth management. Most ISPs purchase bandwidth from Indosat, the Indonesian international telecommunications firm. While the cost of connection to the Internet backbone (bandwidth) is paid in US dollars, the subscriber fees for local ISPs are in rupiah. With the historic volatility of the rupiah/dollar exchange rate, the ISPs are usually cautious about buying more bandwidth than they can afford given their subscriber base.

Both Telkom and Indosat are massive conglomerates quoted on foreign stock exchanges. However, it's as if the pen is mightier than the writing because they are more concerned with marketing 'profitable' services such as cell phones technology on behalf of their stockholders rather than investing in the technology that will benefit the population at large.

According to the Economic Review no. 204 published in June 2006, at the end of 2005, there were (only!!) 336,000 Internet subscribers, which still represented a 230 per cent growth in five years. Another three million had CDMA access, although there are very few wi-fi hotspots in Jakarta, let alone elsewhere.

---

**Update**

For current information visit the website of the Indonesian Internet Service Provider Association, http://www.apjii.or.id

---

On 27 December 2006, an earthquake in the ocean off Taiwan prevented any access to the wide world beyond as it caused a 'disruption' to the connecting undersea cable. Because of the lack of reciprocal rights to use foreign satellites,

During the historic floods in early February 2007, Telkom's main Internet hub was underwater, so there was more frustration.

alternative access to the international telecommunications web was not available and the government was slow to react. A day later, a spokesman at the Communication and Information Ministry's Post and Telecommunications Directorate General told the *Jakarta Post* that his office had yet to decide what steps were to be taken by the government, saying that it needed 'more time to grasp the urgency of the situation.'

If you are Internet savvy and you've got really good eyesight and very small fingers, you can access your emails and web pages on your cell phones. In fact, if you only know how, there are many things you can do with these easily lost and disposable gadgets. In this regard, Jakarta is apparently as 'modern' as, say, Singapore. However, per capita, Singaporeans are four times richer than Jakartans and investment in telecommunications infrastructure was started much earlier there.

Here, IT is a popular study option among school leavers and most of them focus on programming and the creation of flashy websites. It's a shame that it will be years before their services are needed.

## HARSHER REALITIES

For city planners, the nature of Jakarta's topography and bureaucracy means that installing efficient drainage is a nightmare. On each side of most streets in Jakarta are *gots*, drainage ditches which can be as much as a metre deep. The general content of a *got* is rain water and household waste water from sinks and the *mandi*.

If the street slopes, then the contents can flow away quickly. If not, then the *got* quickly fills with discarded wrapping, building rubble and the other detritus that a city generates. This blocks the water which stagnates and becomes, unsurprisingly, the home of mosquitoes, rats and even little fish. Although toilet waste is usually fed directly into a septic tank under the house, the combination of humidity and heat results in some memorable *got* smells. And the contents of septic tanks, after being emptied by official trucks, may be dumped untreated and unceremoniously into rivers.

If you live in a middle class or upmarket area like Pondok Indah or Bintaro Jaya, you need not worry too much, except when you venture out. In the wet season when flooding is common, the *gots* overflow, turning streets into rivers. You have to be very careful then because many unwary pedestrians have fallen in. At all times of the year, you need to be careful when parking; it's very easy to get the wheels of a vehicle struck down one. And a further word of warning: many *gots* along main streets are covered with concrete slabs. Be careful walking along these as they might be missing or extremely fragile.

Rubbish is a problem in Jakarta: it's more or less everywhere. People chuck it out of car windows, burn it, pile it, sift it, recycle it and deal it. This isn't to say rubbish is lying all around the floors of Indonesian homes, but it does seem that any area beyond the confines of one's allotted few square metres is an acceptable place to litter. Outside Jakarta, the picture is much the same: rubbish tipped with complete abandon down hillsides and embankments for all to see. Fancy a weekend sailing trip to Jakarta Bay? Think again. Outboard motors face the grave danger of being clogged up with plastic bags, so dense is the pollution. It's no joke, and a condition not just confined to Indonesia. Sadly, this blatant lack of awareness of efficient rubbish disposal control seems to be symptomatic of the human condition. Much of the rubbish in Indonesia has been 'exported' by wealthy countries operating so-called recycling schemes.

*Pemulung*—or, in plain English, scavengers—are the characters in the stereotype 'Chinaman' hats who poke around in the cement rubbish box outside your house. They make the rounds with large wicker baskets on their backs and picking stick in hand. Some pass by pulling carts and crying "*barang, barang*". They will pay a few rupiah for your pile of old newspapers, kid's broken tricycle or fan. No one knows who they are, or where they come from, but *pemulung* are Jakarta's unsung recycling heroes. They spend their day sifting through everyone else's domestic waste for metal, plastic, cardboard, paper and glass. (Perfume bottles are a particularly prized find—they can be refilled and resold). Families of *pemulung* amass huge backlogs of stock at home. This is their capital, in both senses of the word.

Higher up the social scale is your friendly *tukang sampah*. He is a 'professional' rubbish-man, employed on a salary by the local RT. He routinely collects the trash from each house, although he might refuse, or charge extra, for moving awkward things like tree trunks or building rubble. Precisely where he takes the garbage is a different matter altogether. In the first instance, it gets taken it to the designated neighbourhood dump from where it's taken to a dump outside the city, maybe in Bekasi. Here, it may be piled up or buried, flattened, bull-dozed or burned. Disposing of what 12 million people throw away isn't easy. Space is limited in Jakarta and it has to go somewhere.

Much of the rubbish which doesn't enter the recycling chain gets thrown into the streets from where, in the rainy season, it gets washed into the *gots* which feed the canals and rivers which are already prone to overflowing because Jakarta's flood plain has been built over. As elsewhere, the packaging industry is to blame for much of the waste disposal crisis. In the past, banana leaves were the all-purpose wrapping paper. When thrown away, they decompose and give back nutrients to the soil. Not so those plastic bags with the thousand-year guarantee. Everytime you buy anything in Jakarta, edible or non-edible, is wrapped, tucked,

## Better Attempts Please!

In recent years, coloured rubbish bins have appeared in pairs on the main streets. Supposedly, the green one was for organic waste and the orange one wasn't. We are unable to confirm this because City Hall didn't 'socialise' the reason for plonking them in the streets and they got stolen anyway for personal use outside houses. Then there was a half-hearted distribution of very thin plastic bags so that households could separate their waste. Great idea, but, again, without the necessary 'socialisation', especially amongst the *tukang sampah*, everything ended up mixed up in the same dump.

taped, pinned, stapled and wrapped again before you are free to touch it.

The general public has a general lack of discipline regarding rubbish, but then it's not as if the 'authorities' have made a concerted effort to educate the public.

Education is the key and this can only be achieved by small scale examples. A number of *kampungs* have been encouraged to set up local compost schemes using their organic waste. The compost is then used to make the area 'green', which engenders a feeling of communal pride. Elsewhere, neighbourhoods are encouraged to keep the area in front of their houses clean and the *got* free-flowing. So bit by bit, areas of the city are indeed exhibiting pride in their appearance. Unfortunately, the city keeps growing.

## WILDLIFE
### Rats
Rats (*tikus*) are a common sight in the streets of Jakarta, but that's because the streets drainage systems are open and the climate is tropical. You may think that money would guarantee a vermin-free life, but this is not so. Ironically, it seems the richer the area, the bigger the rat. Rich areas may have better draining systems than the average *kampung*, but they also have better quality rubbish outside. And rats love rubbish. The largest may be as big as a foot in length and in such menacing cases, it's not uncommon for cats, chickens and other street-dwellers to give way to these giant vermin; to stand to one side while they pass. Not all rats are the giant variety, but there are still enough of them to make you squeamish.

You could spend your time preparing traps, laying down *lem tikus* (rat glue) and even shooting them with a pellet gun, but as long as your dwelling is open to the elements at some point, and inevitably it will be, you are going to have your work cut out. The effort might be worthwhile when you assess the damage *tikus* cause: chewed electric cables, food, shoes and furniture. You name it, they sharpen their teeth on it. Just one or two troublesome rats who keep you awake at night playing football in your roof are definitely worth doing something about.

Mind you, there are rats and there are rats. You have no need to be put off by the tiny, blind voles Indonesians call *cecurut*. They are known as 'wall-huggers' (for obvious reasons) and are harmless and vulnerable. Only the most cold-blooded among us could kill a wall-hugger as it squeaks in horror at your presence, and starts running on the spot in its panic to get away. Their panic sometimes gets the better of them, however; shut all the doors and exit points on a panicked *cecurut* and it might well dive down your toilet in desperation. This leaves you with an appalling dilemma: attempt to remove the spinning rodent from your bowl, or simply lift the handle and flush it? Tricky.

## Cats

Cats are everywhere. Many of them have no tails or at best only half a tail. There are two conflicting reasons for this. One has it that the cats are simply built this way; i.e., it's genetic. On the other hand, it's rumoured that tails are systematically broken off at birth by whoever is first to come across the litter (a *pembantu* probably). The belief is that by doing this, there will be more room in the afterlife for human souls, and we could avoid having lots of *kuching* (cats) everywhere, cluttering the place up again.

**Cat Lover**

The prophet Mohammed by contrast would not have minded the large number of cats; he was a cat lover and was said to have rather cut a hole out of his prayer mat than disturb his sleeping pussy.

Coming down to earth a bit, you are more likely to be plagued by random litters in your roof than in the Next World. Stubborn as cats are, your attempts at getting the feline family to keep moving only results in the cats reappearing the next day. From here on, as the kittens mature and the mother trains them in street life, expect to find rats' tails and entrails which the kittens played with and puked up. Further disasters follow as the runt dies and you can't remove its stinking carcass and the others crap everywhere, get stuck in drainpipes and, worst of all, come crashing through your ceiling when you're lying shut-eyed on the bed. Cats born in the roof do not go away. They hover around your house and live permanently upstairs, flitting from roof to roof and never coming downstairs. But these are the lucky ones; Jakarta's more unfortunate victims are born in the rubbish box outside the house. What a great start in life that must be.

But maybe you're a cat lover and can get the feral cats to stay put. You'll have to feed them with Whiskas and train them to use kitty litter though, and in so doing they'll lose their natural instinct which is to catch all those rats and cockroaches you don't like.

---

**Civet Cats**

Consider yourself lucky if you spot a civet cat, as they are rare but welcome visitors which prefer to wander among the night-time roofs. They have a yellowish spotted fur—difficult to make out at night—and a lengthy tail and are larger than the feral cats which are markedly less nocturnal.

---

## Cockroaches

Cockroaches are virtually a way of life in Indonesia. They live behind cupboards, in drains, in the garden, in storage areas and in cracks and crevices all over the house. With every house open to the elements at some point, there's really no escaping them. Obvious precautions, such as covers on drains and keeping a clean house, will discourage a few cockroaches from entering. While no one loves them, it's better to turn a blind eye to the odd *kecoa* than spend your time chasing every one back outside. If you suffer a plague of them, which can easily occur when a neighbour puts insecticide down their drain and causes the cockroach community to 'make a run for it', you are more than justified in enjoying a game of cockroach football.

A popular place to come face to face with a cockroach is near the drain-hole in the *kamar mandi* (bathroom) where they have probably just spend the last 10 minutes watching you shower. Naked as you are, the feeling of helplessness is overpowering. Cockroaches are terrible flyers. When one has been cornered, its only getaway is to take off on a wonky flight across the room and flop onto the nearest person.

It has been said that cockroaches would be the only things to survive a nuclear holocaust. The point is certainly proved when you see how resilient they are, how they seem to eat anything—soap, clothes and cement. And when you think how repulsive they are.

Measures can be taken to keep you home relatively *kecoa-*free. The best option is to use one of the many brands of stick-on cockroach killer. These are small, flat plastic things which you stick behind doors, in corners and near drains. Baygon's Roach Bait Station is a particularly effective one. The cockroach is attracted to the chemical inside and chooses to go in for a rummage round. The effects of the chemical are not immediate, however, and the cockroach is given time to get home first and have a babble with its friends—so passing the chemical on to the others—before dying.

More immediately, you might like to whack them with a shoe, which is a satisfying experience but it does leave such a mess across your floor. And it's altogether possible for a lone, twitching leg or other cockroach part to turn up later somewhere on your being: in your pocket, in your shoe or in your hair. Not to mention the appalling gunge which is inside a cockroach and which is now all over the floor.

Aside from a crunching sound, cockroaches have a distinct smell about them, a kind of rancid, aniseed smell, which only becomes evident once the cockroaches have been and gone. Furniture, which has remained unmoved for a while, or piles of untouched laundry in a drawer, for example, are susceptible to this smell. Some say it comes from their urine, others say from decomposition. Either way it's a unique smell which must be experienced to be recognised. Once smelt, never again.

Part of the problem is that cockroaches are actually quite big things, up to as much as 5 cm (2 inches) long and it can seem inhumane to stamp on them. Spraying them with insecticide is also a saddening experience: the creature squirms and spins around alarmingly on the spot, clearly in great discomfort. A cockroach in the throes of a chemical

182 CULTURE**SHOCK!** JAKARTA

seizure is even harder to catch as it jerks, stops and jerks like a piston around the room. The chemicals seem to actually speed them up; you can only wait till later to look for the corpse, which will inevitably be on its back somewhere under your bed, legs twitching. Awful.

## Mosquitoes

Say the Indonesian word *nyamuk*, lengthening the first syllable—*nyaaaa'muk*—and you have the sound of the tiny dive-bombing mosquito. Newcomers to Jakarta are fresh meat for the little suckers and until you build up a degree of immunity, you are going to feel that you're in hell. The only solution, ultimately, is to try your best to ignore them. Good luck.

*Nyamuk* don't care who they bite, where, when or how often. Indonesians, although not totally immune, do seem to possess a certain degree of sangfroid as do many long-term expats, some of whom suggest that it's the Bintang beer in the bloodstream which offers the best prevention against insect bites. The ankles and elbows are especially prone, but in truth any area of exposed flesh is vulnerable. Certain times of the year do seem to be worse than others; mosquito larvae are to be found in stagnant water so the onset of the rainy season causes them to go elsewhere.

In theory, you should be safe from malaria in Jakarta, but in the dry season, it's possible to catch dengue (*demam berdarah*—blood fever) which is carried by a different, daytime mosquito. One weekend or on a public holiday during dengue season, as recorded by the *Jakarta Post*, and just when you're feeling pleased that you're not stuck in a noxious traffic jam, you discover that your RT, the head of your neighbourhood, has hired a fumigator who carries a two-stroke engine with which to pour exhaust fumes into your home and the drainage ditch in front.

And, to add insult to the injurious fog, you've been really careful to regularly change the water in your *mandi*, to recondition your air conditioners and to ensure that there are no little perpetual puddles which can offer a safe haven for the little breeders. But, hey, at least you live in a community that cares. Beware the bogus fumigators who come round offering to spray your garden. You'll know them because they don't have a *surat izin* (letter of permission from your RT or RW) and they want to use your water.

When you get bitten, get fast relief from the irritating itch by rubbing enough balsam or mentho-eucalyptus preparation (*minyak kayu putih*) on the affected area; this certainly works for most people and also keeps further *nyamuk* at bay.

Some might say that prevention is better than a cure, yet none of the preventative measures offer a permanent solution and some are downright dangerous in the long term. There are any number of locally produced aerosol sprays and green incense coils, which are okay if you like a smoke-filled room. A 'good' brand is Baygon, which is produced by the German company Bayer and yet curiously banned throughout most of Europe itself.

Make sure that the room you want to be bug-free is relatively airtight with windows shut. Spray copiously, including in the dark corners, under the bed and in drawers, exit and shut the door behind you. This should be done several hours before you intend to sleep in the room so it doesn't smell and also because the chemicals are reputedly carcinogenic. There are electric devices which burn a small tablet of *obat anti-nyamuk*, but none offer long lasting protection. Perhaps marginally better are the anti-*nyamuk* ointments such as Off or Autan which are effective but tend to make you feel hotter and smell something rotten.

## Lizards

*Cicak* are lizards that occupy a space in every self-respecting Jakarta home. They are bashful creatures, preferring to hide behind pictures, books and furniture and in corners. They are everywhere—they don't care where they stick. How they stick has only recently been worked out. Their feet are covered in thousands of electro-magnetic filaments which operate as a force field. Apparently.

Anyway, what is important is that these little creatures, which are seldom more than 10 cm (4 inches) long, nose to tip of tail, eat mosquitoes and other creepy crawlies. They are particularly partial to the flying ants that emerge at the start of the rainy season. So think of them as your friends.

They make clicking sounds, presumably to warn off intruders so as to protect their bit of wall, and rush zigzagging after each other. Sometimes they will drop off the ceiling with a propensity for landing in your half-drunk mug of coffee or your hair. If you startle a *cicak*, they are prone, as a shock tactic, to release their tail, which then wriggles about disturbingly on its own for a while. Apart from little birdlike droppings everywhere, there are few drawbacks with these domestic lizards. Even when they die behind a wardrobe, the only way you'll know is by observing a line of ants crawling up the wall carting bits of dried lizard meat.

Twenty years ago, there used to be another lizard in Jakarta, the onomatopoeically named *tokek* (pronounced 'toh-kay') which elsewhere is known as the gecko. The growth of the city with its overwhelming pollution means that you only hear *tokek* in rural areas. You are even less likely to see one; they are light blue-grey with a red back and pink spots underneath, and although much larger than *cicaks*, they don't scamper up and down walls but live just under the roof. To make its distinct call, a *tokek* builds up a head of steam which is then expelled loudly, breath by breath. In Indonesia, the *tokek* plays the same role as the 'she loves me, she loves me not' routine. The more times it grunts, assuming it's an odd number, the more luck you will have.

## SOUNDS

It wouldn't be accurate to describe Jakarta as a quiet place. In fact, noise exists at a tremendously high level of decibels almost everywhere. Clearly, with so many people living in one place, there is bound to be a racket. Houses are usually built with the emphasis on ventilation, as opposed to soundproofing, and it often seems that the street itself is in the room with you. And perhaps it is because most front doors are left open. For maximum space usage, houses tend to be built to the very edges of their plots. With little left in the way of a garden, you are instead given the chance to hear a variety of *bajaj* (motorised rickshaw), *bemo*, *ojek* (motorbike

taxi) and other means of Jakartan transport, especially the
'hell's cherubs' on their souped up 80cc machines, in aural
close up.

Worse still are those *sombong* (arrogant) SOBs who park
outside your house in their SUVs with their engines running
so they get the benefit of AC and you get to hear and feel the
bottom bass notes of their in-car boom boxes. Letting the air
out of their tyres or putting a potato up their exhaust pipe
relieves your stress and increases theirs. But if you want to
live in peace in your community, don't do it.

As well as chickens, dogs and cats, there are lots of children
in Jakarta, all of whom possess great noise potential. People
like to listen to their TVs and stereos at full volume, the
obvious compensation that you too are able to enjoy music
for free at full volume. In the *kampung,* it's popular to hire
a *dangdut* band to play at a wedding party. If you like live
*dangdut* music, then this will come as a real treat. But if
you don't...

In the *kampung*, noise starts early: the tannoy on the
mosque is one of the first to get going, once the cockerels
have had their say. Jakarta's mosques are a club of their own.

By definition, they have to make noise. Apart from five daily prayer calls made through what sounds like a tin bucket, regular sermons are given according to the needs of each *kampung*. There is a wail of feedback as the local boys pass the microphone among each other, do a lot of coughing, "testing, 2, 3" and improvisation on *dangdut* classics. All this before the speaker has even started his sermon or Koran recital.

People are up bright and early. Once they have splashed themselves clean in the *mandi*, they start switching things on. Early morning music (which sort depends on individual tastes and the regional bias of the *kampung*) resonates through flimsy connecting walls. Pity the neighbours of a family with massive speakers who turn *jaipong* or house music up loud at six in the morning. And every *kampung* has such a family. The low ends are the worst of offenders, the bass sounds more felt than heard. Even industrial earplugs are rendered obsolete as the sound of a bass instrument vibrates through the ground and up into the bed.

Outside the window, someone dragging their feet is overtaken by a twittering gang of SD (elementary school) kids. Passing in the opposite direction is an overexcited clack of chicks led by a neurotic clucking hen. A neighbour puts a *dangdut* tape on. Others start 'warming up' their vehicles: revving over and over the engines of a car and a motorbike respectively.

The neighbourhood's *pembantus* are suddenly out in force; sweeping to death front yards and porches. The telephone rings; wrong number. More school kids pass. A cat fight breaks out. The fruit, vegetable and meat sellers set up shop outside your window, inviting everyone to come and buy. The *bajaj* stops outside your house. Its engine is left running as the driver and your *pembantu* wrestle with a new gas bottle, which is dropped on the floor on the way in: there are no lie-ins in Jakarta.

Noise is, of course, generally a negative word. There are some sounds, however, that you may actually welcome. Jakarta street cries are quite distinctive, if only because regular routes are patrolled, so you might listen out for, say, the shoe repairman. But don't be too agitated when you hear the mournful cry of the man calling for his Daddy. "Papa, papa," he goes. Actually he's selling *bak pao*, dim sum with sweet green lentils inside.

Then there's the guy cycling past with enamelled containers strapped to his rear mudguard. He cries out, "s'all mine" to which you may invariably reply, "keep it, keep it". His edible delight is *sio may*, steamed meat dumplings—pork in China, but generally beef or chicken in Muslim Jakarta.

The acoustic click clicks and bang bangs are generally food; you know it's the *bakso* (meatball) man because his distinctive 'jingle' is to whack the side of his kettle with a metal rod. There are amplified sounds too; listen out for the pedalling ice cream vendors and the bread vans. Then there's the high-pitched whistle of the steamed coconut cake salesman. Ask yourself if you could do a job with such unremitting headache-inducing noise.

Some folks are even more annoying. There's the loudly amplified collector of alms for his mosque. It's generally a sermon which is being broadcast with a message which could well be at odds with your local congregation. Other irritants are the *pengamen*, the buskers who come to your gate to serenade you with what they believe is a melody you really want to listen to. If you feel obliged to make a contribution, do remember that word will get out on the grapevine and others will come with increasing regularity.

And in the rest of Jakarta, the traffic makes a racket in a variety of ways: honking horns, silencer-less two-strokes, rumbling buses, and more honking horns. Go shopping and get a headache thrown in for free. Setup at the front of each department store are massive and weighty amplifiers playing raucously loud pop music. That's when the store's in-house DJ isn't letting all and sundry within the neighbourhood know about the store's BARGAINS.

## SMELLS

Although the same can be said about many places, Jakarta offers the world's nostrils some of the world's richest odours. There's a densely packed daytime population of more than 12 million people, moving about in exhaust-belching vehicles, consuming food from throughout the country and the rest of the world, smoking highly aromatic *kretek* cigarettes and

Marlboro Light, rubbing eucalyptus oil on various body parts, washing themselves and their clothes and generally doing what people with smell do, which is to spray on perfume and deodorants.

It's only when you get to spend a weekend out of the city and realise that fresh country air exists that Jakarta's olfactory experience starts to make some kind of illogical sense. One word, *mencium*, means both to smell and to kiss, and, no, this is totally unconnected with the Inuit practice of greeting each other by rubbing noses.

Perhaps the smell of Indonesia is *kretek* cigarettes, a strong, sweet smell of burning cloves. However, there are belated moves to make Jakarta a 'smoke-free zone', which basically means that folks who are addicted to the evil weed are to be isolated. Buses and trains are increasingly fug free and work places have to provide specific rooms for those unable to quit.

Early morning or just after a rain shower on a Sunday are the best times to notice isolated smells. Wander through one of the flower or fruit markets as the sun rises and enjoy a revitalising experience: smelling freshly watered orchids and compost and every kind of tropical fruit in one go is something worth doing. Among the other good smells floating about the Jakarta air is the neighbourhood bakery. The bread itself is sweet and not exactly worth recommending, but, aah....this is an aroma you want to follow to its source.

Come early evening and the air fills with the aromatic smoke of *sate* and fish cooking on charcoal. If you are hungry, it's a genuine appetiser. If you're not, then it's just the smell of burnt flesh.

Bad smells abound, but in the all-pervading smog of the pollution from traffic and industry, smelling is rarely a conscious activity. Petrol and diesel fumes mix merrily with the reek of the city's chemical rivers and open drains. General background smells like these become almost forgettable and, after a while, not really a problem.

But there are particular, individual and really terrible smells on offer. For some, the crème de la crème is that of the durian fruit. Eat it and it repeats and repeats for up to eight hours, and it can be smelt on the breath. It is truly an acquired taste and smell and you are not allowed to take one on board a plane as hand luggage, and not just because if thrown it would be a truly lethal weapon.

> Nice smells, such as orchids, are *wangi* whereas horrible ones, such as dead rats, are *bau*. (The main town on the island of Buton off south-east Sulawesi is called Bau-Bau; it has a Hotel Wangi.)

The truly terrible smell Jakarta has to offer is the sickly-sweet stink of dead rats. This doesn't become apparent until some time after the animal has died, although those with hypersensitive noses will soon pick up on it. The smell is transitory at first, growing more potent all the time. And just like cockroach urine and deceased *cicak*, it's not necessarily a bad smell at first. So subtle is the aroma that you may be wondering what 'that smell' is for days before the truth dawns. And once identified, something must be done.

## CRIME

For a city with such a swollen population, Jakarta is a relatively safe place to be. You are probably safer walking the streets of Jakarta than, say, the streets of London or New York, but as you would anywhere, be careful.

Snatch thieves and pickpockets are genuine threats facing foreigners in Jakarta. Keep your money and handphone out of sight when in public. Be careful of distractions when travelling on public transport and don't trust anyone, even ladies dressed in full Muslim garb. Gangs are known to operate on buses and trains and it's possible to be confronted, distracted and robbed before you realise what has happened.

Stories of people being hypnotised by thieves regularly crop up in the press. These poor fools say they've handed over jewellery, gone to an ATM and withdrawn all their cash. It's more likely to have been a straight con, as in the stories of supposedly respectable businessmen handing over a few hundred million rupiah in the expectation that there is some magic process which will double their money before their very eyes. Gullible or culpable?

Reports of violent crimes against foreigners are, on the whole, comparatively rare, perhaps because most take sensible precautions. Those who flaunt vivid displays of gold and glitter are asking for trouble. When driving around town, it pays to get into the habit of locking your doors—many taxi drivers habitually do it as soon as you get in. Intersections and markets are crowded areas and it's no surprise to find your vehicle surrounded by hawkers while you wait for the lights to change.

Should you be approached in the street by someone you don't know, you needn't assume they are going to con you out of every last rupiah. Perhaps they want to practise their English or want to know where you're going.

You are more likely to be a crime victim at home. Although con artists are not that common and people are unlikely to try and sell you Monas (but if they do, tell them you've already got one), they may take the domestic approach. Going from house to house with an envelope and a mysterious list of names and donations to the charity of their choice, these may be genuine appeals for help and quite often are. This makes it hard to distinguish when to give and when not. If you do give, you can expect to become known as a 'soft touch'. Far better to ask if they have a letter of permission from the RT. You will also be visited by door-to-door sales people who are working on a commission basis to sell yoghurt drinks or vacuum cleaners. But beware the customer survey people. Armed with a clipboard and a questionnaire, they may well have an ulterior motive—to have a good nose around to see if it's worth coming back later that night to steal your TV and car.

And finally, consider who you do allow in your home. Car theft is the most common crime and far too often we hear of drivers not returning with their bosses' BMW or Kijang. Then there's the *pembantu* who disappears one afternoon before you discover that the 2 or 3 million in cash you'd hidden in the sock drawer has also gone, along with four table knives.

## DRUGS
Some 70 per cent of the country's 213 million people smoke, which is why Philip Morris International—owners of the

Marlboro brand—bought out Sampoerna, Indonesia's third-largest cigarette maker, for US$ 5.2 billion. Although smoking is the most addictive drug of all, tobacco in Jakarta's public places is now technically illegal; stiffer penalties, including publicity, await those indulging their private addictions.

There is no open drug use in Jakarta; people are far too wary of the consequences to make a display of it. Rumours of police supplying pushers who turn informer are not without a grain of truth, and hotel and restaurant owners are required by law to turn in anyone using drugs on their premises.

Arrest rates, surveys and media reports all point to increased drug use in Indonesia. As elsewhere, the drugs 'of choice' vary according to market forces. While *ganja* (marijuana), ecstasy and *shabu-shabu* (methamphetamine) are widely used, it is low grade heroin (*putaw*) that has caused an increase in the number of deaths resulting from overdose, as well as higher rates of HIV infection.

In Indonesia, the war on drugs takes a two-pronged approach, targeting both supply and demand. Defending the nation against drugs has involved broad-based education campaigns, increased powers for the judiciary and a high-tech crime fighting capability, or so we are lead to believe. The media regularly reports arrests of councillors and other middle-ranking bureaucrats in some seedy hotel room with a few mates. They were generally gambling for a few thousand rupiah whilst high on a few tabs of *shabu-shabu*.

Less well known is that being convicted and sent to prison for dealing in drugs is no deterrent. High-cost, high-security prisons are being built to segregate inmates with drug convictions from the rest of the prison population.

In prisons, a lack of x-ray machines, easily bribed wardens and perfunctory checks mean that heroin is rife. Syringes, however, are bigger and harder to smuggle in and harder to hide during block sweeps. Ex-convicts report that a couple of needles

## Five-star Facility

The first correction facility for illicit drug crimes opened in Cipinang (East Jakarta) in 2003; two more have since opened and ten more are planned, yet it is reported that drug rings are being operated with seeming impunity from within the secure walls. Prisoners have cell phones in their cells.

may service an entire prison. The syringes are frequently so worn that the plastic plunger breaks and is replaced with a home-made bamboo equivalent. As cleaning needles adds another step in the process (requiring extra time, sterile water and bleach), the spread of disease through intravenous drug use in prisons is rampant.

It is a holy war, complete with propaganda posters that are thick with symbolic imagery. Visions of Satan, death, anguish and deception attempt to deter young people from experimenting with illicit drugs. It is, perhaps, unfortunate that the Indonesian website 'Just Say No To Drugs: Narkoba, Narkotika, Napza.. Those All Shits!!' (http://www.anti. or.id) carries Google ads for anti-anxiety medication and 'non-prescribed sleep solution—without the next day side effects'.

Like all of South-east Asia, source of so much of the opiates, the possession of narcotic drugs in Indonesia is considered a particularly serious offence. There are currently (2006) about 30 foreigners on death row for attempting to smuggle heroin or amphetamines through Indonesian customs. Fools. There are also a few folks sentenced to 20 years imprisonment in Bali for attempting to smuggle *ganja* into Indonesia.

**'Justice' Prevailed!**
There's the Australian model caught with two tablets of ecstasy as she was about to go into a Bali party. She was arrested and sentenced to a lengthy jail term in 2005, only to be released because, it was alleged, she was going to implicate her companion for the night—the son of a very prominent government minister.

Rich or poor, drugs are an expensive addiction and best to be avoided unless you want a real culture shock.

## GETTING AROUND

In order to get anywhere in Jakarta, you have a number of choices, the wisest and easiest of which is probably to stay in your hotel and use room service. After all, it can take longer to get from one side of Jakarta to the other than it does to get to Bogor, some 60 km (37.3 miles) south of Jakarta.

So, what do you do? Firstly, consider the following criteria:
- Is your meeting really necessary?
- Have you used up all your sick days?
- Can your date meet you somewhere local, to you that is?
- Why go to a cinema when you can watch a pirated DVD at home?

If you must go somewhere, consider the logistics and plan ahead, even if you're merely going to your local supermarket. Ask folks for the best way to get from A to B. Ask many folks so you know the range of choices; then you'll have backup plans for your journey. If you're stuck somewhere, lost even, keep an eye out for shopping malls. These air-conditioned oases will have cafés. If you're really lucky, you'll be stuck near an air-conditioned hotel with a bar.

Finally, consider your mode of transport. If you must go out, then is looking cool and suave important or will having sweat stains on your shirt or blouse be acceptable? Option one leaves you with your own transport or a newish taxi. Option two is everything else.

Above all, take it easy and remember this simple mantra: don't blame me; it's the traffic.

## Walking

Jakarta is hot, very hot. If you like walking around cities, pop over to Singapore which is also hot but has footpaths and, for Americans, sidewalks.

Jakarta's streets may have footpaths too, but you'll be lucky to find a stretch which affords you a dozen paces. In fact, a cursory glance will show you that the best-laid footpaths are little used. This is where you won't find, as everywhere else, the potholes, trees, lampposts and road signs, giant plant pots and bollards to stop motorcyclists driving along them or cars from parking on them, parked cars and motorcycles, restaurants, newsagents, tobacconists, garden centres, groups of people doing what groups of people do—seemingly nothing but getting in your way.

If you must walk, say from a taxi to the kerb, make sure that your good shoes are in your bag because you wouldn't want to get them mired in the trash and sodden gutter would you? If you want to cross a road and there's a footbridge, then allow plenty of time to look where you're going. There may be holes to fall through, a missing railing or an obstruction, such as an *ojek* (motorbike taxi) or snacks seller at the bottom. There will certainly be someone selling something you'd forgotten you needed, such as shoelaces, baby turtles or a pink cover for your phone.

Usually there isn't a particular place for you to cross a street; whatever you do, ignore those wide white stripes painted in the road like the pedestrian crossings you see in other countries because all drivers do. Clearly, the safety of the pedestrian in Jakarta is of little importance, and you really do need to look both ways before crossing a one-way street. Having said this, you may be surprised by the way many Indonesians, particularly in crowded areas, cross the street seemingly oblivious to the traffic, leaving drivers to swerve around them. It has been suggested that the reasoning behind this lies in the potential trouble that would befall anyone unfortunate enough to run down a pedestrian, a lynch mob emerging from nowhere in a matter of seconds. This ever-present threat is, apparently, sufficient reason to walk across the road, whilst flapping the hand nearest the onrushing traffic

## Traffic

There is only one topic of conversation in Jakarta: the traffic. It determines where you live, where you shop, where you work and how many meetings you can get to in one day—one, if you're lucky. Traffic is a more important topic than the weather; a downpour will bring the streets to a standstill. Yet, although newcomers to Jakarta are generally bewitched, bothered and bewildered by the seeming chaos on the roads, understanding that all drivers throughout Indonesia follow the same rules to varying degrees should make life easier.

## Jakarta's 'Highway Code'
- Four-wheeled vehicles usually have steering wheels on the right. This means that they are generally driven on the left

side of the road unless there is a white line painted on the road surface. This functions like a monorail: keep your tyres equidistant each side of it. If you are a motorcyclist, then try to drive along it.

- That bus stopped in the outer lane of a toll road (*jalan tol*) isn't parked and nor has it broken down. It is letting off passengers.
- If a vehicle hits yours, then remember that the other driver is at fault. Unless his vehicle is bigger.
- You've heard that street crime is rampant, so do not stop for àny pedestrians, especially those trying to cross the road.
- There are frequent power cuts in Indonesia, so save electricity by not using your indicators. However, if you are affluent, then feel free to illuminate your car like a Christmas tree, especially in daylight hours. Also, use your emergency lights, the left and right indicators, to show you intend to drive straight ahead.
- When approaching a road junction, flash your headlights and drive straight on. That way, you'll reach the next traffic jam (*macet total*) much quicker.
- Do not stop at intersections.

## Parking is Easy

- If you can find a space on a sidewalk unoccupied by street stalls (*warungs*), trees, telephone or electricity poles, advertising boards, and without holes, use it. Oh, and drop us a line about its location.
- Leaving that space and joining the traffic is easy. There is always someone with a whistle and the familiar street mating call of *kiri* (left), *kanan* (right) and *terus* (straight). You can safely ignore these cries; most drivers do, but do be generous with the Rp 1,000 notes. You will be helping to keep *preman* (hoodlums) off the streets. Or, in this case, on them.
- A special rule operates for special functions such as weddings and the annual celebration in front of the headquarters of the traffic police. You can use three of the four lanes for parking. No permit or notification is required, and local

people can be hired to redirect you through the back streets (*jalan tikus*—translates as 'rat run') and alleys (*gangs*).

## Rules For Motorcyclists

- This means of transport is convenient for the whole family. Your three-year-old can sit on your lap and your wife can ride side-saddle behind you whilst breastfeeding your newborn.
- Any motorcycle, especially a cheap Chinese 90cc one, is versatile enough for commercial use. You, or your pillion passenger, can comfortably carry 50 live chickens and/or 3 televisions and/or plate glass for your shop window and/or 100 kg (220 lb) of used plastic bottles. If you don't have a pillion passenger, place the load on the back seat, drape it over the rear wheel and tie it securely to the exhaust pipe with that colourful plastic twine.
- Do not wear a crash helmet; otherwise you cannot smoke a clove cigarette (*kretek*) or use your handphone.
- If you see someone leaving a bus or car stopped by the curb, do try to squeeze through the gap. It will save you a lot of time. In fact, any gap in the traffic is yours for the taking.
- When available, use the sidewalks.
- Carry an umbrella in case it rains.
- Special rules apply during the rainy season.
    - Use your umbrella to keep your *kretek* and/or your handphone dry.
    - Drive as usual along the white lines with no lights on.
    - Park anywhere on the road under a footbridge. If you cause a traffic jam, do not worry. At least those car drivers, who cannot squeeze through the one remaining lane, are dry.
- There are no parking rules for motorcycles.

## Rules For Pedestrians

- Use your handphone so you do not have to notice and give way to other pedestrians.
- Never walk alone. It is best to walk three abreast, slowly. That way it is not you who has to step into the path of motorcyclists.

Fantastic balancing skills are often displayed by Indonesians.

- When waiting for a bus or taxi, form a crowd. There is safety in numbers.
- Cross the road near a pedestrian crossing or footbridge. Flapping your hand by your side is sufficient to warn on-coming cars and buses about your intention to walk in front them. They usually stop, although motorcycles don't.
- Do not think of using the sidewalks.
  Have a safe journey.

## TRANSPORT—PUBLIC AND OTHERS

Three million folks commute into the city every work day, thus swelling the population by a quarter. Jakarta only has 7,500 km (4,660 miles) of roads, many in appalling, if not downright dangerous, condition for the 5 million plus vehicles. If the average vehicle length is 3 m (9.8 ft), and only 35 per cent of those vehicles are on the road, it's a *macet total* (gridlock) situation. And when it rains, fewer are needed to bring Jakarta to a standstill.

Jakarta's traffic jams are phenomenal, legendary even. Engines are turned off; windows unwound and all hope lost. Even the city's many toll roads are jammed to the back teeth. Giving drivers the option of buying a few hundred metres of freeway simply doesn't work. The root of the trouble lies in the fact Jakarta is based around a single main arterial road, running north to south. Jakarta's concentric 'design' means that the centres of public activity are right in the middle of the city. There isn't necessarily a lack of roads; it's just that everybody wants to get to more or less the same place at the same time. Jakarta's administration has, it seems, given Jakarta's public a city which simply invites traffic jams. It certainly hasn't provided an integrated transport plan.

The situation is exacerbated further by the seemingly random way traffic regulations are chopped and changed. It's quite possible to drive down a road one day, only to find it running in the opposite direction the next. To add to the confusion, it's common for one length of road to go through several name changes before it comes to an end. No one is sure which road ends where and which starts where—best of luck. Sometimes, too, 'they' will change the name of a road without informing the residents, so everybody except for strangers continues to use the old name. And why not?

## Driving

Having your own transport, preferably with a hired driver, is an option for the well-off. Having access to a company car is the next best thing, especially one with CD plates which may entitle you to a police escort.

At first glance, short distance travel in Jakarta is a nightmare scenario. One option is to use a motorbike with which you can weave in and out of traffic and overtake the worst jams, but entirely at your own risk. It may be the fastest, but a motorbike is quite definitely not the safest. Keep your legs flush to the bike or risk having one wrenched off by a bus.

Being the smallest vehicles on the streets, motorbike riders have no option other than obeying the pecking order of Jakarta's traffic. Smaller vehicles can only give way to bigger ones. In theory, a pedestrian must give way to a motorbike, which in turn must give way to a *bajaj* (motorised rickshaw), which has to give way to a sedan, which in turn submits to a *kijang* (van), which has to make way for a Metromini (mad orange bus). The problems start when you have, for example, two Metromini heading towards one another. Which one is supposed to give way? Tricky. One of them certainly should, and at the last millisecond one of them nearly always does. People with pace-makers are warned.

This seems to be the prevailing logic of Jakarta's traffic. While it appears nothing short of bedlam to the casual observer, it should be pointed out just how few major accidents do actually occur. You might expect to be involved in a minor car crash on a daily basis when you first experience Jakarta traffic, but this is not the case. True, there are an awful lot of dented vehicles to be seen in the city, but nowhere near as many as might be expected.

---

**Things to Look Out For**

Keep your eyes open at all times. One-way signs, white divider lines, no-entry signs and other road regulations are often meaningless to drivers in Indonesia. And look out for the police. Jakarta is one of few places in the world where you can be stopped for driving carefully.

---

Never assume you have the right of way in Jakarta; there is always someone, somewhere taking a 'short cut' the wrong way down a one-way street. Keep your eyes peeled too for the many makeshift 'roundabouts' intended to slow traffic at crossroads. Basically unlit oildrums, they make a horrible sound upon collision. Be wary also of Jakarta's alarmingly high curbs. Certain roads, like Jl. Buncit Raya, are 'dual carriage-way' and have certain sections of lane separated by foot-high dividers. Driving over one in the dark, which unknowing drivers are prone to do, completely wrecks the undercarriage. Also in place are umpteen '*polisi tidur*' (speed humps aka 'sleeping police'), there solely to wreck a car's suspension. They are only occasionally painted to show their presence, the assumption being that you've already travelled along this section of road.

It's said that driving unleashes the devil in everyone, and Indonesians are no exception. Fortunately, there are more passengers than drivers in Jakarta. Some drivers honk their

One of the few things that will slow traffic down is the colour yellow. It symbolises death and is a sure sign that a funeral procession is imminent. The traffic slows for a hearse, but not an ambulance.

horns constantly in Jakarta, especially when approaching corners, but this noise pollution is, thankfully, a lot less than some major European capitals. Use of the horn means only, 'I am hurtling towards you, watch out because I might run you down'. When drivers flash their headlights, they want you to give way. This is particularly alarming in the case of vehicles which are moving rapidly towards you. You move.

Attempts by the government to stem the terrible traffic jams have included the introduction in 1992 of a 'three-in-one' system. This meant that any vehicle wishing to travel on the main roads of Sudirman, Thamrin, Rasuna Said and Gatot Subroto had to have at least three passengers inside. The irony is that drivers resorted to hiring extra 'passengers' to fulfil the quota; drive down any of the roads approaching the main thoroughfares before 10:00 am and see dozens of potential jockeys waiting to be hired. Invariably children, they charge a minimal amount depending how far you are going.

Various alternative schemes have been touted to ease the traffic chaos. These include a congestion charge, new toll roads into the centre of town, extra traffic lanes (necessitating the removal of umpteen banyan trees), a monorail, currently derailed due the lack of financial guarantees, and a subway. There is no long-term transport policy for the city. Perhaps the most effective bandaid solution has been the Busway.

But no matter. Because all in all, being given a licence to drive like a nutter on a regular basis is surely nothing less than liberating.

## Getting a Licence

Neither of the authors has an Indonesian Driver's License (SIM), although Terry had one back in 1990 or thereabouts. By all accounts—with thanks here to Miko in Jakarta and Oigal in Kalimantan—the system isn't so different now, except that the cost for expats is considerably higher. You still need a KITAS (work permit) or other residence permit; tourists can only use an international licence so you can skip this section. The actual cost could be US$ 50–US$ 100 rather than the posted 'official' rate (Rp 125,000 in 2006). If you use an agent, often a moonlighting policeman, to pay the 'admin' fees, you can get the one day service and won't have to take the test. After completing the initial form, you may be asked to produce a copy of your passport, a letter in *bahasa Indonesia* confirming your employment, a doctor's letter verifying good health, your 'blue book' (STMD police book), your international or home licence, and, of course, money.

Jakarta is a good place to learn to drive. If you can drive unscathed in Jakarta, you can drive anywhere. Guaranteed. Just don't take those appalling driving manners back home with you.

Presumably because expat work and residence visas and permits are renewed every year, the SIM is only valid for 12 months, whereas for Indonesians it's five years. It is worth having, however, as it identifies you as a long-term resident and not a tourist ripe for plucking. International licenses are nothing but trouble as the local cops don't see enough of them to understand the concept. At the very least, you can be held up for hours as he tries to contact his superiors. I should add that here in boonies, local regulations outlaw use of international licenses for KITAS holders. This may be the same elsewhere."

## Owning a Vehicle

Non-Indonesians are not allowed to own registered property in the country so any investment you make in something which requires a signature, such as land, the house you want to buy, a car or motorbike, etc. has to be in the name of a local partner.

## Cars

Here's an account of the complicated process of car-buying from Dominic in Surabaya:

'My friend bought a car but wanted to put it in his wife's name. This is a mysterious process, one that for us mere mortals is far too intricate to be understood. We discussed this with the company driver and arranged with him to get the paperwork sorted.

That morning we found him having breakfast at one of the food stalls on the side road beside the school. Handing him the papers, we went through what we wanted again, he wiped his mouth, nodded, then called over a fellow who was sitting on a motorbike nearby. Once again we went through the explanation, and he seemed to know what we wanted, nodding sagely and telling us what he needed in order to put through the paperwork. Each form photocopied in triplicate, and a few hundred thousand to get the wheels rolling. We asked what would be the final cost and were assured it wouldn't be any more than Rp 500,000. We were pleased at this and left him to it.

Later that afternoon, we chatted again to the driver whose minion was organising the process and he pulled out a bit of paper.

"Now, let's see," he says. "The cost of the tax is Rp 700,000, the stamps, Rp 100,000, the something or another Rp 50,000 and this is Rp 100,000 and that is Rp 75,000 and oh, don't forget, the processing fee is Rp 400,000. Grand total is Rp 1,375,000."

We looked at each other then back at the fellow. "Hang on! You told us this morning it would cost about Rp 500, 000!"

"Oh yes," he said triumphantly, "and look, I got the processing fee down to Rp 400, 000!"

"Yes, but," we spluttered, "what's the rest of this?"

"Oh that!" he said, "well that" (smiling benevolently upon us like a kind uncle explaining the simplest facts of live to two dullards), "that is all the rest of the costs."

"I see," we said weakly.

"But," he added, smiling even more, "you don't have to pay the balance until it's all fixed!"

"Oh, well, that's good then," we say and stagger away.

We held an earnest powpow under the shade of the motorbike park awning.

"So, what'll we do?"

"Look mate,' I suggested, fixing him with what I hoped was a knowledgeable look, 'you've two options.

Pay him, and put it down to experience, or stop the process. However, if he is telling the truth about the costs, it's loss of face to you. If he's not, then nothing is harmed except possibly an unhappy driver and his eager minion."

My friend ruminated and finally spoke the magic words that all we married men say when we are faced with an impossible decision and have no idea what to do: "I'll ask my wife." Relief flowed over both of us.

"Good idea!" I cried, clapping him on the back. "I'm sure she'll know what to do."

To be fair, his wife is Indonesian and thus has a better insight into the whole thing; we foreigners are just way too unsure of the intricacies of the bureaucracy.'

Cars are cars are cars. As this is a guide to culture shock rather than a consumer's guide to motoring, all we need to tell you is that you can buy big SUVs and very small Japanese and Korean city runabouts. You can pay a lot for a Ferrari—yes there is at least one in Jakarta—or a Jaguar or BMW. There are loads of different types of sedan, predominantly locally-assembled Asian models, but the most ubiquitous are people carriers such as the Toyota Kijang which are robust and can carry four adults and a couple of kids in reasonable comfort.

Whatever you buy, remember that you won't get anywhere fast in Jakarta and aren't actually allowed to own it if you're not an Indonesian citizen.

## Motorcycles

According to a *Dilintas Polri* (Traffic Police) estimate, there were around 35 million motorcycles on Indonesia's road in 2006, with about 5.5 million of those on Jakarta's roads. That is 70 per cent of the total population of vehicles. The number is double that of 2002, and 2.33 times higher than that in 2001.

This astonishing growth is due to a number of factors, not least the appalling state of public transport. Within the major conurbations, incomes have slowly risen and with the rise of middle class aspirations for family independence, a family vehicle comes pretty high on the list of essentials. An 80cc motorbike, based on the familiar Honda and Suzuki models, are remarkably cheap. Even a locally produced Honda costing US$ 1,500 can be bought for a deposit of Rp 500,000 (US$ 55), with payments spread over four years.

Now an increase in purchasing power may be good for the economy, but the resulting traffic jams are certainly not. Nor are the medical costs.

### Robo-man!

An expat we know came off his 180cc Honda Tiger one night. It had been raining and one particular puddle covered a pothole. He was operated on in a Singapore hospital which put his arm together with nuts and bolts and bits of Meccano. Now, when he goes through the many security check points in buildings and airports, he sets off the metal detectors.

Another factor which can lead to injury is road rage because this vast army of Hell's Cherubs has no road sense. Their parents weren't drivers so there aren't any models to emulate. When driving, expect to meet hordes of bikes buzzing towards you in your lane. Your only defence is to wind down your window and to stick your arm out. This will be at the head height of the oncoming motorcyclists and it's a joy to watch them hurriedly veer back into their proper traffic lane. As an added deterrent, hold a machete.

In 2006, the traffic police finally got around to enforcing a couple of traffic regulations first promulgated some 15 or more years ago. Motorcyclists are expected to keep to the left lanes and drive with their headlights on. It is unlikely that these rules will still be followed by the time the next edition of this book is compiled.

If walking along one of the few navigable sidewalks, expect to be beeped by a bike or two. If you're big and assertive, you can block their passage and force them back onto the road. You won't receive much encouragement from other pedestrians, but they will secretly admire your efforts on their behalf and wish their culture enabled them to stick up for their rights.

Naturally, if you do decide to drive around on two wheels, you won't have followed your authors' advice and we disclaim all responsibility for your expected hospital costs. You may not have an accident, a statistical probability, but you'll certainly have an extra coating of tar in your lungs, gulped in from the bus you can't get past.

## Buses

On the face of it, Jakarta's bus system appears nothing less than absolute mayhem, and to an extent it is. It is reputed that you can purchase a printed guide telling you which bus goes where at bus terminals, although the authors have never seen one. However, behind the apparent chaos, a certain structure prevails. If you don't mind the packed conditions, the heat and hard seats, the risk of being robbed, the pollution and the generally painfully slow progress from A to B, then buses are a good way to move around town.

The main fixed destination services operating in Jakarta, in descending order of comfort, size and speed, are the Busway, the *Patas* (express) AC, the single-decker PPD, Aja, Steady Safe, Mayasari and sundry others, orange Metromini or cream and green Kopaja, and *mikrolets* and *angkots*. These all have fixed fares although '*dekat atau jauh*' (near or far) doesn't apply to all services.

The Busway is a limited stop service which runs in special lanes mostly down the middle of the roads. Access is by footbridges to the ticket booths and waiting areas in the median. At the time of writing, the fare is Rp 5,000 for any distance, although variable distance rates are being considered. Unless you board at a terminus, it's unlikely that you'll get a seat and will have to strap-hang. This shouldn't be too much of a bother because you'll be standing under a blast of cold air and can gaze at the backed up traffic, denied the road space given to your bus, whilst you speed to somewhere close to your ultimate destination. Your only problem is likely to be navigating the sidewalk once you've descended from the footbridge.

The Busway drivers are the only ones with a salary, in 2007 Rp 2,500,000 (US$ 310) per month, and this system is the only one to issue 'tickets'. These are in the form of credit card-sized plastic tokens which you insert into a slot in order to get into the waiting area.

---

### TransJakarta Busway Routes

The following Busway *koridors* (routes) were in operation at the time of going to press—mid-2007.

Interchange between *koridors* is possible at Kampung Melayu, Harmoni, Dukuh Atas, Halimun, Matraman and Senen.

- Blok M—Kota
- Pulo Gadung—Harmoni
- Harmoni—Kalideres
- Pulo Gadung—Dukuh Atas
- Kampung Melayu—Ancol
- Ragunan—Dukuh Atas
- Kampung Rambutan—Kampung Melayu

The following routes are planned. Maybe.

- Ciledug—Kalimalang
- Senayan—Tanah Abang
- Warung Jati—Imam Bonjol
- Pasar Minggu—Manggarai
- Tomang—Harmoni—Pasar Baru
- Lebak Bulus—Kebayoran Lama
- Pulo Gebang—Kampung Melayu

---

'All other buses, from large to small, are hired by the driver and his conductor(s) who take their wages in cash from fares collected. They have to pay fleet owners and various *preman* (hoodlums) on the route a fixed amount each day. Naturally, this leads to anarchy as the bus crew are understandably keen to pick up as many passengers as possible, no matter how close the destination. with conductors almost force-feeding passengers into the innards. The conductors are too busy collecting from passengers to bother with the hawkers and musicians who also pile on to pick up a few stray coins from the passengers who are generally stoic.

A bus ride incurs a fixed fare (Rp 2,000 + in 2007) *dekat jauh* (near or far), which is very reasonable. However, the drawbacks with bus travel are many. The discomfort is exceptional, even if you do manage to get a seat.

After a few minutes, when it's clearly hot enough to fry rice, you start wondering why no one has opened a window, only to be reminded how very fearful Indonesians are of anything remotely draughty. The belief is that any lengthy exposure to wind results in untold health problems known primarily as *masuk angin* (entered wind), but what we call breathing.

The number of people that can be crammed into a single bus is beyond belief. People are stuffed in to the point where the bus leans over so much, it practically moves forward on two wheels. And still people continue to pile in, many of them transporting enormous chest-high parcels, sacks and boxes of bed stuffing and prawn crackers. Passengers end up hanging out of the door and holding their breath inside. And still a couple of buskers manage to squeeze on and start jamming. Indonesians are extremely resilient it seems; old people, heavily pregnant women and knee-high schoolkids alike are thrown around the bus with the same blank abandon. Buses generally go as fast as possible; they make no concession unless they aren't completely full. In which case, they'll dawdle interminably at traffic lights and anywhere else they expect to find an extra passenger. For your comfort, we advise you to board buses at the terminuses.

One of the people hanging out of the bus is the 'conductor' who, when not collecting fares, spends his time counting a wad of bank notes and hollering their destination to the world. Some of their cries have become legendary: "Blok M", for example, when said at a hundred times a minute becomes "blemblemblemblemblemblemblem". It's not uncommon for conductors to leap off the bus and 'round up' passengers, some of whom had perhaps no intention of getting on that particular bus. So a hundred metres down the street you will hear either *"kiri pak"* ("left here mate") or the sound of a coin tapped on glass, and off they get again. Sometimes the passengers can't make up their minds whether to get off or not and wait uneasily at the door, blocking access. The progress of all city buses is marked in this way; stopping and starting, stopping and starting, all done as hastily as possible.

Sometimes the bus takes a totally different route, depending on the traffic ahead. If the bus is stuck in a jam, or word comes through that the area ahead is *macet total* (gridlock), the driver might endeavour to do a three-point turn in the middle of the madness or get onto the adjacent toll road. Naturally, this only adds to the confusion and disappointment of those passengers who had hoped to get to the destination displayed on the front of the bus.

The pollution emitted by most buses is immoral. You do not want to be behind one of these monsters if you are travelling on an *ojek* or even in a taxi where, although spared the brunt of the thick, black exhaust smoke, a ton still gets through the car's AC system, though somewhat chilled.

There used to be a fleet of old Volvo and British Leyland double-deckers and a few Chinese bendy-buses, but due to a lack of servicing, these regularly caught fire and were withdrawn from service.

## Laws That Don't Work

The government regularly attempts to clean up the bus service. In 1994, it introduced a strict table of conditions with which buses were expected to comply. Buses producing too much smoke were threatened with massive fines, far beyond the pocket of any Metromini driver. And because nearly every bus on the street failed to meet these conditions, the implementation of these laws was impossible, and a year later nothing had changed, although a lot of drivers were missing their licenses. Another new law was aimed at cutting down the number of people on a single bus (after a glut of death-by-falling-out-a-bus-in-motion reports), and stated that buses had to be able to close their doors. The way round this was simply to cram the usual amount of people in and then shut the doors. This, of course, resulted in perhaps the single most uncomfortable bus ride of all time.

## Taxis

Taxis are abundant in Jakarta and come in a variety of colours. The vast majority are now clean and efficient with polite and honest drivers and very few are the not-very-fondly-remembered 'Taxis From Hell'. Until you are familiar with the different liveries, you'd be wise sticking to the blue ones such as the highly recommended BlueBird. This is a generally reliable service with a GPS system enabling a fairly quick pick-up service. However, they are more expensive than the majority of the others.

At the time of writing, there were two tariffs, the new and the old. In early 2006, with an oil supply crisis caused by geo-political factors in Iraq, Iran and elsewhere, the government, still trying to recover from the Asian economic meltdown of 1996/1997, took the tough decision to cut the fuel subsidies. Fares inevitably rose and the more expensive travel option of a taxi became less desirable. All taxi companies found that passengers became much scarcer. Some decided to keep to the tarif lama (old rates) and prominently displayed this on the windscreens and rear windows. At the same time, it seemed that, through peer pressure perhaps, service increased, drivers became more civil, which is not to say servile, and it is now rare to find a driver whose driving scares you or tries to con you into going the long way round.

You might still be asked to leave the taxi if the driver thinks a particular area is too jammed (*macet*) or flooded (*banjir*), while on a bad day they refuse to even stop. But this is increasingly unlikely because any fare is income earned.

Occasionally, it becomes clear after being in the taxi for a few minutes that the driver is *baru* (new) to the job and doesn't actually know where he is going. This may be a genuine lack of knowledge because taxi drivers are employed solely on the basis of having a driving licence. Even the highly recommended BlueBird taxi drivers can be clueless. More than likely, if it's a Sunday, he's a visiting relative who has agreed to give the taxi's regular driver a day off. If you do encounter problems, you are entitled to command him to stop (say 'stop' in a commanding tone of voice), and exit. Most drivers are pleased to receive a foreign customer and inevitably have all sorts of questions to ask. Prepare to talk.

Not only should a taxi offer efficient service, it should also smell good. Since Jakarta's streets are no perfume-garden, many vehicles are equipped with powerful air fresheners, the resulting scent of which is often more overpowering than the smells outside. Rare now is the taxi with the aroma of yesterday's *kreteks*. It is rare, too, to find yourself in a taxi with inefficient air conditioning. Although AC (pronounced 'a'—as in 'hat'—'say') recycles the pollution from the bus in front, albeit with the grit filtered out, it also spreads germs. Jakarta's taxis can also be colder than your fridge back home, which is why the driver wears a jacket and you freeze.

There's an initial 'flag fall' fare which inevitably increases from year to year. In 1990, it was Rp 500, five years later it had doubled and now it is Rp 4,000

## Travelling in Style

Occasionally, such as getting a taxi at, say, the Sultan Hilton, you may find yourself in a SilverBird. This is an upmarket BlueBird and a black limo affair, an Australian model rather wimpishly called Cedric. It has darkened windows, decorous drivers and a higher tariff. It's the height of luxury so enjoy the fact that you are stuck in yet another traffic jam, but that this time you're doing it in style.

(*tarif lama*) or Rp 5,000 (*tarif baru*) with a differential in the charge per metre travelled., The length of time spent with the taxi is also a factor; witness how the meter continues to rise even when busy going nowhere in a traffic jam.

It's best if you know where you are going. If you don't, you should at least try and sound as if you know where you are going. It helps if you can beat the driver to the punch and tell him which way you want to go before he asks. For example, if you were travelling from Pasar Minggu to Blok M, you could '*lewat* (go via) Kapten Tendean', or you could just as well '*lewat* Kemang'. If in doubt, you should state that you just want to go there '*langsung*' (directly).

There was a time when travelling by taxi was a lottery. You'll rarely find one now with inefficient air conditioning or a driver who refuses to use his meter. Although you are not usually expected to tip the driver by much—round up the fee to the nearest couple of thousand—you may decide to pay more than you would be expected to. Why not? All in all, taxis are an inexpensive way to travel about the city and the next best thing to having your own chauffeur

*Becaks* are three-wheeled pedicabs, two at the front (over which passengers are seated) and one at the back where drivers work their sinewy legs. Sadly, there are hardly any *becaks* left in Jakarta although there are still a few operating in the occasional pocket of resistance in back street areas of Bintaro, which is actually in the satellite town of Tangerang, but on the whole they are a thing of the past. It was decided in City Hall that *becaks* were 'inhumane' and that death among *becak* drivers from expanded heart and lungs was high. It was decided also that *becaks* didn't do much to enhance the modern face of Jakarta. Far too '*kampungan*' (unrefined) apparently, even though they were restricted to the back streets of the *kampungs*.

A lot of jobs were lost. Some found work driving *bajaj*, some opted to quit the city for good and *pulang kampung* (go home), while many more became responsible for the million *ojek* that currently meet the continuing demand for cheap short distant travel around Jakarta. Others became Walls Ice Cream or bread vendors endlessly pedalling their

A fast disappearing sight in Jakarta, the *becak* can now only be found in certain places.

way around the back streets on tricycles which appear to be converted *becaks*.

Go to Yogya for the best *becak* in the land.

*Bajaj* on the other hand, are cheap taxis. Three-wheeled and usually orange, *bajaj* (pronounced 'badge-eye') are two-stroke motorised rickshaws which get you from A to B for a negotiated fee. The competition on the streets is fierce; while the bulk of Jakarta's *bajaj* are run by co-operatives, many are privately-owned. They are the cockroaches of Jakarta transport: the noisiest, hottest and possibly the dirtiest things on the roads. Get stuck behind one in a traffic jam and watch your vehicle slowly fill up with nauseating blue exhaust.

*Bajaj* are not permitted on big roads like Thamrin and are restricted to working in one mayoralty. Drivers may refuse to go somewhere if they think it's too close or too far, or they think it might be *macet* (jammed) ahead. You can get two people comfortably inside, and probably up to four if pushed. Ensure you have agreed on the price beforehand; some hard bargaining may be required. Tip the driver enough and he may even let you drive.

An illustration of the *bajaj*. A convenient and relatively fast way to travel.

*Bajaj*, which are made in India, were first imported in the early seventies and were an instant success. Television adverts at the time warned pregnant women to think twice before using one, due to the extremely pot-holed condition of Jakarta's back streets, not to mention the bouncing, 'trampoline-style' bridges in certain parts of town. The risk of whacking your head on the roof of the *bajaj* every time it hits a pot-hole is high. Suspension, like AC, is not part of the design.

Since *bajaj* do not have any air conditioning, they can get very hot. Don't grumble too much, though. Think of the drivers who have to contort themselves just to fit on the front seat. Most suffer from excruciating backache.

### Hot! Hot! Hot!
There's the story of a man wearing plastic shoes while stuck in the back of one for over an hour in a traffic jam. When he finally arrived, he found his shoes had melted to the floor of the vehicle, and he had to be cut free.

The city government has hoped to rid Jakarta of all its *bajaj* for nigh on 20 years, just like it did with *becaks*. Schemes have been announced to develop hybrids or to import a new generation of *bajaj* from the Bajaj Corporation in India. The only evidence of these schemes and dreams is the small four-wheeled *Kancil* which means mouse deer and is not to be confused with the Malaysian people carrier nor the Indonesian equivalent, the *Kijang*, which means big deer. Yellow, very slightly bigger and quieter, it has a 404cc engine, seats four, can reach a maximum speed of 80 kmph (49.7 milesph) and gets 17–20 km (10.6–12.4 miles) to the litre. A small fan is provided for the comfort of the up to four (small) passengers. Some 500 are apparently on Jakarta's streets, but sightings are rare because, at a cost of Rp 40 million (US$ 3,500), few *bajaj* operators can afford them.

Mikrolet and Angkot are the two principal names of the mini-buses that serve set routes on smaller main roads. They are either light blue or rich red and seat 9–12 people, depending on the type and greed of the drivers. Fares run from Rp 1,500–4,000, depending on the distance; there should be a fares chart on display somewhere. Students pay Rp 1,000 if in uniform—for any distance. The beginning and end points of the routes are visible on the front and back of each bus, along with a route number. For example, Tanah Abang–Meruya M11.

## Ojek

After *becak* were finally banned in 1994, the *ojek* (motorcycle taxi) service began as a people's initiative to provide a transport option for people to use from main roads into and around housing complexes. The majority are the small 80cc Japanese bikes, or the cheaper Chinese clones. Westerners may have difficulty sitting comfortably on these small velocipedes, so keep your eye open for the much rarer Vespa motor scooters. There is no government licensing for or control over *ojek*. By law, all motorcycle passengers must wear helmets, so *ojek* drivers should have a spare for you to wear but probably don't. Ladies have a careful balancing act if wearing a dress and wishing to sit side-saddle on the back of the vehicle. Bargain before you get on, preferably having asked a local for the going rate.

## Trains

If you want to leave Jakarta by train, and the journey to Bandung is one of the world's most scenic, depart from Gambir station near Monas in the centre of town. There are a few commuter trains in Jakarta which use the same tracks, but confusingly, none of them actually stop at Gambir, so you'll have to go to the station by taxi.

Commuter trains run between Bogor and Jakarta's historic Kota station stopping at every station in between (except Gambir); this is useful if you live in, say, Tebet, Depok or Pasar Minggu. There is also a commuter line between Serpong, in the township of Tangerang, and Tanah Abang, As they bypass traffic jams, they are both reasonable routes to take if you are reasonably stoic. You have to be because the trains are filthy, the doors don't shut (or can't be opened), the fans don't work, the carriages are overcrowded, both inside and on top, and you're unlikely to get a seat. Mind you, for Rp 1000 or Rp 2000, you mustn't grumble, unless your pockets are picked or someone steals the signal cable—a regular occurrence, and you're stuck for what seems to be forever somewhere you don't want to be whilst dripping sweat onto a stranger.

There are also newish express trains to Bogor and Bekasi which don't stop at every station, cost a little more and have very cold air conditioning—unless this is an old copy of the book, in which case please refer to the last paragraph. There don't seem to be any timetables so don't promise to meet anyone at a particular time at the end of your journey.

The cattle class rolling stock is gradually being updated with cast-off Japanese carriages. Initial trials show that they are totally unsuitable for physically disadvantaged folk, but then this is true of all Jakarta's facilities. Other improvements include double-tracking which will presumably allow the use of more second-hand carriages on certain lines. There is also promised a token system as used by the Busway. This may actually increase the available space in the carriages as KAI (Kereta Api Indonesia) reckon that at least 25 per cent of their passengers ride for free.

Ah, but if only the city hall would invest in more railways instead of inner city toll roads ....

## Airport

Allow plenty of time if you're hoping to leave Jakarta from Soekarno-Hatta Airport, particularly in the rainy season, November to April, as the ever-sinking access toll road tends to flood. Not all taxi firms are allowed to pick up passengers there but given that a one way journey out there is a substantial sum towards the daily rental of the cab, few drivers would refuse to take you.

If you have enough time and are travelling alone, the Damri bus service which leaves every half an hour from Blok M, Gambir, Rawamangun and Pasar Minggu, is fast and efficient and the fare saving is about the same as the airport tax.

Terminal 1 is for domestic passengers and Terminal 2 for international arrivals and departures. By the time you read this, there may well be a Terminal 3 for passengers on low cost no frills airlines, unless efforts to save the planet's climate have drastically reduced these people carriers.

In 2005, 27,947,482 passengers used the facilities at an average of about 100 per plane. They will have paid an airport tax Rp 100,000 for international flights and Rp 50,000 for domestic departures. Residents and expats with residence permits are expected to pay *fiskal*, which is Rp 1 million and supposedly can be reclaimed from the income tax authorities. We have been unable to trace anyone who has successfully done this, nor can we find a government source prepared to explain how much of this income actually reaches the treasury.

# FOOD AND ENTERTAINING

## CHAPTER 6

'For the novice, one word is vital: *pedas*. It means
the spicy and pungent hotness that burns the
beginner's mouth. Remember that Indonesians
chewed chillies when you sucked boiled lollies.'
—Ivan Southall, *Indonesia Face To Face*

## EATING IN

If eating at home in Jakarta, you have a fantastic choice of meals to have your *pembantu* (housemaid) cook you. Yes, more than likely it's the servant of the house (or of the month) who prepares the food you eat at home. It's no great sin in Indonesia to be clueless about cooking: the men of the house are never expected to lend a hand in the kitchen, and women are under little pressure either, most having grown up with servants around. So let's assume your food is being cooked for you. Since the average *pembantu* in Jakarta is from the island of Java, there's more likely to be a profusion of Sundanese and Javanese dishes appearing magically on the table, as opposed to such rare Batak specialties as dog-meat, which a servant from that particular region might be tempted to dish up. Fortunately for dog lovers, there are few, if any, *pembantus* from North Sumatra.

Indonesian dishes are rice-based, with a side vegetable, meat and chillies. Pork is not generally popular, since most Indonesians are Muslim, but it does crop up in Chinese dishes. Vegetarians are shown little sympathy in Indonesia. The very concept of 'no meat for me, thanks' is something quite alien to the average cook, and even so-called vegetarian dishes probably have some diced chicken thrown in somewhere. To an outsider perhaps, Indonesian food is pretty much the same: rice, something *pedas* (hot), and covered in *kecap asin* or *manis* (salty or sweet soy sauce). Of course, when you look at cooking in closer detail, you become more aware of subtle differences in method and flavour. Only time will tell. Best keep eating.

You could be served up any one of a million of dishes. Here are some of the more common ones: *nasi goreng* (fried rice), *cap cai* (a Chinese-style mix of veg and bits), *bakmi goreng* (fried noodles and things), *nasi rawon* (plain rice, black spicy veg and beef soup), *nasi rames* (plain rice, veg, eggs, meat, coconut), *lontong* (sticky rice wrapped in banana leaf 'sausages'), *gado-gado* (steamed and raw bean-sprouts, veg, hot peanut sauce), *gulai ayam* (yellow, curried-chicken broth), *gulai kambing* (same but with goat meat), *pisang goreng* (fried banana), *tempe* (fried fermented soya cake), *tahu goreng* (fried tofu), *bistik* (fried beef with gravy, sounds like 'beefsteaks'—get it?), *ikan pindang* (yellow curried fish), *telur pindang* (same but with egg instead of fish), *fu yung hai* (vegetables and shrimp omelette with sweet and sour sauce), *kari ayam* (curried chicken), *kari ikan* (curried fish), *sop ayam* (chicken soup), *sop apa saja* (any soup you want), *sayur bayam* (spinach soup), *sayur asem* (sour vegetables), *lalapan sayur sama ikan goreng* (fried fish, fresh veg and chilli sauce), *sayur lodeh* (veg in coconut soup), *oseng-oseng* (fried veg and optional tahu bits). Lack of food is definitely not one of Jakarta's shortcomings.

> Although some families adopt 'Western' style sitting in front of place settings at a table, most adopt a buffet style arrangement. Also, a fork and spoon are the general cutlery sets. Table knives are a rarity, not least because your *pembantu* is liable to take one home to her kampung to demonstrate the exotic lifestyle she has in Jakarta.

## RICE

Rice is currency in Indonesia. You don't talk about the weather in Indonesia, you talk about rice. You talk about the quality of it, the size of the grain, the taste. It comes in several colours including *beras merah* (red) and *beras hitam* (black), but the most recognisable form of rice is the generic *nasi putih* (white).

There are lots of words in *bahasa Indonesia* to describe different states of rice. *Gabah* is the real, just-picked thing. *Beras* is the dehusked item. Cook it, and you have *nasi*. Cook

The rural areas in Indonesia are dotted with rice paddies.

it incorrectly and you might have a sticky matter known as *ketan*. Don't cook it long enough and you will have an unappetising bowl of *biji limau*. Cook it perfectly and it's *nasi pulan*. Get served a ration of rice in prison and it's known as a *pelabur* or *ramsum*. Fry it and you have *nasi goreng*; cook it with coconut and it's *nasi uduk*. Sticks of squeezed, wrapped rice-sausages are called *lontong*. Rice porridge is *lecek* or *bubur*. Cook it for a banquet and it's *nasi angkatan*. The equivalent proverb to the one crying over split-milk is *nasi sudah jadi bubur* (the rice has already turned to porridge).

If your poster of the President falls down, glue it back up with a dab of *lem nasi* (rice glue). If things are getting you down, why not turn to sake? This pleasant and potent rice-drink works wonders for your outlook.

Rice is truly a political issue in Indonesia—the basis upon which governments may rise and fall. Indeed, it was after a 1973 shortage that former President Suharto pledged national self-sufficiency in rice—a move which, perhaps being so intimately linked with the Indonesian psyche, overshadowed his other, more questionable policies. The administrative body behind this immense task was the State Logistics Board—or Bulog—which, through supplement and subsidisation, managed to stabilise rice prices, achieve self-sufficiency, reduce poverty and seriously enrich the directors charged with overseeing the accounts.

In hindsight, however, this achievement led to a degree of political complacency which, when the economy collapsed in 1998 causing rice prices to rocket, culminated in some of the worst social unrest in decades—and the ultimate demise of Suharto's government.

The contested issue of rice has continued in the wake of Suharto's resignation when, after months of crippling economic crisis and the drought-induced failure of crops that year, it was revealed that the Jakarta Logistics Agency was siphoning off half Jakarta's 5,000 ton daily requirements. The arrest of the

Civil servants and the like are given a sack of rice as part of their salary which, in their bids to find the purest rice, is subsequently hawked around the neighbourhood like dope. The best rice in the land is a particularly refined strain known as Beras Cianjur.

agency's former head, Ahmad Zawawi, centred on allegations that subsidised rice was being sold for personal gain—a crime of corruption which carried the death sentence.

With half of the population officially below the poverty line at the time, the news that donations and subsidies from Japan, Pakistan and other countries were being resold at profit brought further social uproar. However, with the big boys seemingly protected in a tangled web of legalities, it was the ethnic Chinese of Indonesia who again bore the brunt of the forces of resentment.

## FRUIT

As long as you are in this country, you must take full advantage of the fantastic range of fruit available. Fruit keeps you healthy. Fruit keeps you working. What better way to line your stomach in the morning than by drinking an entire liquidised mango?

Clearly, since the climate is tropical, the emphasis is on soft, juicy, exotic fruit as opposed to unexciting second-leaguers like apples, oranges and grapes.

*Jeruk* is the generic word for all citrus fruits. *Jeruk* Bali has been described as the fruit you are given when you wake up for breakfast on your first morning in Heaven. It's like a user-friendly grapefruit: sweet, segmented, self-contained. *Jeruk nipis* is lime and *jeruk limon* is lemon. *Jeruk manis* (sweet oranges) often aren't so; perhaps the best oranges are imported.

There are rumoured to be 24 varieties of banana alone in Indonesia: red ones, long thin ones and strange, small, three-sided ones. Not all are edible, mind you, and some even have big hard seeds. The best ones to eat are the short and sweet *pisang emas* and the larger classic *pisang Ambon*. Indonesia is one of the world's major growers of bananas. Unfortunately, as quality is not guaranteed, it is not one of the world's major exporters—its share of the world market in 1996 was a meagre two per cent.

Malang, in East Java, is famous for its apples (*apel*). We aren't quite sure why as they are rarely to be found amongst the standardised tasteless imported ones in the

supermarkets. Perhaps it's because they are misshapen and have a bit of a flavour.

Another classic tropical fruit is, of course, the *nanas* (pineapple). If you are used to the canned variety of rings and cubes in a sweet syrup, then you must check out the fresh variety. The *nanas* is unbelievably sweet, tangy and juicy. In Indonesia, *nanas* is often eaten with salt to take the edge off, while a lot of women avoid it altogether, believing that it makes them *gatal* (itchy). Cutting a pineapple is nothing less than an acquired art-form; ask someone to show you how it's done. Pineapple bought from a vendor, however, will have been pre-peeled, sliced and bagged, so there's no need to carry a *golok* (machete) around with you. If you like to grow your own, few things are easier: simply cut off the top, plug it in the ground and wait.

A favourite fruit is the *mangga* (mango), best eaten from June onwards. Indonesians seem to like eating these before they are nice and ripe, when the juice pours down your fingers. Peel and slice them, and slurp them down. Then suck on the large flattish white seed inside until it is clean and hairy. Now draw a face on it. Alternatively, slice lengthwise either side of the stone and scoop out the flesh from within the skin with a spoon. It's a sad day when the season is over.

There are some crunchy fruits which are also very refreshing. *Belimbing* (starfruit) is one such with a cool, earth-watery flavour. Cut a slice crossways to see its five-pointed star shape.

*Jambu air* are crunchy, bell-shaped numbers, full of water (hence the name air) and commonly eaten as *rujak* with a chilli, peanut and palm-sugar sauce. Fruits like *jambu air* grow in Indonesia with the same free abandon that conkers (horse chestnuts) do in England. They grow like weeds, the season starting around September. If there is a tree in your yard, make yourself popular by filling plastic bags with the harvest and giving them away.

These are not to be confused with *jambu*, which are called guava elsewhere. You'll be lucky to find a soft one as they are popular as crunchy bits of a plate of *rujak*, the mixed fruit platter with the chillified peanut sauce.

*Manggis* is the love-fruit of Indonesia. Available between November and February, manggis is the most sensual, the most erotic of all fruit. The purple-brown outer shell cracks open to reveal a thick, rich mauve, almost marzipan-like, flesh beneath. Finger your way through this, and you reach the edible part; an exquisitely flavoured tight, white cluster of dribbling segments. *Manggis* is a notoriously difficult fruit, its ripeness easily misjudged. Often only half its inner charms are edible; the other half having already over-ripened into darker bits.

### Worth a Queen's Ransom

And over a hundred years ago, Queen Victoria offered her royal favours to whoever could get her some of these fruit to her in good condition.

*Duku* is a marble-sized lychee type fruit. In Jakarta, they are piled up for sale by the roadside: *Duku* Palembang—*yang paling manis*. A thin pale skin peels back to reveal a sweet, segmented flesh with a stone in the middle. Eat too many and you urinate a lot.

Rambutans are the bright-red, softly-spiked numbers which appear in the wet season; they are not dissimilar in taste to *leci* (lychee). Buy them in clusters on stalks.

*Alpukat* (avocado) are another good thing. For a truly fulfilling *minuman* (drink), liquidise an *alpukat*, add palm-sugar, a dollop of chocolate or vanilla ice cream and you have a very special *jus alpukat*. Fantastic.

*Salak* (or snake-fruit) are distinctive for the perfect snakeskin that covers them. Peel carefully and it comes off whole to reveal a nutty, crunchy, dry flesh of three, maybe four, stoned segments. The sweetest ones are *salak Bali* and *salak pondok*, each fruit with three segments: two large and one small, two sweet, one not so.

Some people have a passion for *marquisa*, which could be why they're known as passion fruit. The size of a pear, inside the leathery skin is what appears to be a mass of frog spawn. The globules of snot-like jelly encase a seed which is crunchy and quite tasty. Some folk prefer to slurp the contents without actually getting the full benefit of the flavours. This is not very passionate, less erotic, more exotic perhaps.

And last, but by no means least, there is what to local folk is the 'King of Fruits'. Durian (thorny fruit) is the name of about 25 varieties of a tall tropical evergreen tree native to Southeast Asia. These trees bear fruit of the same name which have a hard thorny outer husk and can individually weigh 1–5 kg (2.2–11 lb). Inside, there are sections of yellow curd-like flesh that surround a seed. Reams have been written about this fruit which drops to the ground with an almighty thump when ripe. Don't stand under a tree during a thunderstorm or in the durian season, around the turn of the year. Both can have fatal consequences.

We googled 'quotes about durians' and got 666 pages—seriously. It is the smell which causes most interest. In 1856, the British naturalist Alfred Russel Wallace provided a much-quoted description of the flavour of the durian: "A rich custard highly flavoured with almonds gives the best general idea of it, but there are occasional wafts of flavour that call to mind cream-cheese, onion-sauce, sherry-wine,

and other incongruous dishes. Then there is a rich glutinous smoothness in the pulp which nothing else possesses but which adds to its delicacy."

Wallace further cautioned that 'the smell of the ripe fruit is certainly at first disagreeable'. More recent descriptions by Westerners can be more graphic. For example, travel and food writer Richard Sterling says: "Its odor is best described as pig-shit, turpentine and onions, garnished with a gym sock. It can be smelled from yards away. Despite its great local popularity, the raw fruit is forbidden from some establishments such as hotels, subways and airports, including public transportation in South-east Asia."

The English novelist Anthony Burgess famously said that dining on durian is like eating vanilla custard in a latrine. The taste is certainly something you'll never forget, for at least eight hours anyway as you burp your way through the day.

Enjoy.

## COFFEE

For drinkers of coffee, Indonesia offers arguably the best in the world, once you are used to it. While European approaches to coffee are either in the style of the mini expresso or the particularly disgusting 'instant' variety favoured in England, the Indonesian approach is neither. Order *kopi* in a *warung* and expect a large glass of sweet brown stuff. A large spoonful of ground coffee is put in a glass with a large spoonful of sugar. Water that has just boiled, as hot as it gets, is poured from a thermos and everything is stirred together. Now comes the hard part. First, the glass is too hot to hold, so you wait. And wait. But when the glass is just about cool enough to hold by the rim, you'll find that the grounds have settled and you are able to sip the sweetness. Don't gulp it unless you don't mind mouthfuls of sludge. And don't stir it with the spoon conveniently left in the glass.

After a while, you'll get used to drinking coffee this way—the naturally percolated way. You won't need filters. Of course, you could make it in a jug, leave it to brew for a minute or so and then pour it into your mug once it has settled. If you really can't adapt to the local custom, then get yourself a percolator.

Those of you who will only drink instant coffee powder, check out your local store.

Those of you who like a cup of 'real' coffee but are not gourmets, then check out the big packs of *Kapal Api* or *Tora Bika* which are mixes of Arabica and Robusta beans and cost just over a dollar for about 350 g (12.4 oz), which is less than a cup of a Starbuck's fancy brew.

---

**For the Coffee Connoisseurs**

Coffee connoisseurs looking for fair traded Arabicas from small communities in Sumatra, Flores, Bali, Papua and Toraja in Sulawesi, check out Merdeka Coffee (http://www.merdekacoffee. com/), a company run by a New Zealand expat, Alun Evans, with his Indonesian wife, Arlini.

---

## EATING OUT

Eating out is better than eating in because you don't have to feel guilty about having someone cook your food and you don't have to look hard to find it. Much of Jakarta's food comes looking for you. Little parcels of food are paraded past you all day long, pushed through car windows at every set of traffic lights in the city. But beware of some of these snacks; don't be surprised to find a sausage running through your cup cake, or some other weird combination like cheese and chocolate.

People eat like it's going out of fashion. The Indonesian style of eating is 'little and often' with the emphasis on 'helping yourself'. People prefer a selection of smaller dishes to choose from. A ton of rice is cooked up early in the morning and, along with other things, stored below a plastic cover to keep flies off. The best example is in a Padang restaurant where the instant you sit down, a dozen or more small dishes and bowls are spread over the table. They contain some recognisable dishes and the others may be bits of meat you wouldn't usually eat. Every sauce is extremely *pedas* (spicy hot) which disguises whatever you are chewing. At the end of the meal, you pay for the bits you've eaten and the rest gets returned to the window display where it's protected from flies. You pay whoever's at the cash register near the door for whatever the waiter thinks you've eaten.

Indonesian food alone has enough varieties to keep the most dedicated eater busy for years. Food from the 27 provinces is fully represented. It's on sale everywhere: from the *kaki lima* (mobile vendors) and *warung* (street stalls) to an amazing assortment of restaurants; some cheap and basic, others posh and expensive. There can be no excuse for going hungry.

### Like People, Like Food

After eating one's way around the archipelago, you become aware that with so many different places accounted for under the one name come the regional differences in the people themselves. We are truly what we eat. Just as Padang food, with its blend of dry and fresh spices, is hot and fiery, so is the reputation of *orang Padang*, who are considered to be just as fiery and outspoken. And just as *orang Jawa* are considered the most subtle, sweet and innocuous people of Indonesia, so is their food, which uses fresh spices with sugar to take the edge off, albeit with a hidden fire.

If you need to, and an awful lot of people do, you can fill your belly on a fantastically low budget, or you can choose to spend a near fortune on cooked food—Jakarta has it all. The cheapest, and arguably the most authentic Indonesian food, is that sold by the *kaki lima*. These are five-legged, two-wheeler, mobile restaurants—meals on wheels—which hawk their wares day and night, albeit by a schedule. Fast food is not an American concept and never has been. Order a bowl of meat balls (*bakso*) from a passing vendor and you can be slurping away within a minute.

Commonly offered dishes from the *kaki lima* include *sate* (pronounced 'sa-tay'), which are skewers of goat or chicken cooked over charcoal and served with rice and a fiery peanut sauce, *rujak* (unripe fruit salad with a chilli sauce), *soto ayam* (chicken soup with rice noodles and veg), *bubur ayam* (rice porridge with chicken), *mie pangsit* (a ravioli-style dish), *nasi goreng* (fried rice), *mie rebus* (boiled noodles), *mie goreng* (fried noodles), *ketoprak* (cooked and chopped noodles, beansprouts, tofu, peanut sauce and more), *gado gado* (mixed fresh and boiled vegetables, also with a peanut sauce), and even hotdogs and hamburgers. Unfortunately, quality is not guaranteed with a *kaki lima*, but if you take a few chances, you'll soon get to know who's got the tastiest dishes.

The *kaki lima* washing up facilities are never very advanced, limited usually to a bucket and any running water there happens to be nearby. Supplying your own plate and seeing the food cooked with your own eyes should dispel any major fears you may have about hygiene. Of course, much of what you see paraded past your home can also be found in restaurants. For example, visit one of the city's established *sate* houses such as Sate Pancoran on Jl Raya Pasar Minggu, which also serves excellent seafood.

The next step up from the *kaki lima* is the *warung*. These offer the same dishes as above and a whole lot more. The emphasis at the *warung* is on home-cooking. Seafood and fish dishes like *ikan pecel lele* are rarely sold by a *kaki lima*, but are readily available at a *warung*. The same is true for *nasi uduk*, Padang food, *tempe*, *martabak* (a rather weighty pancake: sweet or savoury), *tahu* (tofu), *sayur asem*, *burung dara goreng* (fried pigeon) and umpteen varieties of *rendang* (a hunk of meat slow cooked for ages in a coconut-based spicy sauce).

At the most rudimentary level, a *warung* is simply a *kaki lima* that has come to a standstill, while at the most sophisticated level, they offer steak and Italian dishes. Some *warungs* have chairs and tables, some just a plank of wood to seat everyone, although many people are happy to simply *jongkok* (crouch down) to eat. You may even find yourself sitting on various car-body parts and tyre-piles; many *warungs* are makeshift affairs converted by night from garage workshops. Depending on your upbringing, however, you may find the entire experience less than appetising as you settle down to eat next to an open sewer with rats. Maybe. But this is Jakarta street food—what do you expect? The *warung* offers home-cooking at down-to-earth prices.

---

### Exotic Food for You?

Indonesians will eat parts of animals that Westerners would not normally consider. Ask for some fried chicken and you can expect the entire fried animal, head and all. Offal is popular stuff to eat; brains, lungs and intestines being essential ingredients in many Indonesian dishes. Fried, dried chicken-blood is a good appetiser, as is goat's head soup. You might follow this with a dog or catfish sandwich, or maybe some snake blood soup. Okay, so these aren't the average *warung* dishes, but then again, not entirely out of the question.

---

At one point, it was possible to sample the delights of food from every province in Indonesia simply by walking down Jl. Asia Afrika, opposite the Senayan sports complex. Perhaps because it was considered too rough-and-ready for the forthcoming Visit Indonesia Year promotion, the whole *warung* collection was moved to a location which was hard to access, next to a dual-carriageway, and slowly but surely the lot of them disappeared. It is still possible to experience much of the nation's food under one roof by visiting a shopping mall, but their food courts are just as likely to feature franchises of Western chains such as A & W and KFC.

However, nearly every area of Jakarta has a selection of Padang, Batak, Sundanese and Chinese restaurants, to name

A *kaki lima* can be found everywhere, even by the beach.

## The Rich and Famous

Some *warungs* are actually renowned and visited by the rich and famous. At night, in Jalan Kebon Sirih just north of the Sarinah department store, the street may well be virtually blocked with Mercedes and BMW limousines. If you can peer through the darkened windows, you'll see *ibus* and *bapaks* tucking in to mounds of *nasi goreng* with goat meat. At the other end of Jalan Sabang, there is a *kaki lima* which sells a special *sate*—or so Terry's wife says. She and the 'recipe' of the skewered meat *sate* both come from Medan in North Sumatra.

but a few. Many have impossibly long menus which, dish by dish, would take years to get through. The point being that they could, if they wanted to, cook up these dishes; they are within the chef's capabilities, that's all.

Rumah Makan Sunda (Sundanese restaurants) are good. The food is fresh—you choose a fish from the tank on your way in. *Ikan gurame* is a particularly tasty Sundanese dish: a deep-fried, fresh carp straight from the tank. That's it: just a great big, deep-fried goldfish. Former keepers of goldfish will get to see their pets in a new light; they will be able to eat them. Hygiene need not be so much of a worry in these restaurants. Sinks, or wash basins, are dotted strategically around every restaurant.

The fruit juices served in a good Sundanese restaurant are impeccable. While Padang restaurants have the monopoly on good *jus alpukat* (liquidised avocado, vanilla and sugar), the rest belongs to Sundanese restaurants. If you're lucky, you will eat your food to the accompaniment of Sundanese *degung* music to help with the digestion. (The choice of music can sometimes make or break the meal in a restaurant, particularly if you're in a *warung* in Blok M and a man made up like a courtesan is serenading you.)

## NON-INDONESIAN FOOD

There is such a wide variety of foreign food for sale in Jakarta—Italian, Indian, Chinese, French, Dutch, Japanese, Korean and Mexican cuisine—that it's difficult to know where to start. If your dietary needs can only be catered for with American-style fast-food fare, then you'll do OK. Bastions of the American Empire include McDonald's, Dunkin' Donuts and Starbucks and you'll be able to forget you are in Indonesia in these plastic emporia—not many order a cup of Java in Starbucks. Elsewhere, there is Planet Hollywood on Jl Gatot Subroto and Hard Rock Café in Jalan Thamrin. Where the Hard Rock used to be in the Sarinah building, there is a Manchester United themed café/bar. (Being a Charlton Athletic supporter, I refuse to darken its doors. TC)

For a 'safe', albeit generic, meal, visit any of the major hotels in the city. Check the *Jakarta Post*, a daily newspaper, or the *Jakarta Java Kini*, a monthly magazine, for reviews of new restaurants in town and news of special culinary promotions to be found around town.

## Recommended Restaurants

Some excellent Indian food is to be found notably at the popular Shah Jahan restaurant in the Sahid Jaya Hotel on Jl Sudirman and the Hazara restaurant on Jl Wahid Hasyim, Kebon Sirih, which serves distinctly north Indian cuisine and is popular with a young mixed crowd. In Jl.Veteran 1, beside the Mesjid Istiqlal, the Grand Mosque near Monas, you'll also find good restaurants popular with Indian businessmen who keep a bottles of Johnny Walker Black label whisky ready for their evening visits—a sign of good fare.

For a really *mewah dan mahal* (posh and expensive) Italian meal, visit Ambiente within the Hotel Aryaduta on Jl Prapatan, Menteng.

---

### History and Food

There are two restaurants housed in historic buildings which are certainly worth a visit.The Café Batavia is in historic Kota, on the opposite side of the pedestrianised square to the National Museum. It is open 24 hours and the place to go whenever you want to impress someone. It is in a beautifully restored and furnished 2-storied building with a comfortable ambience to remind you of Dutch colonial times.

---

If you want to spend a fortune on the type of food you could have cooked at home for about 1 per cent of the price, visit the Oasis restaurant in Jl. Raden Saleh, Cikini. This historic restaurant is in a large old Dutch villa and its menu features 'classic' Indonesian dishes. However, if you can assemble a large group and want a real treat, then pre-order *rijstaffel*, a Dutch banquet brought to your table(s) by a team of waitresses whilst you are being serenaded by a group of, admittedly very good, Batak musicians.

Naturally, restaurants come and go in Jakarta and even seemingly popular ones can disappear overnight, so we can only recommend a couple of restaurants which are likely to still be here for the life of this book.

## DRINKING

In recent times, a few Islamic leaders have imposed rules and restrictions regarding alcohol. To the west of Jakarta lies the township of Tangerang, which has imposed some *sharia* (strict Muslim) rules on its residents. These include a ban on the sale of alcoholic drinks except in 3-star or more hotels (of which there are very few). For a while, the Jakarta's City Hall followed suit and decreed that not even beer could be sold in supermarkets. However, as with most displays of intemperate rules, they are now largely ignored.

And Jakarta residents and visitors can again freely imbibe whatever makes them drunkenly convivial.

*Bir Bintang* and *Bir Anker* are the most popular and reasonable tasting locally-produced pilsner lagers. Heineken and San Miguel can also be found in some supermarkets, along with Anker Stout. It isn't recommended that you buy beer from a *warung* as keeping beer on an open shelf in tropical heat isn't a good idea.

---

**Foreign Taste**

For wines and spirits, visit supermarkets such as Kemchicks and Sogo, which cater for a foreign clientele, with prices to match. They have good selections of imported wines and spirits, as do the Duty Free shops in Kemang and Kuningan. You are supposed to have a card, or a friend with a card, for shopping at these.

---

Ask for a beer in a hotel, restaurant or bar and you find that the price shoots up. A single glass of hotel beer costs at least twice the price a large bottle of beer does. It might be useful to remember that all bars and restaurants are subject to closure on Indonesia's many national holidays, whereas hotels remain open.

## Watering Holes

There are a proliferation of bars, ranging from the near-respectable to the plain seedy, to be experienced in many areas of the city. The major hotels offer stress-free drinking; usually to the accompaniment of some form of entertainment, usually in the guise of a Filipino group offering cabaret-style performances of songs their audiences are familiar with. Other hotels, such as the Sari Pan Pacific, feature attempts at 'pubs' such as the obligatory kit-form Irish pub, O'Reilly's.

Parts of the town get redeveloped, there are political or economic events which change perceptions, a bar manager moves on or popular barflies gad off elsewhere, so the 'in' places to be seen in are wherever you feel comfortable. You are free to drink with abandon in Jl. Peletahan in Blok M, Kemang and Cilandak Town Square, to name a few places popular with expats.

Jalan Jaksa is an admirably self-contained unit in the centre of Jakarta, around the corner from the Sarinah Department Store and Jalan Thamrin, not far from Gambir railway station.

Jl. Jaksa used to be Jakarta's equivalent to Bangkok's Khao San Road and Bali's Kuta beach, where all the backpackers went. There is of course no beach, just the cheapest hotels, guest houses and restaurants in the city, offering 'international' cuisine and other budget-travel requirements such as second-hand book exchanges and cheap beer.

There are fewer backpackers now thanks to the introduction in 2004 of a one-month tourist visa. This kind of restricts the amount of time available to climb volcanoes or go *batik* painting, diving, jungle trekking, surfing or sunbathing. But the street continues to thrive although on some days, you can be hard pressed to find any foreigners along the street!

Jaksa is now just a low-cost accommodation area used by both foreigners and Indonesians. The dirt-cheap dives of the past are pretty much gone, thank goodness, and the few tourists who go to Jaksa these days in any case want more than a US$ 1 a day flea-pit.

It is also a night life area, frequented by locals and foreign 'residents' of Jakarta. These residents include teachers of assorted varieties, journalists, oildudes, consultants, traders and business people. Tourists of any sort are very much in the minority.

As a meeting place of sorts, Jaksa's cheap and cheerful approach makes it a stress-free place for everyone to sit about eating, drinking and sweating. It's not the greatest food in the world, but it's excellent value nonetheless. With cold beer sold in the large bottles at a very reasonable rate, an entertaining evening is easily had.

The seedy scene of yore has passed now that backpackers no longer have the time to linger. There are suggestions that a 120-day tourist is going to be introduced as a means of boosting the tourist industry (and sales of this book). If that happens, Jalan Jaksa could well see a return of the illicit drugs trade and the *cewek nakal* (naughty girls) that it was once renowned for.

## SMOKING

If you are returning to Jakarta after a number of years away, you will notice an immense change: Jakartans smoke a lot less. Travel by bus or train and those who do light up may well be told to stub it out. It's the law, you know. In fact, if you get caught smoking in public in the main thoroughfares, you could be fined. Could be, but law enforcement is still weak. However, public buildings such as office blocks now provide a specific smokers' area.

And the major cigarette companies continue to sponsor every music gig and sports event they can use to plaster their ads all over. Philip Morris, the American cigarette giant, bought out Sampoerna, a major manufacturer of the ubiquitous *kretek* (clove) cigarettes, for a couple of billion dollars, so although mandatory health warnings on packets were introduced in 1992, Indonesia is still a fertile ground for smokers unable to give up their addiction.

There are a number of varieties of *kretek*, which are filtered cigarettes with a mix of locally grown tobacco and cloves, the most popular being Gudang Garam and Djarum. Garam means salty, hence the flavour, whilst Djarum (needle) are sweet. If you are bold enough, try Dji Sam Soe, the king of the *kretek*. These mammoth, conical, hand-rolled numbers take an estimated 20 minutes to smoke. Ironically, since cloves have anaesthetic properties, smoking them effectively numbs the lungs to any damage done. They're probably good for toothache as well.

---

**Tip for Smokers**

One final hint for nicotine addicts: when leaving Jakarta for another country, buy your tobacco allowance in your local *warung*. Cigarettes are far cheaper than in the duty free shops.

---

You can also smoke local versions of most American brands and an assortment of imported brands. Pipes are not common and neither are hand-rolled cigarettes, although Drum, the Dutch rolling tobacco, is produced and sold here, along with gummed papers—local papers are gumless. If you do like roll ups, the markets of central Java are a good source of mild rolling tobacco.

Although smoking is on the decrease in Jakarta, one growth area is in the establishment of specialist cigar lounges. Unfortunately, we can tell you little about these as neither of us would dream of spending US$ 30 on an upmarket stogie.

# CULTURE AND TRAVEL

## CHAPTER 7

'In all probability, Indonesia can still offer the
greatest variety of primitive scenes and
entertainments of any country on earth.'
—Norman Lewis, *An Empire Of The East*

## PURSUING CULTURE

It is possible to come to Jakarta and live what is termed an expatriate lifestyle. Probably the only adjustment you need to make is to the equatorial climate, which also means that days and nights are generally of equal length. You don't intend to stay for long so you don't have to expose yourself or your family to Indonesian life. Your children can be enrolled in an international school and sit for internationally acceptable subject exams. You can find food from home and eat international cuisine in fine restaurants and pay less or more than you would back home. You can watch familiar TV programmes on satellite or cable TV or on pirated DVDs. The music you listen to can be downloaded to your iPod, assuming you can get a good Internet connection—which you can't!

But, hey, why should you? The joy of being away from home is brought about by experiencing different sights, sound and smells. And in Jakarta, that is what you can get if you have the sense to allow your senses to open up.

So, you think you are a cultured person because you like art, you're a music lover and you have an online photographic portfolio. But then, your cultural background comes from where you do. There's nought wrong with that because we all need our comfort zones, so perhaps your pursuit of culture could start with the familiar. To help you, and those Indonesians who are interested in your country's

## Cultural Organisations

- British Council
  Jl. Jend. Sudirman Kav 52 -53
  Tel: (21) 515-5561
  Website: http://www.britishcouncil.org/indonesia.htm
  A much diminished presence, with its main focus on educational fairs, supporting 'future leaders' and modern pop culture.
- CCF—Centre Cultural Francais
  Jl. Salemba Raya No. 25
  Tel: (21) 390-8585
  Website: http://www.ccfjakarta.or.id
  Annual French film festival.
- Erasmus Huis
  Jl. HR Rasuna Said Kav. S-3
  Tel: (21) 524-1069
  Website: http://www.erasmushuis.or.id
  Regular itinerary of lectures and shows on Indonesian arts and history. It also boasts some 22,000 books, mostly in Dutch.
- Galeri Nasional Indonesia
  Jl. Medan Merdeka Timur 14 A
  Tel: (21) 348-33954/5
  Website: http://www.galeri-nasional.or.id
  Galeri Nasional Indonesia represent one of the functioning culture institute for the protection, development, and asset exploiting as education-cultural medium and recreation and also creativity development and artistic apreciation.
- Gedung Kesenian Jakarta
  Jl. Gedung Kesenian Jakarta No. 1
  Tel: (21) 380-8283.
  Website: http://www.gkj-online.com
  The 'Jakarta Building of the Arts' in Pasar Baru is a beautifully restored 19th century colonial building

offering more refined notions of 'culture'—orchestral performances, ballet and theatre.

- Goethe Institute
  Jl. Sam Ratulangi no 9-15
  Tel: (21) 2355-0208
  Website: http://www.goethe.de-jak.com
- Istituto Italiano di Cultura
  Jl. Hos Cokroaminoto 117
  Tel: (21) 3392-7531
  Website: http://www.itacultjkt.or.id
  Movies and exhibitions.
- Jawaharlal Nehru Indian Cultural Centre
  Jl. Imam Bonjol 32
  Tel: (21) 315-5120
  Website: http://www.embassyofindiajakarta.org/
  Music and dance recitals, photographic and painting exhibitions, workshops and dance, tabla and yoga classes.
- Jakarta Convention Center
  Jl. Gatot Subroto
  Tel: (21) 572-6000.
  Website: http://www.jcc.co.id
  Major venue of conferences and trade expos.
- Taman Ismail Marzuki
  Jl. Cikini Raya 73
  Tel: (21) 31934740.
  Website: www.tamanismailmarzuki.com
  A complex worth an afternoon's browsing with its art exhibitions, second-hand book shops, planetarium and theatre. Also houses Institut Kesenian Jakarta, the city's leading arts training institute.
- Jakarta Java Kini
  Website: http://www.jakartajavakini.com
  Monthly listings magazine; you can either subscribe or check online.

culture, there are a number of organisations part-funded by their respective governments. Many of the city's embassies regularly show films or give talks, invariably in the language of that embassy. There are a number of 'cultural centres' associated with various embassies in Jakarta, and many have their own libraries and archives for those delving into the history of their country's relationship with Indonesia. In 2005, the British Council gave its library to the Department of Education in Jl. Sudirman. They still have a good selection of books, much to the surprise of local cynics.

Check the local press for details of current activities, or give the centres a ring to request a monthly programme.

Contact the respective embassies of other countries, including Australia and the USA, for information about their cultural activities.

The longer you spend in Jakarta, the more you'll become aware of local TV. The poorest shack in the most crowded slum has a set, or the neighbour does. Their favourite programmes, as elsewhere, are soap operas (*sinetron*); here the settings are in rich people's homes, in a high school or in a ghostly graveyard where kung fu adepts fight black magic fiends with the help of the local Islamic preacher. Radio can also give you an insight into local culture, if only because the music enjoyed by your taxi driver can tell you what part of Indonesia he comes from.

Perhaps unsurprisingly, radio and TV are good sources of Indonesian music and culture. TVRI, the state-run TV station, in particular regularly features a 'traditional performance' slot late at night, which might be anything from a *wayang* performance (shadow play) to a display of razor blade-eating black magic to a traditional song or two sung by a woman in a traditional *kebaya* (dress). Until a few years ago, TVRI was funded through a licence fee, but now it has to compete for a slice of the advertising pie to supplement its subsidy. Their programmes are broadcast throughout the nation so there is a need for some 'unity in diversity', and what better way to appeal to the masses than by offering a diet of 'family entertainment' suitable for the older generations.

Fine art is big business in Jakarta, and exhibitions and galleries are all over the place. Aside from the aforementioned places, fine art can be viewed and bought in Pasar Seni, an outdoor art fair in Taman Impian Jaya, Ancol. Artists are generally working 'on site' and it's a good chance to see *batik*, *ikat*, *wayang* puppets, and other Indonesian indigenous art-forms in the making. There is also an abundance of private galleries around the city: Kemang is one such area.

Taman Mini Indonesia Indah is the probably the most comprehensive crash-course to Indonesian culture under one roof—except of course there isn't a roof, only the widest selection of Indonesia's great diversity in one place. Just off the Jagorawi Toll road in the south-east of the city, it was completed in 1978 to accusations that it was nothing more than an extravagant playground for Ibu Tien Suharto, the former President's late wife.

It has in fact turned out to be Jakarta's most visited attraction, and although it may have been expensive to construct, and the land clearance was resisted violently, Taman Mini is actually very good. The nation's 27 provinces are represented by 27 full-scale traditional houses, each replete with the handicrafts, clothing and, quite often, 'traditional' music and performances of that province. Museums, insect-houses, a bird park, cinemas, lakes, mini-Borobudurs and the general feeling of open space are what make this flamboyant project such a success. A cable car ride will give you an impressive aerial view of the spectacle; look down at the lake containing small islands—this is a map of the country. Note that the authors have not had a chance to check its accuracy, so please let us know if East Timor is still depicted.

Particularly on weekdays, this is a hassle-free and spacious place to stroll about and well worth the visit.

## STREET FURNITURE

When you're stuck in a traffic jam and you don't have a good book to read or a good game to play on your cell phone or laptop, then you're forced to gaze at the world outside. We have taken a look at the people of Jakarta in the

A visit to Taman Mini will give you interesting insights into Indonesian culture.

previous chapters. Other visual delights and eyesores are considered here.

## Billboards

The culture of Jakarta is making money and those with the most flaunt it by erecting towering billboards, by which we mean above the tops of the remaining trees.

## Statues

Spend any time in Jakarta and you'll come across some distinctive statues. Described by some as 'hideous lumps of concrete representing little more than the propaganda of Indonesia's eager first government', and by others as mere 'lumps of concrete', there's no denying that they are essential features of Jakarta's street furniture. To Indonesians, they are a concrete reminder of those first flushes of independence. And for a country that was under colonial rule for almost four centuries, independence is something worth celebrating— preferably in concrete. It was conveniently forgotten during Suharto's New Order that many were a present from the then communist Soviet Union.

At the Pancoran road junction in South Jakarta, at the bottom end of Jl Gatot Subroto, stands the tallest of them all: the Dirgantara statue. He represents the Hindu monkey-god Hanuman and appears to be standing on an enormous number seven. Long-term expatriates and frequent visitors know this landmark as the '7-Up Man'. In the middle of the roundabout at the bottom end of Jl Sudirman, is a statue of similar execution, the Sermangat Pemuda. It is likened to a 'Flaming-Pizza Man', but also known more familiarly known as 'Hot Plate Harry'.

Perhaps the most brutal of all is the Lapangan Banteng monument in Banteng Square near the Hotel Borobudur. Representing the battle for independence of Irian Jaya against the Dutch in 1963, it appears to have hands twice the size of its head.

In the centre of the city, by the fountains in front of Hotel Indonesia, are 'Hansel and Gretel', the official welcome statue of Jakarta. They were erected as a symbol of the 1962

Asian Games held in Jakarta; again, both characters possess oversized hands.

Of course not all Jakarta's statues are so tasteless—see the Arjuna statue on the edge of Plaza Merdeka or the Henry Moore-ish one in Taman Surapati, Menteng. Not all are made of concrete: see the Petani monument by Gambir station—and not all have big hands.

## MUSIC

The Equator runs through only ten countries on earth; Indonesia is one of them and the only nation in Asia with the equatorial stripe impaling it. There are so many different cultures spread-out on these islands that it would take several lifetimes to experience them all properly. Within this umbrella of diversity is one of the world's richest and most dazzling sound museums.

Each region of Indonesia offers a distinct dialect, dress, food and attitudes, and its own special way of making music. And with so many fiercely-proud people from all over Indonesia in Jakarta, regional music is for sale in many outlets. And sell it does. People like their music—it reminds them of home.

If you have any interest in 'world music', then there's a universe of sounds available here, but catch it while you can. The clear-cut line between popular and ethnic music is rapidly fading as the advances of technology deem it fit to place electronic instruments and computerised beats alongside the more wholesome sounds of the traditional instruments associated with much of Indonesia's music.

Nonetheless, changing times aside, there is some wild, wacky and downright weird music to listen to in Indonesia. Listen to the music of Bali. Listen to a CD recording of the *kecak* and indulge yourself in a sound experience like no other. Listen to the tranquillising, hammered bamboo music of the *anklung* or try the full-blown bongo-fury of Balinese bamboo percussion, *jegog*. Listen to *rindik*, which is two *anklung* and a *suling* (bamboo flute). Listen to catchy *tarian* music, the original sound of the dancing Minang people in West Sumatra. Listen to *dangdut* music. Listen to all of it.

## Shopping for Music

Most malls have at least one shop selling CDs and cassettes, By far the best in terms of range of music and sheer quantity are Aquarius, which can be found in or near malls in Pondok Indah and Blok M. Jl. Sabang in Central Jakarta has a few shops which are worth browsing in. For mainstream music at lower price than you would pay at home, have a look in your neighbourhood hypermarket.

While tapes of Western music are less than half the price they are back home, imported Western CDs are at an equivalent price. Indonesian music is still far cheaper to buy than any other. For second-hand LP records, cassettes and CDs, go to Jl. Surabaya in Menteng. Bill Clinton did when he popped over to Jakarta for a presidential visit. (But George Bush junior didn't.)

If you have a curious ear for indigenous music, obviously your best sources would be in the specific regions. However, give yourself time to explore the racks of Indonesian CDs and cassettes, listen to a track or two and who knows what gems you may unearth.

You may wish to download music. This is not really feasible given the abysmally narrow bandwidth, even on so-called broadband connections.

## Gamelan

*Gamelan* is perhaps the defining sound of Indonesia. For the Javanese, it's the music of royalty; for the Balinese, it's played for the gods. *Gamelan* is the music Indonesia would send into space if it had a space programme to go with its space agency. So far, *gamelan* is the only Indonesian music to have gained any sort of worldwide recognition and over the years, it has been scrutinised, copied and adapted to the point of near confusion, prompting concern from the purists who believe that its cultivation outside Indonesia is somehow missing the point. In Holland, for example, they'll give you a grant to study it, and there are sets of *gamelan* instruments in London and several cities in the USA. But foreign interest isn't all bad. Indeed, it was the Dutch who in 1990 came up with *kepatihan*: the written notation of *gamelan*. Yet the purists have a point; for so tied up is *gamelan* with the lifecycle rituals of Indonesian life that its practice so far from its place of origin is certainly a bit *aneh* (odd).

The orchestra itself takes on a variety of forms: featuring an array of perhaps 80 different gongs, a few drums and a couple of *saron* (xylophones) to provide melody, all of which are 'answered' in turn by optional *suling* (flutes) and vocals. An expanded form of *gamelan* is *legong*, which combines dance, singing and drama—a truly multi-cultural art form.

The profusion of simultaneous melodies in *gamelan* can play tricks with the hearing. Sometimes it's possible to focus on a single melody, but like all good things, as soon as you put your finger on it, it's gone, the floating melody instantly buried in the overall cacophony. At times, the sound seems chaotic and random, and just when you want to give in, everything is brought down to earth with a bang on the drum. In *gamelan*, the drummer keeps the show together, controls the tempo and introduces new phrases and melodies.

*Gamelan* might not be to everyone's taste: the sound is too metallic, too harsh, too alien, the tempo changes too

sudden for many Western ears. Scholars of the music argue differently: its shimmering, multi-layered, charisma-charged melodies are an acting medium between the human and the spirit world. The average sweating tourist, however, sitting in a hotel lobby watching his complimentary 'genuine traditional cultural performance' might not be so aware of the cosmological virtues of *gamelan*.

This is part of the problem. The influx of tourism means that many traditional musical forms like *gamelan* get modified, abbreviated and commercialised simply to appease foreign audiences. It doesn't have to be this way. When in Bali or Yogya, keep an ear out for the sound of a *gamelan* orchestra rehearsing. Like the smell of bread baking, the *gamelan* sounds waft over the rooftops and you find that you have to get to the source. It may be in a *kraton* (Sultan's palace) or temple; enter quietly, sit and give yourself time to get with the groove, to enter the music, to meditate. You may have found the ultimate 'chill' music.

## Dangdut

*Dangdut* is the music of Jakarta's *kampungs*. If you need to know what Jakarta sounds like, listen to *dangdut*. True, it spreads right across Indonesia, but Jakarta and West Java are where this music is made, performed and developed. You hear it playing in an awful lot of taxis and many non-expat bars—everywhere in fact.

It is basically blues music as it deals with the tribulations of Indonesian life: infidelity, poverty, bad rice harvests and other domestic mishaps, although like the blues, it just as often deals with lighter subjects. Described as '*kampungan*' (unsophisticated, working class) by some, very few wealthy Jakartans will admit to liking it, although they all seem to know the lyrics.

*Dangdut* first emerged in its most recognisable form in the 1960s and has progressed steadily ever since. Traditionally, the sound is characterised by wailing vocals, flutes, mandolin, electric fuzz guitar and *tabla*-type drums. This is where the name *dangdut* originates: the *dang* and the *dut* are the sounds produced by beating the drums in a certain way. It has a heavy rhythm section, dominant bass and very 'Asian' percussion. *Dangdut* has Arabic, Malay and Indian influences: indeed, early recordings routinely featured a sitar in the line up.

Such is its crowd-pulling potential that no election rally, celebration of New Year, Independence Day, etc. is complete without a *dangdut* band on hand. Dancing to *dangdut* is easy—you simply try not to move. You can put your arms up in the air if you want and sway a bit, but you shouldn't start doing the jitterbug. When the music plays, couples have to dance (or rather sway) in rows, doing their best not to touch each other.

The Arabic and Malay influences are most strongly felt in the *dangdut* of Rhoma Irama who, through numerous film appearances in the 1980s, helped popularise *dangdut* beyond mere pop music and into a way of life. He became '*si Raja Dangdut*' (the King of Dangdut) in the 1990s, although his aura was tarnished when he left the fold of the Islamic political party, PPP, in the 1997 election and joined the Suhartoist grouping, Golkar, apparently in return for a franchise to set up another taxi company. His mother's house in Tebet was trashed and for awhile he became *persona non grata* with the people.

More recently, Inul Daratista has taken centre stage, but not so much for her singing. Although her fans may identify with the themes of her songs, which identify with the 'little people', she has become an instant icon.

More controversially, Inul has forced Indonesians to confront the increasingly sharp struggle in their society between conservative, closed and fundamentalist forces and those that are open, liberal and progressive in their quest to advance democratic principles and practices. Interestingly, Rhoma Irama is one of the conservative voices, perhaps because he is jealous of Inul's sales, and said that she wasn't to sing any of his songs. The free publicity helped her enormously.

What has stirred the controversy is her dancing, which she calls 'drilling', a sensuous gyration of the hips. As social commentator Julia Suryakusuma pointed out, "Various aspects of Indonesian culture are very sensuous. They predate the arrival of Islam and can be seen in carvings in the various Hindu temples in Central Java and in many traditional performing arts. Compared with the *jaipongan* dance of West Java, the *tayub* of Central Java, or indeed, other established *dangdut* singers, whose movements are slower but more suggestive, Inul's dancing is much less erotic."

Those who defend the right of artistic free expression find it hard to imagine how Inul's hip movements could be more devastating in corrupting the nation than unemployment, gambling, drug abuse, pornographic videos and the trafficking of women and children. All are widespread and on the rise in Indonesia.

It is the conservative forces, unwilling to accept that their ways of the Suharto days are coming to an end, who are behind the proposed anti-pornography law.

*Dangdut*, the music of love and hate.

## Degung

Upon the seemingly infinite variations on the theme of *gamelan* is *degung*, one of the traditional sounds of Sunda (West Java). A truly hypnotic experience, *degung* is like a musical form of valium, and features only the basic selection of *gamelan* instruments with flute and bass drum to the fore to emphasise melody. It's an extremely leisurely-paced affair. If *gamelan* is the multi-tracked studio production, then *degung* is the stripped-down, unplugged, acoustic version. One of the finest exponents of *degung* is the group Gentra Pasundan, conducted by the blind flute player and songwriter, Ujang Suryana. Away from its traditional form is a more dynamic pop version of *degung* as practised by the wonderful Nining Meids among others. Nano Suratno is a highly prolific writer and performer of all-things musical in Sunda, including *degung*.

## Jaipongan

Also to be found in West Java is *jaipongan* music. The uninitiated again might think it sounds like more 'plinky plonky' *gamelan*-type music, and while it does use some of the gongs and drums of the *gamelan* line-up, *jaipongan* is far more humorous and punkier than formal *gamelan*. *Jaipongan* isn't just music, it's an attitude. Its lyrics are suggestive; sometimes rude, sometimes not. This difference in music is as obvious as the difference in the people themselves: the overly-polite, formal Javanese and the sassy, nudge-nudge, wink-wink Sundanese. A woman starts the show off: whispering, 'oohing' and 'aahing' as the rhythm accelerates, slows and speeds up again. Drums are to the fore, and scraping away in between is the *rebab*, a two-stringed bowed instrument producing a distinctly wonky sound. She might have a couple of 'friends' there to chant harmonies, ask questions and elicit answers from the singer. When it's going flat out, you start wondering how long they can keep this furious pace going. Then it suddenly stops and everyone starts chatting and joking, until reminded to continue. Listen to any recording by the accomplished Jugala group from Bandung for an introduction to the delights of *jaipongan*.

## Keroncong

Listen also to *keroncong*, one of the original sounds of Jakarta. Strictly speaking, *keroncong* is strings-only music, a reminder of the earliest Portuguese merchants who presumably packed violins, mandolins and guitars on board with them all those years ago. Add further influence from China and Holland, give it to Indonesians to play, dub a Betawi dialect on top and you have *keroncong*. These days, this music is the mainstay of the middle-age, or the seriously downhearted. When it's good, *keroncong* is very good: rolling, floating, moving music. Listen to virtually any recording by Hetty Koes Endang, who in the 1980s was responsible for single-handedly reviving the *keroncong* tradition in Indonesia. But sometimes it's dreadful—you are just as likely to find a *keroncong* version of Tie a Yellow Ribbon Round the Old Oak Tree as you are the real thing.

## Recommended Recordings

- Various: Music of Indonesia (CDs 1 to 20) Smithsonian/ Folkways

Perhaps the most comprehensive beginner's guide to Indonesian music, this 20-CD set dips a toe into the local music scene in all the right places. Much of this music is utterly unheard of outside Indonesia, and so well recorded too. Disk 2 is the pop CD and features essential recordings of *dangdut*, *keroncong* and *jaipongan*, unavailable elsewhere. Discs 3 and 5 concentrate on some of the truly peculiar (and rapidly disappearing) sounds of Jakarta, featuring several tracks in the style of *tanjidor*—arguably the wonkiest music you will ever hear. All in all, a superb round up of the Indonesian music scene, but ultimately only the very tip of one enormous iceberg.

## Incomplete Glossary of Musical Forms

While a lot of Indonesian music happily bounces around between styles, there are still a great many distinctions to be made.

| From | Local name | Sounds like |
|------|-----------|-------------|
| Jakarta | *Ajeng* | *Gamelan* with attitude, gong, 'milk bottle' frenzy. |
| Jakarta | *Keroncong* | Stringed instruments. Ballads. |
| Jakarta | *Topeng Betawi* | Bed springs and sink plungers. Men at work. |
| Jakarta | *Gambang Kromong* | Plinky-plonky, drums, gongs. Wonky. |
| Jakarta | *Tanjidor* | Brass band gone wrong. |
| Jakarta/Java | *Dangdut* | Indian and Arabic pop. Slow or fast. Fat and fun. |
| Sunda (W. Java) | *Jaipongan* | Dance music with attitude, drums, sassy vocals. |

| Sunda | *Degung* | Musical valium. Drum, gong, flute. Introspection. |
|-------|----------|---------------------------------------------------|
| Sunda | *Pop Degung* | *Degung* with words. Haunting. |
| Sunda | *Pop Sunda* | Pop music from ... erm....Sunda. |
| Sunda/Java | *Tembang Sunda/Jawa* | Zithers, gong, drum, very slow, haunting. Vocals. |
| Java and Bali—mainly | *Gamelan* | Haunting or furious. Metallic bits banged. |
| Bali | *Jegog* | Bamboo *gamelan*. |
| Bali | *Kecak* | Male vocal *gamelan*. |
| Bali | *Legong Bali* | *Gamelan* as opera. Frighteningly wild vocals. |
| Bali | *Rindik* | Bamboo percussion and flute. Tranquillising. |
| N. Sumatra | *Lagu Batak* | Surprisingly straight folk songs. |
| W. Sumatra | *Tarian Minang* | Cheap but catchy instrumental. Clap along. |

## Pop

Pop music is as popular in Indonesia as anywhere else, but who's in and who's past it are determined by market forces. Lovers of esoteric music might get in a huff with the predominance of apparent 'slush' on the airwaves, but that's the norm everywhere. The Indonesian fondness for soppy Western pop music has spawned an entire genre of sickly-sweet balladry in Indonesian music. The lyrics to these syrupy recordings often depend solely on the words *cinta* (love) and *hati* (heart) being repeated every other word. But when Indonesians want lyrics to mull over, they still listen to Iwan Fals' old albums. There is also a thriving rap scene; the moves and the clothes are spot on.

## Foreign Acts

There was a time when Western music was banned outright, even that performed by local acts. The first president, Sukarno, was particularly worried about the mayhem which the influence of the Beatles and their ilk might wreak within his newly indoctrinated generation, and so he banned Western music altogether. Instead, he encouraged Indonesia's musicians to look at their own extensive musical heritage for inspiration. Thus the emergence of *jaipongan* and *dangdut*.

Following is an interview with Leonardo Pavkovic—CEO of MoonJune Records:

TC.: Leonardo, for a number of years you have been organising tours of Asia for the groups and musicians involved with MoonJune. Given that Jakarta and Bali are surely convenient stopovers, what is it that's putting off promoters like you from booking acts to play in Indonesia?

L.: I guess the major problem was that the Indonesian economy wasn't doing well after the crash in the late nineties. This meant that subsidies were unavailable. For quality foreign music, there are promoters, but then they have to rely on sponsors and sponsors only want commercial music.

Another factor is that there is total misinformation about Indonesia after the bombing incidents in Jakarta and Bali in recent years. Somehow, it is wrongly thought that Indonesia is not a very safe place to be and to put on shows. This is rubbish. I feel more secure in Jakarta than in downtown Washington D.C. or some areas of Detroit. Indonesia, as a very moderate Muslim country, is suffering the consequences of the confusion in the world and the current worldwide political situation. Unfortunately, insurance companies often cancel already booked shows for 'security reasons'.

Apparently, things have been getting better lately and I hope it can continue.

TC.: Which Indonesian bands do you think will still be listened to when the next edition of *CultureShock! Jakarta* is written, say in 2012?

L.: That's difficult to say. I count on a few very talented bands, like Simak Dialog and Anane, but I'm also closely watching Discus, Nerv and Tomorrow People Ensemble.

Simak Dialog's early albums are 'great'. Just OK, but great musicianship. Then, the third album, the previous one, is very good, but just very good. Anyway, the last album, *Patahan*, that came out last year and which I am launching now, is VERY VERY VERY GOOD!

TC.: Are there any Indonesian musicians you feel could have a career outside Indonesia?

L.: There is an amazing guitarist, Dewa Budjana, who has just made a great record featuring Dave Carpenter and Peter Erskine (drummer with Weather Report); the music was played and performed brilliantly, with great compositions, but the sound is a bit too 'American'. Too polite. I wish he could do more 'unpolite' music, but he has a great career with Gigi and makes money.

Riza Arshad of Simak Dialog is definitely the greatest musician I have discovered in Indonesia and I know the best of him is still to come. He's an amazing pianist with a great touch and ECM sensibility. I am talking to him to liberate himself and challenge his artistic ego with evolutionary and free music spirit, without being afraid to experiment more, which he will do, and to express himself musically and say what he wants to say.

From the early 1970s onwards, major acts included Jakarta in their world tour schedules, so Deep Purple, Steve Wonder, Mick Jagger, BB King, Sting and Diana Ross and have all played to great fanfare in Jakarta. But it can get out of hand: Mick's show incited a riot in which a number of people died. Nowadays, many performers will only play as part of special

American Express 'clubholder' deals, at high ticket prices and in five-star hotels to the must-be-seen crowd as opposed to the riffraff of the general public. Sometimes, posters appear around the town for foreign acts who are totally unknown in the West but who have somehow made it 'big in Jakarta' via a fluke of popularity, such as teenybopper acts who are far too short-lived to merit a mention here.

## Crossover Music

A number of Western musicians have incorporated strands of Indonesian music in their recordings. These include David Bowie and Andy Summers of the Police. There are also whole albums of 'new age' or ambient music to be found, particularly in Bali.

Sha'aban Yahya's *Return to Yogya* is a perennial seller, although for the authors it stirs no nostalgia.

Jalan Jalan's album *Bali* has an 'ethno-electronic sound' with the traditional instruments of Bali alongside synthesisers.

*Kaleidoscope of Rainbows* by the late British jazz composer Neil Ardley also features the pentatonic scale, with five notes to an octave.

---

**Crossing Over**

Sabah Habas Mustapha is British and his friends know him as Colin Bass of the group Camel. With the *Jugula All-Stars*, his Indonesian group, he has toured abroad and recorded a number of albums here. Check out *Jalan Kopo*, recorded at Jugula Studios. This album is primarily Sundanese but with a bonus track from his *dangdut* album recorded in Jakarta. Colin also wrote the song *Denpasar Moon* which was an enormous hit for the Philippine singer, Maribeth.

---

## Indonesian Musicians With A Foreign Following

Anggun was a child star, a teen pop idol and now, following her marriage to a Frenchman or two, has a career as a soulful and sultry singer in a similar vein to Sade and Annie Lennox. On her albums, she mostly sings in English, with French and Indonesian lyrics on a couple of songs for her fans.

Karimata is a now disbanded jazz group. Their album *Jezz*, which featured American musicians such as Lee Ritenour, Bob James and Ernie Watts, is an interesting exploration of Indonesian music such as *jaipongan*, *kendong*, *gamelan*, *giring-giring*—a Kalimantan dance—*kecak* and Minang sounds.

SambaSunda is a group of mainly percussionists who can be seen and heard at 'world music' festivals. Their base is the Jugula Studios in Bandung.

Simon Grigg, as an interested observer, offers a few thoughts on the Indonesian music scene:

"It's tricky arriving in a vast nation like Indonesia and being able to rapidly get a handle on the popular music of the country. For a person with only a limited grasp of the local languages and dialects, the indigenous pop culture is both fascinating and impenetrable. The vast pop concerts on the local TV stations and the sounds coming out of the radio seemed utterly alien. I understand the psyche a little more now but I still see myself as little more than a voyeur.

"Getting a handle on the pop music, for the first 12 months, was the least of my priorities. Indonesia was a great unknown to me. Not only its music, but the country as a whole is an often misread enigma to most of us bought up in the West. I knew nothing of the indigenous popular music and still know very little. I'm still not comfortable commenting on much of it, especially the transnational fusions that constitute so much of what is pop here. That said, it intrigues me, so.....

"I come from a country which, like Indonesia, is a musical non-starter internationally...we have had Crowded House and OMC but that's it. But at least we have the advantage of language and a relatively supportive government, plus some access to the international market.

"Indonesia has none of these and consequently its Western styled pop / rock music has developed in some sort of strange isolation. Its perception of the styles it's emulating are both pure and slightly warped, but the limited access the country has had to the popular media has driven an industry that is, thus, stylistically its own.

"Genres that are largely forgotten elsewhere have thrived and survived in Indonesia, mutating as they go. Watching a band stylistically and visually like The Clash circa 1981 performing killer rock'n'roll tunes in Balinese is a wonderful thing. Quite invigorating in a strange way. It's the essence of what music is all about, the fusion of different, often clashing, styles together. After all, the music that took over the world in the 1950s was simply a mutation of the various styles of West Africa, the British Isles and the Russian Jewish songwriters that flooded NY in the early 20th Century.

"And the mutation and the isolation is a wonderful thing. My problem in NZ is that so many musicians simply ape whatever they see. You can point to our U2, or Fiona Apple, etc. Indonesian bands tend to ape but, gladly, add something else.

"On the other hand, I see Indonesia as a much larger version of Jamaica. In 1962, nobody could have foreseen the global influence the twisted American R'n'B coming out of the clubs and bars of Kingston would have over the next 40 years. Those misplaced elements assembled in Trenchtown, when put together and marketed by a few visionaries took over the world, so much so that there are now Indonesian flavoured takes on it coming out of places like Jogja.

"The market is also stymied by the vast piracy...there is no money in making records in Indonesia, so the acts have to, as in Jamaica, work incredibly hard to survive, honing their skills and seeming going off on tangents.

"I stood on Kuta beach with my Indonesian friend watching the aforesaid reggae band from Jogja thinking this is reggae but it's not. It's almost ska but it slips and slides around too much. I listened to the album from The Upstairs, knowing what they were trying to do but thinking 'they've got this so wrong', and that is why it is so right."

The future of the music industry globally is niche. The days of the big star acts driven by big companies are ending. The Internet (when it finally hits Indonesia properly...a big when) could drive much of the music being made here out beyond the country's shores, as it has with so much independent and niche music from around the world. Technology has meant that so much more music is being listened to and explored. And providing music that is different is the key to standing out from the mass. The vacuum that provided the breeding ground and the distortion of global pop culture in Indonesia could perhaps provide that difference.

## KITES

*Layang-layang* (kites) are an integral component of the Jakarta sky. Usually handmade in the *kampung* from struts of bamboo and rice paper, the kites don't stray too far from the standard *intan* (diamond) shape. Tails are optional.

---

### The Many Uses of Kites

Kites have enjoyed many uses throughout Indonesian history. In long distance sea fishing, shadow-free kites are used to carry hooks and lines out past the breakers. In West Java, bats are caught by kites, and in Bali, humming kites are flown above homes to promote good vibrations. For examples of the more weird and wonderful-shaped kites flown around Indonesia and the world, try and catch the annual Kite Festival held in Central Jakarta's wide open space of Monas.

---

Stuck in the confines of a city, one way for Jakarta's children to experience a sense of liberation is to fly a kite as high as they can. Since there's little wind in the capital, it takes an effort to get a kite airborne. Some seem to go miles up in the sky before their strings finally break under the pressure. Sometimes, things get out of hand between *kampungs*; glass and razors are sometimes attached to the strings in order to 'down' rival kites. Pedestrians and motorcyclists are known to have been injured by stray kite strings stretched across streets, and tiles are easily displaced. The wrecks of fallen kites are strewn everywhere.

## HIGHLAND GATHERING

This is one of the capital's odder days. Jakarta's Highland Gathering is a well-established part of the expat calendar, and the organisers claim it has become the largest of its kind outside Scotland. It's a chance for 'The Expat World

And His Wife' to relax unharassed and be surprised at just long it is since you met old so-and-so. It may well have been at last year's do.

First held in 1974, the gathering has grown from a small-time act of whimsy into an international extravaganza, capturing the national media's attention every year with its big Aussies massacring logs with chainsaws, parachutists, caber tossers, kilted bagpipers, the likes of whom are, unsurprisingly, unrivalled throughout Indonesia. In fact, so thoroughly alien is the event that when you see a queue of Western children waiting their turn to be knocked off a greasy pole, it's altogether possible to forget that you are actually in Jakarta. Which, of course, you're not. Held for many years in Rasuna Said, then in the Senayan complex, the Gathering is now hosted each year at the beginning of June, thanks to generous sponsorship, some 40 kilometres to the west of Jakarta in the new town of Lippo Karawaci.

### A Caber-Free Event

Indonesia is always well represented at the gathering in terms of traditional dance displays, stone-jumping and rival bagpipe and kilt frenzies from Sumatra. The Indonesian authorities, however, very nearly made the gathering a caber-free event, when in 1975 the caber was refused permission of entry. The way round this minor detail was to fly the caber back to Britain and then ship it out to Java where it could be unsuspectingly tossed overboard and left to drift ashore in north Jakarta.

The Gathering has been cancelled a few times when national events, such as the abdication of Suharto in 1998 and the Bali bombs of a few years later, have dampened spirits or had a scary security dimension. More recently, as a precaution against 'terrorist plots', which may or may not have been illusory, publicity for the Gatherings has been very last minute and largely on the gossip grapevine. Held over a weekend, the authors really enjoy the Sunday when we can be found in one of the hospitality tents waiting for the closing fireworks display, probably the finest in Indonesia. Ooh, aaah. Wow.

## SPARE TIME?

The hard core expat community have a full range of sports and social organisations to help fill the time and to retain roots. There may be a football club which notionally represents your flag; you can play rugby, cricket and softball. If running and drinking is your scene, then join the Hash House Harriers. Want to keep fit? Then check out the major hotels, most of which have a fitness centre.

Visit the offices of organisations you may be interested in joining to begin learning about community activities. Attend the monthly meetings, special events or newcomers functions sponsored by these and other organisations if they fit into your schedule; newcomers are always welcome. Information on upcoming community events can be found in the announcements section of the *Jakarta Post* classifieds, the Living In Indonesia website (http://www.expat.or.id) Community Events Calendar and posted on community bulletin boards.

## NATIONAL HOLIDAYS

The Indonesian calendar offers a generous number of national holidays, or *tanggal merah* ('red dates') as people like to call them. The majority are based on religious calendars, are celebrated worldwide and can vary from year to year. Being in Indonesia where it is still the law to adhere to one of six nominated religions, it means that everyone benefits from a number of days when traffic lessens and those in salaried positions enjoy a national day off work. In January, long-term residents check for those which will fall on Mondays or Fridays as they mean a long weekend trip out of town can be planned.

At least once a year, there is the one big holiday that everyone gets to celebrate together: Idul Fitri (or Lebaran). For those who adhere to the Islamic faith—most people in Indonesia—Lebaran is a particularly significant time: a time to celebrate that every human temptation has been held at arm's length—during daylight hours at least—for an entire month, the Muslim fasting month of Ramadhan.

This is a period of 30 days when everything slows down. Apart from young children, sick folk and menstruating and pregnant women, from sun up to sundown, all good Muslims are supposed to refrain from swallowing anything, food, drink or saliva.

In the build-up to Lebaran, you will notice a gradual slowdown in the general pace of life in Jakarta. The number of beggars in the city seems to increase, however, as do the number of sly requests to bump up any tips you are giving. Lebaran in fact becomes an all-round excuse for all manner of delays: letters take longer to come, anything vaguely 'official' takes forever, and just when you start to get bored of the excuse, it's time for the next one. This holiday is very much a 'holy' day (or week) because it marks the end of a period of self-denial.

Lebaran is significant for Jakartans because it's the time when you realise just how many people in the capital actually come from somewhere else in Indonesia. In what has become a traditionally frenetic exodus from the city, people throw abandon to the wind (as well as seemingly all that famous Indonesian reserve) in their fight to gain their place as one of Jakarta's Lebaran escapees. Shedding fresh light on the concept of 'packed like sardines', public transport is pushed to its limit and beyond. Anyone who doesn't need to travel by coach or train out of Jakarta during this time is advised to make alternative plans. Or better still, stay in town.

Following this mass departure from the city, streets, shops and restaurants suddenly seem to cease all activity, and, when all the drums have stopped beating, you feel that you can breathe a sigh of relief. Then you notice the shop shelves seem empty because the shelf-fillers have all gone home too. More than likely your *pembantu*, if you have one, will be among the sardines, leaving you to either enjoy the relative privacy for a few weeks, or go bananas because you have forgotten what the word 'housework' means.

But with the experience of your first Indonesian Lebaran under your belt, you will be all the more prepared when it comes round next year. Being based on the lunar Hijah calendar, they do come round sooner than you think, some ten days earlier each year. This means that it's possible to experience more Lebaran than the actual number of years you might spend in Jakarta.

Aside from Lebaran, there are other significant Islamic holidays. Hari Raya Idul Adha (or Lebaran Haji) poses similar shocking scenes for those with no experience of living with Islam. You may have wondered, in the week before the celebration, why so many goats and cows can be seen tied up together around the city, in bus shelters and on every vacant plot. You are advised not to get emotionally involved; in a ceremony symbolic of Abraham's willingness to sacrifice his own son, so the sacrifice of animals is undertaken and the meat distributed to the poor. Hari Raya Idul Adha falls on the 10th day of the 11th month in the Hijrah calendar.

On the 12th day of the third month is Maulud Nabi Muhammad SAW; the birthday of the prophet Mohammed, again a national holiday.

On the 27th day of the seventh month comes the Isra Miraj holiday, which celebrates the ascension of the prophet Mohammed.

Other Hari Raya (or 'Big Days' as national holidays are also called) are more 'traditional':

There's Tahun Baru (New Year's Day) when hordes of Jakartans head for the fireworks and *dangdut* concerts on the coast at Ancol or in Monas square.

Apart from Christmas Day, other Christian holidays include Good Friday (Jum'at Agung or, on your desk calendar, Wafat Isa Almasih) and Hari Raya Kebangkitan (Ascension Day).

The Hindus give us the Balinese New Year, or Hari Raya Nyepi (Day of Silence). This is a day off work in Jakarta, but in Bali it is a very serious holiday which traditionally sees people taking a vow of silence for the day. Strictly speaking, followers of the Hindu faith should not eat, speak to anyone, use anything electrical, make any journeys or light any fires for a solid 24 hours. Parts of Bali will be in temporary blackness on Hari Nyepi. The evening before, however, is the complete opposite. People intentionally make as much racket as they can: in doing this, the malingering sprits of the land will be roused into curiosity, but when they find the island

Imlek, the Chinese New Year, is now a major holiday in Jakarta, particularly in North Jakarta's 'Chinatown'. Many stores close for the day as the owners take an official day off to celebrate and the rest of us go shopping in the few stores left open.

in absolute silence the next day, will hopefully panic and flee the island. That at least is the belief. And accompanying the racket on the day before Nyepi is a parade of *ogah*, which are demonic mannequins designed again to scare off evil spirits. Traditionally, they are representations of generic villain-types, but in recent times they have become an outlet for wider social comment: effigies of presidents, both home and away, are cropping up more and more.

Buddhism gets its Hari Raya Waisak, a day which celebrates the Lord Buddha's birth, death and enlightenment. Celebrations are held during a full moon in April or May of every year to a somewhat surreal fanfare in Central Java's magnificent Borobudur temple.

## Other National Days

There are a number of other national days which are celebrated, but not always as an excuse to go to the beach. The most important is 17 August, Hari Kemerdekaan RI (Independence Day). Naturally, this is a 'big one', a *hari raya merah* (red calendar day) when offices and schools shut, with celebrations occurring throughout the archipelago—parades, street-parties and recitals of the original Proclamation of Independence made in Jakarta by Sukarno in 1945. Everyone, including you, is expected to fly the flag. Obviously *orang asing* (foreigners) are generally forgiven if you forget the first time round, but don't be surprised when your *pembantu* eventually asks you to invest in a flag and requisite bamboo pole. If not, the RT may be round for a chat.

There are other holidays which get celebrated in the government offices and schools, if not by the populace at large. The first, on 21 April, is Hari Raya Kartini which commemorates the birthday of Raden Ajeng Kartini, the founder of the movement for the emancipation of Indonesian women.

Next, on 22 June, is Hari Ulang Tahun Jakarta, the official birthday of Jakarta.

Hari Pancasila on 1 October celebrates the introduction of the state philosophy, Pancasila, by President Sukarno. Four days later, the Army has its turn with Hari Angkatan Bersenjata RI (Armed Forces Day); the attendant and televised military muscle-flexing is much less than it used to be as the TNI (*Tentara Negara Indonesia*) has much to live down.

Lastly, on 10 November, the nation's many heroes, past and present, are honoured on Hari Pahlawan (Hero's Day). This day is a kind of New Year's Honours List where the 'ordinary' people can be awarded by the President himself for their charitable work, or other outstanding achievements for which they will have been nominated.

## WEEKEND RETREATS

White sand, coconut palms fringing the shore, multicoloured coral reefs, abundant shoals of unique, colourful fish, a golden sun setting in clear blue skies...does that fit your image of Jakarta?

Pulau Seribu (Thousand Islands) is a group of small islands scattered in Jakarta Bay. There are actually only 126 or so, but all are within easy reach from Jakarta by private speedboats, inter-island ferries or charter flights which land on a grassy strip on Pulau Panjang. Several islands have been developed as tourist resorts or for recreational purposes, where there are bird and marine sanctuaries. The northern part of these islands have been zoned as a national marine park to preserve its underwater resources and beauty. About 90 km (60 miles) from Jakarta are Pulau Putri, Pulau Pelangi, Pulau Melintang and Pulau Petondan, which have upmarket accommodation, restaurants, a dive shop and boats for hire. Nearby, the islands of Melinjo, Papa Theo and Sepa have been developed for divers and budget tourists.

Other popular destinations for Jakartans include Puncak in the hills to the south, an area of cool air, tea plantations and villas built by Jakarta's élite. There's

Other popular weekend retreats for expatriate families include Pelabuhan Ratu on the south coast and Anyer on the north coast to the west. Both are about a three- or four-hour drive away, depending on the time of day. Midway between the two on the Sunda Strait is Carita. All have a mixture of hotels and villas for rent.

also Bandung, newly accessible with a toll road. Both are incredibly crowded and far from relaxing at holiday time.

## PHOTOGRAPHY

Since the first edition of this book, digital photography has taken off in a big way, if only by the exchange of snaps taken on a cellular phone. More serious photographers will have a whale of time in Indonesia, as visual treats are available to the visually aware around every corner.

In terms of taking pictures, you have an endless choice of subject matter to photograph, both day and night. The sunlight bleaches out a lot of colour from photographs. Because it sits so high in the sky, the sun robs your pictures of nearly all the shadow. A polarising filter will bring back some of the shadow and darken skies. A fill-in flash is a good idea on these occasions to avoid too much contrast. And you have about an hour in the evening before it's dark when shadows get long.

Jakarta looks particularly photogenic at night, particularly the night markets. Streets are lit entirely by gas lamps—an excellent light source—and which, in combination with a high-speed black and white film, make for very effective pictures. If you put a tripod up, some weird and wonderful colours are had after a few minutes on *film berwarna* (colour film), particularly low ASA films, with the B shutter.

People in Indonesia are generally very receptive to being photographed, but it's only polite to check first. In tourist areas, you may be asked to pay before you shoot.

The dominant photo shop in Jakarta is the green Fuji Image Plaza shop. Using fast, automated printing machines (for all C41 films), they claim to be able to print films in a record 22 minutes, although the average wait is rarely less than an hour. Their cheap and cheerful approach is not without its drawbacks, staff often having little idea about such basics of film-handling as not treading

Some Javanese are superstitious about being photographed in groups of three, believing it tremendous bad luck and that one of them will soon come a cropper. A lot of Indonesians don't smile in photographs; perhaps smiling is associated with a lack of self-control or perhaps because they have bad teeth.

on negatives. Fuji staff also have the infuriating habit of only printing the pictures which they think we would like. Pictures that look a touch 'arty' or blurred or several frames of a similar picture get ignored, so ask them to '*tolong, cetak semua*' (please print the lot).

The larger branches of these photographic emporia can also process your digital takes on the world.

# COMMUNICATING IN JAKARTA

## CHAPTER 8

'It's a profitable language; for French translation exercises at school you got marks, sometimes for Indonesian translations you get rupiahs.'
—Ivan Southall, *Indonesia Face To Face*

## LANGUAGE

*Bahasa* is the Indonesian word for language. This book, for example, is written in *bahasa Inggris* (English). For the purposes of this section, we use *bahasa* to mean *bahasa Indonesia* (Indonesian).

Not everyone in Indonesia speaks *bahasa*: some 20 per cent of the country won't know what you're saying if you use it. To the population at large outside Jakarta, the national language is still a second language, with their regional language taking precedence. At best, people learn *bahasa* alongside their local language. The people in Irian Jaya, for example, are not used to the idea of *bahasa* at all: they speak some 240 local dialects. They haven't exactly been impressed with the government's sincere efforts at modernisation and schooling either: images of foreign-looking Javanese and rice paddies are simply too alien for their imagination. The implementation of regional semi-autonomous status may mean that *bahasa* will not make great inroads. What will aid the propagation of the national language is an increase in access to communications technology.

Jakarta is unique in that it has a small percentage who were born here and therefore only speak *bahasa*. However, new arrivals from the villages may have to think twice before speaking. Perhaps because the risk of someone not getting your gist first time is quite high, language is kept brief and to the point.

On a basic level, *bahasa Indonesia* may seem quite easy, unsubtle and blunt even. This is because just a couple of words need be used to convey what might be a lengthy sentence in another language. But then, that is the same with most languages. On a higher level it's as complex as any; it is, after all, an entire language. Great works of literature are written in *bahasa Indonesia* and there's no limit to the range of vocabulary to be learned.

---

### Intricacies of Bahasa Indonesia

One word in this language can have several radically different meanings. An obvious example of the language's polysemy is *jalan*, which can mean 'road', the verb 'to function' or the verb 'to walk'. Meanings also change with the addition of affixes at the beginning and ends of words. Further nuances in meaning are achieved through context, intonation and body language. Thus implication becomes a test of the listener's interpretation skills which, for non-native speakers, can take a while.

---

Another factor to bear in mind is conceptualisation. 'Rice' is not a key word in English, although we may be familiar with various varieties such as brown, white, Bismati and pudding. Here in Indonesia, rice can make or break governments; such is the population's dependency on it. It's a farmer's means of livelihood and the population's staple food.

*Padi* is the rice plant (which comes in different varieties), not the wet field (paddy in English) in which it grows. *Gabah* is the unhusked destalked seed (*biji*). *Beras* is the dehusked item. Cook it, and you have *nasi*. Cook it incorrectly and you might have a sticky matter known as *ketan*. Don't cook it long enough and you will have an unappetising bowl of *biji limau*. Cook it perfectly and it's *nasi pulan*. Get served a ration of rice in prison and it's known as a *pelabur* or *ramsum*. Fry it and you have *nasi goreng*; cook it with coconut and it's *nasi uduk*. Sticks of rice-sausages wrapped and cooked in banana leaf are called *lontong*. Rice porridge is *lecek* or *bubur*. Cook it for a banquet and it becomes *nasi angkatan*. The equivalent proverb to the one about crying over split-milk is *nasi sudah jadi bubur*—the rice has already turned to porridge and you can't turn the clock back. And talking of time, everyone knows the expression 'Time is money', yet those two nouns rarely have a Western connotation in Indonesia.

Ask someone for the time—*Jam berapa*? And they may answer '*jam setengah sebelas*', which you correctly translate as 'hour half eleven' and therein lies a major problem, because it's actually half ten, a one hour difference. You see, whereas we think of half past the hour, Indonesians think of half before. If that is difficult to grasp, it becomes much easier to use the language of digital time and say ten thirty—*jam sepuluh tiga puluh*—which both can understand.

And money? Put simply, the concept of saving for a rainy day is not that common here. A windfall is likely to be spent as soon as possible, but then when that's gone something else will probably turn up, *Inshallah* (Allah willing).

*Bahasa Indonesia* was first put forward as the national, all-encompassing language in 1922 by Sukarno and the freedom-fighters of the time, and its use was eventually sanctioned by the Japanese in 1945, partly because few people could understand Japanese.

Standard *bahasa* is derived from the Malay language and is littered with Arabic, Dutch, Portugese, English and other loan words, many of which were introduced by the country's colonial masters. *Topi* (hat) is usually spelt 'topee' in English and was originally a Hindi word. *Amok* was originally an old Javanese word which entered both English and Malay, from whence it entered *bahasa*.

There are lobbyists for a pure *bahasa* and maybe they have a point. To hear *sok tahu* (know-all) pseudo-intellectuals cramming as many English phrases as possible into their press statements is genuinely annoying, especially when there's a perfectly good

Conversations in *bahasa* are often kept deliberately vague and indirect for fear of upsetting someone and losing face. Speakers often fall over themselves to use the correct title of respect—all this before they have even started saying anything. For many Westerners, the indirectness of speech is annoying. For Indonesians, it's a sign of great social proficiency that they can interpret the meaning of the most convoluted conversation, and give an equally convoluted response. It's also worth bearing in mind that no-one likes being the bearer of bad news.

## Football Language

Local football commentators can be just as bad. To the unknowing ear, it sounds like "mumble mumble mumble goal kick, mumble mumble penalty, mumble mumble handball" and so on, proving that football commentaries are boring the world over.

equivalent in *bahasa*. Words like *protes* (protest) and *krisis* (crisis) have perfectly valid equivalents in *bahasa* (protest—*menyanggah* and crisis—*masa gawat*), yet are consistently used in a pseudo-English way, as if the very concepts have been newly-imported with the word. Which, come to think, with the forced abdication of Suharto in 1998, they have.

However, a language which doesn't change is a dead language and, thankfully, *bahasa* is undergoing changes as we speak. The 'd' of the old spelling of 'Djakarta', for example, is rarely seen these days. Likewise, the 'e' in the old spelling of 'Sumatera', and the ex-President's name, 'Soeharto' becoming 'Suharto'. *Bahasa* is very much written as it is pronounced and very much a phonetic language; these changes therefore can only be good. But real attempts at standardising *bahasa* haven't met with complete success. As the dust settles and a couple more generations make it their first language, we should see the definitive *bahasa* emerge. There are, after all, a few hundred regional influences to contend with, not to mention the Indonesians' inherent practice of twiddling with their national language as if they were somehow uncomfortable with it. It's almost as if everyone's been told to wear a particularly unflattering set of overalls, and the best they can make of these overalls is to take them in at the sides, roll the sleeves up and sew extra bits on the collars. For Indonesians, it seems the temptation is to modify *bahasa* and make it more comfortable. All signs indicate that this is what is happening. No need to push for its reform, for it is occurring regardless.

It is a sign of a vibrant democracy when variations are tried out. In the 1970s, a new variant of *bahasa* was identified in certain parts of the capital. Presumed to have originated among Jakarta's criminal underground and known as Prokem, it was a cross-mutation of the official *bahasa*, *bahasa Sunda* and various Betawi dialects. Many of its words were acronyms for longer meanings, while many were completely new words. Some were simply standard *bahasa Indonesia*, only backwards. It worked well at first and successfully left the authorities in the dark for a good while, but it wasn't to last long as a secret. The young generations, excited by the idea of a 'private language', eventually popularised Prokem to the point where you could buy dictionaries of it and read novels written in it. Prokem continues to mutate, to be used by the hip young things of Jakarta, but it's hardly a secret anymore.

So now there's *bahasa Gaul* (pronounced 'gow'all').

## LEARNING THE LANGUAGE

If you want to make the effort (and any effort you make will be warmly greeted), there are a number of ways to go about learning *bahasa Indonesia*. The local papers often carry advertisements for language courses, and some are available via the major language schools in the city. The Indonesian-Australian Language Foundation (IALF) in Jl. Rasuna Said and International Language Programmes (ILP) in Jl. Panglima Polim regularly run courses in elementary Indonesian, as do many of the expatriate clubs and associations in the city.

---

**Teach Yourself Bahasa Indonesia**

For self-study methods of learning, you will need a good book or two. Recommended is the Periplus Editions publication *Bahasa Indonesia: An Introduction to Indonesian Language and Culture* by Yohanni Johns. Similarly clear and helpful is *Speak Standard Indonesian: A Beginner's Guide* by Dr Liaw Yock Fang and published by Times Editions. It covers the Jakartan dialect well and has a useful breakdown of colloquial terms as well as more formal ways of communicating. More widely available abroad is the *Indonesian Language Survival Kit*, which is a phrase book and CD, published by Lonely Planet.

---

A good dictionary is also quite essential. Widely used is the *Kamus Inggris Indonesia/Kamus Indonesia Inggris* by John Echols and Hassan Shadily. Highly comprehensive, it covers the gamut of formal words and terms (with examples to illustrate each) as well as a number of slang words. Perhaps the only criticism would be that it edges too closely towards formal Malay in its examples. While *bahasa Indonesia* is of course wholly derived from the Malay language, there are still a number of differences in sentence structure and vocabulary, but then this dictionary is over 30 years old.

*Bahasa* was, and always has been, a user-friendly means of communication. For those prepared to make the effort, it is not necessarily a confusing language. Arguably, the best way to pick it up is by exposing yourself to it. By simply being in Indonesia, you will acquire enough language—seemingly by osmosis—to survive.

And here's a little starter, a sketch of some of the more common multi-meaning words and their usual applications.

Good examples of the one-word-meaning-a-lot are *bisa* (can) and *mau* (want). These are incredibly useful words, and next to *apa* (what), probably the most used words in the language. Consider '*Bisa datang besok?*' (Can you come tomorrow?) and '*Bisa bicara bahasa Indonesia?*' (Can you speak Indonesian?) and the one word answer '*Bisa*' (Yes I can). Sometimes the question is just one word: '*Bisa?*' (Can it be done?) and the reply likewise: '*Bisa*' (It can be done). Look at '*Kapan bisa?*' (When can it be done?) and '*Besok bisa*' (It can be done tomorrow).

As for *mau*, a whole sentence like 'Would you like some?' can be expressed with the one word '*Mau?*' '*Mau minum?*' (Do you want a drink?), '*Mau makan?*' (Do you want to eat?), '*Mau muntah?*' (Do you want to throw up?) '*Mau pulang?*' (Do you want to go home?). '*Mau.*' (Yes).

We can see from *mau* and *bisa* that the words 'yes' and 'no' are used differently in Indonesian. 'Yes' is usually expressed as part of another word. When you answer '*bisa*', you are saying 'Yes, I can', and when you answer '*Mau*', you are saying 'Yes, I want ... (whatever)'.

There is more than one word which means 'no' or 'not'.

*Tidak* and likewise the more informal *nggak* are used with verbs

- *Tidak mau?*—You don't want …?
- *Tidak bisa?*—You can't do it?
- *Tidak bisa, ma'af.*—No I can't, sorry.

*Bukan* is used with nouns.
- *Kamu orang Perancis?*—Are you French? You say *Bukan* (I'm not)—unless of course you are.
- *Saya bukan orang gila* (I'm not a lunatic).
- *Itu bukan mainan* (That's not a toy).

The answer to a question like *Sudah makan?*—Have you already eaten?—is *Belum* (Not yet) and not *Tidak* (No).

There are no verb tenses in *bahasa*. Instead there are 'time words' which indicate past, present and future. When talking about the past, four small words can be used.

*Tadi* is for things which have happened recently.
- *Lagu apa itu?*—What song was that?
- *Yang apa?*—Which one?
- *Yang tadi.*—That one just now.
- *Tadi saya jatuh di pasar swalayan.*—I fell over earlier in the supermarket.
- *Tadi, dia kesini.*—He was here earlier. (This might be misleading as *dia* can mean 'he' or 'she' or 'it'.)

For something that happened yesterday or a few days ago, use *kemarin*.
- *Kenapa hari ini nggak mau? Kemarin mau.* (Why don't you want to today? You wanted to yesterday.)

*Dulu* is for things that went on a while ago, at first.
- *Dulu saya merokok tapi sekarang nggak lagi.*—I used to smoke, but not anymore.
- *Dulu ada banyak orang Belanda disini.*—There used to be lots of Dutch people here.

*Baru* has several uses.
It can be used for things which have just happened.
- *Dia baru dating.*—He's just arrived.

- *Dia baru mau kesana.*—He was just about to go there.

Another use is heard, for example, in a taxi:
- *Ke sini dulu, baru ke sana.*—Go here first, and next, go there.

The most common use of *baru* is 'new'.
- *Sepatu baru?*—New shoes?
- *Kamu punya pacar baru?*—Have you got a new boyfriend?

*Sekarang* means now and *nanti* means later
- *Mari kita pergi sekarang.*—Let's go now.
- *Aku tidak mau. Nanti aja, dong.*—I don't want to just yet. Later will be fine, mate.

*Akan* is generally used with other 'time words' to give a future idea.
- *Nasi ini akan dimakam nanti.*—This rice will be eaten later.
- *Dia akan datang besok.*—He's coming tomorrow.

*Besok* literally means tomorrow which, remember, never comes.
- *Besok pagi saya pergi ke* Bali.—Tomorrow morning I'm going to Bali.
- *Saya kirim uang besok.*—The cheque is in the post.

For congratulating someone, or simply wishing them a good day, use *selamat* plus whatever.
- *Selamat Hari Natal.*—Happy Christmas.
- *Selamat jalan.*—Goodbye, to which the response could be *Selamat tinggal*, literally 'Happy stay'.
- *Selamat makan.*—Enjoy your meal.
- *Selamat pagi / siang / sore / malam*—Good morning, afternoon, evening, night.

*Dong* is a little something many Jakartans tack on the end of a sentence. It's extremely common, although its actual meaning is unclear. It's almost an insult, but not quite. *Hati-*

*hati*, for example, means 'be careful', but *hati-hati dong* means something like 'be careful even though everyone knows you're the most careless individual there is'. It's the closest an Indonesian gets to being sarcastic. Many non-native speakers of *bahasa Indonesia* use it on the end of every word, as if to make up for a general lack of vocabulary, which of course sounds silly.

---

### Indonesian Alphabet Pronunciation

**A** as in 'the cat sat on the mat'

**B** 'bay' (Indonesians have to mind their 'Bs' and 'Ps'.)

**C** 'chay' guevera ('C' is generally pronounced as 'ch' in church.)

**D** 'day' follows night

**E** as in 'egg' and 'heirloom'

**F** 'eff' er pheasant

**G** 'gay' as in gay

**H** 'ha, ha' said the clown

**I** 'ee' bah goom as they say in Yorkshire

**J** 'jay' as in a bird and walking

**K** 'ka' as in 'car'. (Indonesians think k in English is 'key' not 'kay'.)

**L** 'ell' for leather

**M** as in James Bond

**N** 'en' as in 'enpecked

**O** 'oh'—it's the same

**P** as in a short 'pay' (Indonesians have to mind their 'Ps' and 'Bs'.)

**Q** as in 'queue' ('Qs' and queues are both in short supply in Indonesia.)

**R** as in a Highland 'aire' ('Rs' are rolled, particularly by the Javanese.)

**S** as in 'Yes, it's the same' (Plurals are made by doubling the word. e.g. sama-sama)

**T** 'tay' as in a river

**U** as in 'Ooh, isn't she/he sexy!'

**V** 'vay'

**W** 'way'

**X** as in 'ex' girl/boyfriend

**Y** 'yea', verily I say unto you...

**Z** as in the British one, 'zed'

## SWEARING

Calling another person an animal is the worst thing you can say to someone in Indonesia. Shouting '*babi*' (pig) or '*monyet*' (monkey) and especially '*anjing*' (dog) will turn heads and leave you with all kinds of explaining to do. The word '*brengsek*', common in Jakarta, can be used lightly as in 'damn' or can have a much stronger meaning like 'bastard'; it all depends on how you say it. '*Bangsat*', which can translate harmlessly as 'bedbug', carries a far stronger meaning when used to describe a person. The same is true for '*tai*' (shit). Be careful if you wear a bow tie, which could be pronounced as '*bau tie*'—smelly shit. The word '*kontol*', a particularly vulgar word for male genitalia, is to be used with caution carrying approximately the same weight that the 'eff' word does in English.

Of course, swearing in a foreign language, especially if you haven't reached native speaker fluency, is to be avoided at all times. You only sound gratuitously stupid, and you can never be sure how your utterances will be received. So it is also inadvisable to tell a stranger that she/he is *gila* (crazy) or *bodoh* (stupid) even if you think they are.

You will find that a number of well-known English swear words are demoralisingly common in Indonesia. Although TV and cinema have scenes that hint of sexuality rigorously censored, scenes of gratuitous violence and bad language are not. So don't be over-surprised when local schoolchildren use bad language on you. Often, these are the some of the very few English words they know and they are probably trying to be friendly with you rather than offend you. Or maybe they aren't.

| English | Indonesian | Bahasa Gaul |
|---|---|---|
| I | *Saya* | *Gue, aku, aye, akika* |
| You | *Anda, kamu* | *Elu, ente* |
| Good morning | *Selamat pagi* | *'Met pagi* |
| Good evening | *Selamat malam* | *'Met malam* |

| Nice to meet you | *Saya senang berjumpa dengan anda* | *Hai 'bro!* |
|---|---|---|
| Take care | *Hati-hati* | *Titi deejay (fr. 'hati-hati di jalan')* |
| See you | *Sampai jumpa* | *Ketemu lagi yaw* |
| Truly sorry if I made mistake | *Ma'af bila saya berbuat kesalahan* | *Kalo ade saleh maapin aye* |
| I'm sorry | *Ma'afkan saya* | *Maapin aye* |
| Yes | *Ya* | *Iye, yo-i* |
| No | *Tidak* | *Nggak, gak, enggak* |
| Finish | *Sudah, selesai* | *Sutra, kelar 'bo* |

## NON-VERBAL COMMUNICATION

When you first arrive and try to communicate, there are a number of visual factors you must bear in mind.

Think of your physical appearance: are you taller, bulkier, hairier and/or fairer than the throngs who face you? How are you dressed? Only tourists and manual labourers are seen in shorts in public.

Are you used to crowds? Do you enjoy football matches and/or rock concerts? It would certainly help because here not only will you be part of a crowd, you will inevitably stand out in it. At times, you will be the focus of attention in the biggest city on one of the most crowded islands on the planet.

Do you come from a hot country where folks are happiest outdoors or do you come from a temperate clime where your doors and windows are kept shut to keep the heat indoors? If so, you also also keep the neighbours out in the cold.

Welcome to the tropics where if Mother Nature is left to her own devices, she can supply all your needs. Every patch of dirt here can become an orchard in a few short, hot and humid months. The Garden of Eden was definitely not in Iceland. There are places in Indonesia where the climate can be described as bracing, so don't expect an energetic life. After all, only mad dogs and Englishmen go out in the noonday sun. It's far better to mooch around with your friends, gossip a little and wait for the fruits of life to drop into your lap.

However, if you are planning to work in an air-conditioned office, make sure you bring a sweater with you as you can expect to almost freeze. The usual setting is 16°C (60°F), which far from energising the staff, renders them virtually comatose: this is because hyperthermia thickens the blood and life barely ticks along.

Once you have adjusted and made allowances for your differences, there will still arise numerous occasions of total communication breakdown. You feel sick, have a headache and ask for an aspirin and the response is a fit of the giggles. Indonesians seem to laugh in many situations where you don't see the humour, and not merely because you don't appreciate slapstick.

There could be any of a number of reasons to provoke a laugh. Maybe Indonesians laugh because they're not supposed to get angry. Or maybe it's embarrassment at the thought of communicating with someone of a different skin colour, language, culture or whatever. Or, again, no-one likes being the bearer of bad news and laughing it off diminishes its severity. It's really not worth getting aggrieved at what you may consider to be an act of insolence or thoughtlessness.

There is an ingrained acquiescence to what life has in store. It will take at least two generations to move beyond the paternalism and guided democracy of the state philosophy, Pancasila, subverted to his own ends by former President Suharto. Current teachers and parents are products of the then curricula. Their parents and grandparents had the previous colonial masters determining their fate

Suharto also saw himself as a reincarnation of a Central Javanese ruler. Javanese culture is a mixture of Islam and mysticism wherein every person is expected to know his or her place and to have few expectations of bettering one's birthright. At the top of the hierarchical pyramid, Suharto could do no wrong (but his children and cronies did).

So the Javanese may seem to be less assertive than, say, the Bataks of North Sumatra, yet it is the Javanese who have ruled Indonesia in post-colonial times. There are fine social distinctions which not only determine the register of speech, but also the body language. It may manifest itself in a dip of the shoulder so that the underling can demonstrate his or her lower social status.

### Almost Like Limbo Rock

When I first arrived and moved into my house, I furnished it with a low coffee table, mattresses and floor cushions. My *pembantu* had immense problems in keeping below head height and it took me some time before she could be encouraged to not slither past.

There is body language which you may have to learn in order to not give offence. First of all, remember to never use your left hand: do not give anything to anybody, do not accept anything from anybody, do not put food in your mouth with your left hand and, above all, do not make any gestures with your left hand. This is because the use of toilet tissue is not universal and water with the left hand is. Your left hand is, *per se*, dirty. So never ever tell anybody that actually you use your right hand to clasp the toilet paper when wiping your bum.

Shaking hands when greeting people is acceptable, with your right hand of course. Similarly, wave goodbye with your right hand and flag down a taxi with your right hand.

Strangely, writing with your left hand is not stigmatised as it has been elsewhere.

If you are a touchy-feely kind of person, you ought to curb some of your enthusiasm. Although personal space here may be less than you are used to—think how close or far you like to be to the person you are conversing with—don't crowd people unless you already have a fairly intimate relationship with them. Even then be careful where you are and who can see you.

It has been proposed by some self-appointed moral guardians that kissing your spouse goodbye at the street gate be made illegal. Even a husband and wife holding hands in

the street can upset some folk, although if you hold the hand of someone of your gender, that's acceptable.

If you are really want to express your outrage at this, then you should be aware that the British two-fingered salute here means 'two' or 'victory'. Your intended insult is either the one-fingered salute used in most countries or, if you really want to demonstrate your awareness of Indonesian gestures and really offend someone, then protrude your thumb between the middle and forefinger.

Pointing with a finger—any finger—is considered rude, so indicate direction with an open, extended hand held at an angle to the vertical. Don't point with your feet either; this upsets all Asians, particularly Buddhists.

By and large, you will be familiar with most gestures, such as those used for OK, please, sorry and money. If you practise communicating in mime for a week or so before coming here, you won't really need this section on *bahasa Indonesia*.

# DOING BUSINESS

## CHAPTER 9

'If you have knowledge of good and bad,
then logically you know that corruption
is bad. But in Indonesia, sometimes
corruption is considered a good thing...'
—Emha Ainun Najib, preacher and poet

## ADJUSTING TO DIFFERENT NORMS

When Indonesians talk about the future and their role in it, an oft-used expression is 'this globalisation era'. They learn English in order to participate in 'this globalisation era'. They hope that their new business initiative will compete in 'this globalisation era'.

Any unaware Westerner coming to Jakarta to set up business will look at the highrises, notice that the population at large has at least one handphone in constant use, will appreciate the service in his or her five-star hotel and will automatically expect that apart from the usual hassles, it won't be too difficult to get things going.

Later, having spent several hours stuck in traffic, he or she will come the realisation that only one meeting can be held in a day. And that is the least of the problems.

First and foremost is the need to recognise that life in a tropical country has a different pace and energy from that experienced in more temperate climes. We are all products of our environment and culture and, perhaps, Westerners are more 'homogenised' than our Indonesian counterparts who have the home town (*kampung*) factors of religion, ethnic group and class as essential characteristics. An Indonesian will always 'belong' to a quite specific subset; this means that no Westerner can expect to have an instant rapport with a business partner or colleague. Even those who have studied at a university outside Indonesia and have a superb facility with English will not necessarily have a Western mindset.

---

### Problems Galore

A GM for a very large multinational company told a visiting group of 30 business leaders from Holland that he would honestly think twice before setting up a company here. He cited corruption, lack of legal certainty and frustration in dealing with local companies and bureaucracies as the main impediments in doing business here.

As an example, he explained to the visitors that while his company was doing okay, it had taken six months to get the necessary permits and so on to obtain the natural gas required to run his plant after the supplier they were using dried up. He said it should have taken a week at most. The run on effect was a large layoff in his workforce until the necessary permits were issued.

The visitors nodded and then continued on their way to visit Thailand, Vietnam and Malaysia as other places to invest in.

—Dominic Brady

---

One should also bear in mind that until 1950, which is very recent history, Indonesia had colonial masters—fought over by the British, Portuguese and the Dutch, who eventually ruled for 300 years only to be forced out by the Japanese. There is a generation of grandparents who remember those times. Sukarno became the effective president in 1950 and attempted to instil nationalistic pride, a recognition of the cultural differences which has given Indonesia its pluralistic outlook.

Then, in 1965, along came Suharto with his military and imposed a 'New Order'. They removed the recognition of certain religions from the nation's palette and drove the Chinese cultural practices underground whilst benefitting greatly from their business acumen. The bureaucracy was bent to his will, but then to the innately mystical Javanese, the most populous group in the country, he was (and remains at the time of writing) a 'wise king' whose judgement was not to be questioned.

Indonesians will generally say that it was his children who were the greedy ones; they corrupted the country and he never took a rupiah for himself. To date, he remains untouchable, but then that is because remnants of the old New Order remain entrenched in political, business and military circles. And the public at large has yet to raise its expectations to those accepted for generations in the West.

---

**Indonesian Society**

Gary Dean from Okusi Associates (http://www.okusi.net/) offers his insight into Javanese society. "Javanese society is strongly patrician and hierarchical, with what appear to be great power distances between each level within a social structure. Showing proper respect, in speech and behaviour, is an important aspect of Javanese culture. Javanese society is highly inclusive; there is a place for everyone from the most high to the lowliest. Hierarchy ensures that every person in society knows both their place and their obligations within the social structure. Those in high positions should be shown respect; those in lower positions should be treated with goodwill and their welfare guarded.

In traditional Javanese society, the *priyayi* comprised the class of officials, military officers, and intellectuals, and is now strongly associated with the bureaucracy and ruling elite. Whilst in the past *priyayi* were the descendants of nobility, these days *priyayi* can refer to anyone with an academic education or to anyone who simply reflects this particular outlook."

---

It is still rare to find a non-Javanese in a senior position within the bureaucracy, police, military or a state-owned business, so an understanding of what makes them tick should make business initiatives somewhat easier. Should, but doesn't.

Having been entrenched for so long in their positions, positions gained through family and *kampung* connections to which they owe fealty, there is a seemingly inbred perception that the population at large owes bureaucrats a living. They are there to be served. As life and one's position in the world is pre-ordained, then there is no need to hurry or worry. Things will work out okay in the end.

Of course, knowing one's place and paying respect, perhaps with a token of appreciation of those services which will be rendered, will certainly prove beneficial and increase the pace of processing permissions and documentation. None of this will be articulated in plain language, which is why many companies employ a 'Mr (or Mrs) Fixit' who has the relevant societal connections. This is another reason why the entertainment and hospitality budget may seem disproportionately large.

Not going with the flow can prove disadvantageous, however self-righteous one may feel.

## OVERVIEW OF RECENT DEVELOPMENTS

Notwithstanding the foregoing, Indonesia is undergoing a rapid transformation with direct elections becoming the norm for political posts. Whether this will effect major changes in the bureaucracy is yet to be determined. Laws are promulgated with the self-perceived best of intentions, but without the regulatory competence to uphold them. It is a process of 'trial-by-fire', and it is not unknown for presidential decrees to be withdrawn within months following publicly expressed disapproval. Both government and the business sector are now much more accountable to the public.

The new buzz phrase is Corporate Social Responsibility (CSR), which is not to be confused with, let alone equated to, customer service. CSR is about image rather than substance so, for example, the major telecommunications conglomerate seeks kudos from rehabilitating eight elementary schools rather than providing an efficient nationwide Internet broadband service. In other words, corporate governance reform in Indonesia is still very much in its infancy and much remains to be done. Whilst it is relatively easy to enact legislation in this regard, the proof is in the implementation and enforcement. Law-making in Indonesia has a peculiar symbolic quality about it, and lawmakers give very little thought to how the legislation they occasionally enact will actually be regulated.

So the country is on a steep learning curve, but there are strong indications that a more transparent foundation for economic prosperity is being forged. Many of the more fundamental economic and structural changes in the business environment since 1999 have been at the insistence of the IMF and World Bank. All IMF loans were fully paid up in 2006 and at the beginning of 2007, President Susilo Bambang Yudhoyono announced that Indonesia no longer needed the Consultative Group on Indonesia (CGI), formed in the wake of the Asian Economic meltdown in 1996/1997. Any negotiations about debts would be on a one-to-one basis with the then main debtors, Japan, the Asian Development Bank and the World Bank.

This was a reflection of a much improved economy resulting from the removal of fuel-related subsidies, much reduced debt repayments and increased tax revenue. The increase in wealth in the regions with decentralisation has had the benefit of a rise in expenditure on education to 17 per cent. This will naturally bring further benefits in the growth of a more skilled workforce.

With *reformasi* giving the public the freedom to express their concerns, the quest for social justice is a key driving force behind the changes. Government and business sectors are now more accountable to the public, although much remains to be done. As ever, the principal obstacle to business activity and economic development generally remains the government bureaucracy. It is to be hoped that substantial pay rises, particularly for the upper echelons, and the jailing of several prominent public officials for corruption will lessen the incentives to seek extra-legal bonuses.

## INDONESIAN LAW AND LEGAL CERTAINTY
### Owning a Company

Non-Indonesian citizens are not allowed to own property. However, foreign-owned companies can. If you are intent on establishing a small or medium-sized business to operate in Indonesia, you will need to establish a company. It is a common myth that foreign citizens need a partner.

In 1996, the then-government opened the way for establishing 100 per cent foreign-owned companies (referred to as 100 per cent PMAs, short for *Penanaman Modal Asing*, or 'Foreign Capital Investment').

For the most part, there are now very few areas of the Indonesian economy that are closed to foreign investment, with the proviso that some areas may require local equity partnership. Some commercial activities, such as retailing, food and drink manufacturing and animal husbandry, require an Indonesian partner, usually with a minimum equity share of 20 per cent. Some areas are reserved only for locals (*usaha kecil*; small ventures); these are mainly concentrated in the agricultural, handcrafts and informal sectors.

Working alongside local businesses is an important part of nearly every Indonesian venture. Long-term, performance-based contractual arrangements with Indonesian companies may in many cases be a much better option than a Joint Venture (JV).

Establishing a company in Indonesia is a highly bureaucratic process, but nonetheless a process that has become relatively easier over the past few years. The first step in this rather complex process is the obtaining of an Investment Approval from the Investment Coordination Board. This approval process is nowadays relatively quick, and can be completed in as little as 14 days in some Investment Board offices.

Once Investment Approval is given—referred to as the SP (*Surat Persetujuan*—literally, 'Letter of Agreement'), which also permits the investor to establish an Indonesian company, a process that will take about two months—there are a plethora of licences the investor must seek from local authorities. This can take considerable time and is often fraught with bureaucratic Catch 22 situations. For all practical purposes, most projects can commence immediately, without necessarily having to wait for all the bureaucratic processes to sort themselves out.

There are too many tales of wives seeking divorces from their expatriate husbands in order to seize his capital assets. He generally leaves the country with a broken heart and empty bank account. There are stories too of business partners who bleed a company dry to feed a gambling addiction or who in mismanaging the company affairs drive out the capable staff and lose valued customers.

## Contracts

At higher levels of Indonesian business, contracts written in English are common enough, thus present no problems, at least for the Western side. However, for the most part, contracts are drawn up in Indonesian, and where required, an English translation made. For especially critical agreements, it would be wise to obtain more than one translation as a double check.

In the West, the attitude 'a deal is a deal' means that once an agreement has been reached and signed, it is then generally closed for further renegotiation. Western business tends to emphasise textual agreements using the language of law where rights and responsibilities are clearly laid out in writing and binding no matter what the circumstances.

Contracts and agreements in Indonesia tend to be much less detailed, and contain much more 'unwritten text' relying upon the context upon which the agreement was made. Much more emphasis is placed upon flexibility; contracts are 'softer' and rely upon mutual understanding of the discourse that has occurred between the parties over a period of time, and the trust and interdependency that has built up between them. Contracts can be subject to constant renegotiation and reinterpretation.

Securing agreements and maintaining contracts in Indonesia requires more than mere written documents. It requires maintaining relationships at as many different layers as possible: personal, business, government and community. Networks should be maintained at as many levels as is practical, and ideally, these networks should interweave and overlap with those with whom you do business. Social pressure for contracting parties to act fairly and honestly towards one another is of much greater value in securing agreements in Indonesia than a wad of legal documents.

Although many satisfactory contracts can be made without the assistance of a notary (notaris), e.g. employment agreements, it is obvious that the more important a contract, the more important it is to secure the maximum amount of legitimacy for the agreement, whatever it might be.

A contract drawn-up and co-signed by a notary has more weight in the minds of most Indonesians than a contract drawn-up by a non-notary. Signing ceremonies, overly formal though they may seem to the Westerner, have important symbolic power, serving to increase the prestige and legitimacy of the contract.

Given the state of the legal system, one might be forgiven for giving Indonesia a wide berth as an investment or business destination. Embezzlers of vast funds flee with seeming impunity, or outright connivance, out of the country.

## Going to Court

The chances of a foreigner or a foreign company getting a fair hearing in an Indonesian court are not good. Corruption, cultural misunderstanding and a misplaced nationalism, amongst other factors, often conspire to put foreigners at considerable disadvantage should their case ever get to court.

The laws governing business are mostly inherited from the Dutch Civil Code. It's a slow process rewriting them in order to fit into international conventions which Indonesia is a signatory to as well as meeting the demands of a rapidly

evolving society. Entrenched forces within the judiciary and law enforcement agencies do not yet have the needed mindset to enforce these changes.

For example, before 1998, Indonesia did not really have an effective bankruptcy process. The weak bankruptcy laws that existed in Indonesia before 1998 dated from 1906 and technically only applied to non-indigenous Indonesians such as Europeans, Chinese and Arabs. Consequently, the 1906 laws were used extremely infrequently, and 'bankruptcy' as it is generally understood was rarely ever applied to a company or person. Rather than referring to a legal process to assist in meeting obligations to creditors, the Indonesian loan-word *bangkrut* is used to indicate an absence of loss of money, or an inability to pay, So the level of understanding of bankruptcy processes in Indonesia is quite low.

At the insistence of the IMF, Indonesia was forced to introduce new bankruptcy laws, which it did in April 1998. A number of specialist commercial courts were established to hear bankruptcy cases, and judges in these courts underwent training in commercial law. In addition, a number of ad-hoc judges, lawyers who specialise in commercial law, were also appointed to these new courts.

To date, sadly, outcomes from commercial courts have been very disappointing. 'Strange' decisions have been common, partly because judges are still coming to grips with the concept of bankruptcy, there being few precedents naturally. Bankruptcy laws may well have been 'reformed', but it seems that Indonesian courts are still reluctant to protect creditors from debt-ridden Indonesian companies, especially, it appears, when those creditors are foreigners.

## IN THE OFFICE
### Labour and Labour Relations
The Department of Manpower, known by its Indonesian abbreviation, 'Depnaker', is the government body that regulates all employment practices in Indonesia, including conditions of employment and labour-employer relations. These are in line with the International Labour Organisation (ILO) Conventions.

At the time of writing, Act Number 13 of 2003 Concerning Manpower is in force, although certain provisions displease employer federations. This Act governs the issuance of contracts and terms and conditions, the procedures for termination of employment, whether for disciplinary reasons or redundancy, and the payment of compensation. Depnaker is responsible for overseeing this Act and can serve as the official ombudsman in the event of disputes between employer and employee(s).

Companies frequently need to train workers on the job to make up for deficiencies in formal skills or education. Recruiting administrative or professional workers 'raw' from local universities is often an excellent way of inducting talent into an enterprise. However, such recruits may well be a lot 'greener' than, for instance, the average Western graduate.

Remuneration packages for Indonesian workers usually have several components, and are paid on a weekly or monthly basis. The primary component is the basic wage (*gaji pokok*). Commonly added to this are daily allowances for transport, meals, attendance, and, occasionally, productivity. Indonesians frequently expect foreign-owned companies to pay higher wages than local companies. Annual bonuses equal to one month's wages are paid either just before Lebaran (the annual Islamic celebration) or Christmas, depending on the individual worker's religion.

Minimum wage rates for most low to medium-skilled work are set on a province-by-province basis. A limited number of industry sectors also have their own minimum wage rates, varying from province to province. The 'going rate' for a particular trade or skill can usually be found by asking around in the locality concerned. Failing that, regional offices of Depnaker can sometimes be of assistance.

Worker insurance is still very underdeveloped in Indonesia.

Skills considered basic, such as computing and report writing, are often quite poor, and very few graduates would have prior workplace experience. Companies prepared to make relatively small additional investments in education and training will be rewarded with employees who will tend to be more loyal to the company, and, of course, much more productive.

*Jamsostek*, the government-backed insurance scheme provides only a nominal protection for workers, including cover for accident, health and old age pension. Premiums add from 7–11 per cent to the total wages bill. However, in the event of an accident or sickness, the caring employer will top up the insurance, as the payout is rarely sufficient to properly cover medical or living expenses.

Encouraging a family-type atmosphere, remembering birthdays and giving a certain amount of leeway for the celebration of weddings, circumcisions, etc. will encourage greater loyalty. If invited to attend one of these celebrations, then go. The attendance of a Western colleague, especially if he or she is the boss, will greatly enhance the prestige of the worker.

## Working Hours

Indonesians are the earliest risers of any nation in the world, which presumably accounts for the office hours. Mondays to Thursdays, government offices tend to close by 3:00 pm, but they do open at 8:00 am if you're lucky. Saturday mornings are no longer a compulsory working day for bureaucrats in Jakarta, so most offices and all banks are shut. Friday afternoons tend to be quiet because of the exodus of male employees to the mosque, so Fridays are basically half-days. This leaves the weekends for shopping: hours are generally 10:00 am–9:00 pm.

## Language

An ability to speak English is often a point of pride amongst Indonesians, indicating as it does their educational status. It often happens, however, that an Indonesian may seem to be listening to and understanding what is being said in English, but sometimes critical details are missed.

Complicating the matter is that many Indonesians will rarely ask for repetition when something is unclear to them, partly because it is thought impolite, and partly because of embarrassment. These comments also apply to professional Indonesian interpreters who might feel that they will lose face if they continually ask for repetition.

It is very prudent in the Indonesian context to often repeat important details during the course of discussions so that your meaning is completely clear. When you do, speak clearly and slowly, and if you can, paraphrase. Indonesians will often say 'yes' purely as an indication that they are listening; 'yes' in this context does not necessarily indicate understanding or agreement with what is being said. Another approach is to ask a colleague who has good English to summarise the discussion; you then have an intermediary who can probably be relied on to relay the main points in Indonesian.

## THE LOCAL COMMUNITY

Recent problems involving the mining industry in Indonesia invariably have had their roots in a lack of communication between local communities—or in a few cases, provincial governments—and the mining company. Mining companies especially have generally relied too much on legal devices to secure their rights, and have either ignored or paid too little attention to the community in which they are operating.

Concepts of traditional ownership of land are still very strong all over Indonesia, and local communities feel they have a stake in what happens in their environment, regardless of land titles or contractual rights that may have been awarded to a company by a government. Under the Suharto regime, local communities were often bypassed in the consultation process for projects or were pressured to accept very unfavourable terms. Foreign mining companies may often have been unaware of this, and some of them have good reason to feel 'stung' at what has been happening at their mines recently.

But it's not just mega-projects which need to pay heed to the local community. New businesses establishing themselves in any area of Indonesia will invariably come under the 'jurisdiction' of an RT/RW, and relations should be established before operations begin. Similarly, if housed within an office complex or tower, establish a relationship with the building management.

Gestures, gifts, employment and money will not ensure good relations and security if the venture tries to isolate or distance itself from the community.

Businesses must aim to create close and symbiotic relationships with the surrounding community so that the community feels it has a stake in protecting it.

## CONTACTS

If you are intent on setting up in business in Indonesia, you are going to need a supportive network. Your embassy will have a trade attaché who will liaise with local Chambers of Commerce in Jakarta which offer regular networking opportunities. The following is a partial list.

- **Jakarta Chamber of Commerce and Industry (KADIN)**
  Majapahit Permai Block B 21-22-23
  Jl. Majapahit No.18-22
  Jakarta 10160
  PO. Box. 3077 Jkt.
  Tel: (21) 380-8091, 384-4533 (hunting)
  Fax: (21) 384-4549-569
  Email: kadinjkt@indosat.net.id
  Website: http://www.kadin.or.id
- **American Chamber of Commerce in Indonesia (AmCham)**
  World Trade Center, 11th floor
  Jl. Jend. Sudirman Kav. 29-31
  Jakarta 12920
  Tel: (21) 526-2860
  Fax (21) 526-2861
  Email: info@amcham.or.id
  Website: http://www.amcham.or.id
- **Indonesian-Australian Business Council (IABC)**
  World Trade Center, 11th Floor
  Jl. Jend. Sudirman Kav. 29-31
  Jakarta 12920
  Tel: (21) 521-1540, 527-0942, 521-1718
  Fax: (21) 521-1541
  Email: secretariat@iabc.or.id
  Website: http://www.iabc.or.id
- **British Chamber of Commerce in Indonesia (BritCham)**
  Wisma Metropolitan I F/15

Jl. Jend. Sudirman Kav. 29-31
Jakarta 12920
Tel: (21) 522-9453
Fax: (21) 527-9135
Email: bisnis@britcham.or.id
Website: http://www.britcham.or.id

- **Indonesia Canada Chamber of Commerce (ICCC)**
World Trade Center, 6th Floor
Jl. Jend. Sudirman Kav. 29-31
Jakarta 12920
Tel: (21) 2550-7859
Fax: (21) 2550-7812
Email: iccc@cbn.net.id
Website: http://www.iccc.or.id

- **Indonesian French Chamber of Commerce and Industry (IFCCI)**
Jalan Wijaya II No. 36
Kebayoran Baru
Jakarta 12160
Tel: (21) 739-7161
Fax: (21) 739-7168
Email: contacts@ifcci.com
Website: http://www.ifcci.com

- **European Business Chamber of Commerce in Indonesia (Eurocham)**
World Trade Center, 10th Floor
Jl. Jend. Sudirman Kav. 29-31
Jakarta 12920
Tel: (21) 521-1650
Fax: (21) 521-1651
Email: info@eurocham.or.id
Website: http://www.eurocham.or.id/

- **Malaysia External Trade Development Corporation (MATRADE)**
Plaza Mutiara, 12th Floor
Jl. Lingkar Kuningan
Kav. E.1.2, No. 1 & 2
Kawasan Mega Kuningan
Jakarta 12950

Trade Commissioner Direct Line: (21) 576 4322
Tel: (21) 576-4297
Fax: (21) 576-4321
Email: jakarta@matrade.gov.my

- **International Enterprise Singapore**
C/O Singapore Embassy, Jakarta
Graha Surya Internusa, 19th Floor
Jl. HR Rasuna Said Kav X-0
Kuningan 12950
Tel: (21) 522-9274
Fax: (21) 520-1488
Telex: (21) 3 SINGA 1A
Cable: SINGAWAKIL JAKARTA

---

### Special Thanks

We are indebted to Gary Dean of Okusi Associates (http://www.okusi.net) for verifying the factual information. The opinions are largely ours.

# FAST FACTS

## CHAPTER 10

'Life does not consist mainly, or even largely, of
facts and happenings. It consists mainly of the storm
of thought that is forever flowing through one's head.'
—Mark Twain

## Official Name
DKI—Jakarta
*Daerah kota istemewa* (area of special city)

## Location
Jakarta, the capital and largest city of Indonesia, is located on the Indonesian island of Java.

## Land Area
Ever expanding. On a good day, for example at 3:00 am on a Sunday morning and using the toll roads, you can probably cross the city east to west or north to south in about an hour.

## Climate
Tropical, with two hot seasons: one dry, the other wet. Theoretically, the rainy season is from November to April.

## Flag
A red horizontal stripe above a white horizontal stripe

## National Anthem
*Indonesia Raya*

## National Motto
*Bhineka tunggal ika*—Unity in diversity

## Time
GMT + 7 hours in Jakarta (WIB—*Waktu Indonesia Barat*—West Indonesia Timezone) Jakarta is one hour behind Bali.

## Telephone
Country Code: 61
Jakarta Code: 21

## Electricity
127/230V 50Hz

## Population
Probably 13 million people are actually resident within the city limits, but as these are expanding to notionally include the separate administrative areas of Bekasi, Tangerang, Depok and further, it is virtually impossible to quantify. Every work day, the population expands by some eight million commuters.

## Ethnic Groups
Representatives of every group in Indonesia can be found in Jakarta apart from those groups who hold fast to their traditional way of life, such as the Badui of West Java and the Mentawai of West Sumatra.

## Languages
*Bahasa Indonesia*. If you can understand Malay, you'll understand much of what is said. *Bahasa Gaul* is spoken by young people to confuse their elders.

## Religions
Predominantly Muslim, with Christian, both Protestant and Catholic, Buddhist and Hindu.

## Administrative Divisions
There is a city government with a directly elected governor and his deputy.

Below this, there are five mayoralties (*wali kota*), north, south, east, west and central.

Below this, there are *kecamatan* (district), e.g Tebet, which is divided into *kelurahan* (sub-district) e.g. Kebon Baru. These are further divided into RW (*rukan warga*) which is a neighbourhood which comprises lots of RT (*rukan tangga*) which is a street or two of about 40 houses.

New residents are supposed to introduce themselves to Ibu or Bapak RT (pronounced 'air tay') and copies of I.D are passed up the chain so that the authorities can keep tabs on the city's citizens.

## Currency
Rupiah (Rp). US$ 1 is approximately Rp 9,500.

## Economy
It can be said that Jakarta's economy is soundly based on servicing and managing the nation's economy. Major production and manufacturing is generally carried out in the satellite towns and vast industrial estates that ring the city.

## Gross Domestic Product (per capita)
Higher than any other Indonesian city. It was estimated before a measure of autonomy was given to the regions that up to 80 per cent of the country's wealth was in Jakarta. During *krismon*, much of it was sent elsewhere, such as Singapore and China, so GDP is probably lower. There is also, as elsewhere, a disproportionate distribution of wealth with the monthly minimum wage, for a basic nuclear family of parents and two children, set at Rp 1.2 million. Many have to survive on less.

## Imports & Exports
Jakarta, as Indonesia's business centre and capital city, has the major port at Tanjung Priok and the major international airport, Soekarno-Hatta at Cengkareng. It can therefore be stated with some confidence that it imports and exports a lot of everything.

## Icons
Monas—*Monumen nasional*—is on the city badge.

## Famous People

Anybody who is famous inevitably spends some time in Jakarta. They may become famous after arriving or be born here, but very few are actually real Jakartans. Most of the population claim affinity or birthright with their *kampung* which is somewhere else in the archipelago.

# CULTURE QUIZ

## SITUATION 1

You arrive at the house of a business colleague. You see shoes at the front door. What do you do?

**Ⓐ** Greet your host(s) and walk in.

**Ⓑ** Greet your host(s), take your shoes off and walk in.

**Ⓒ** Greet your host(s), leave your shoes on because they say it's okay and walk in.

**Ⓓ** Greet your host(s), take your shoes off although they say it's okay to leave them on.

### Comment

As always, try to fit in. If your hosts are bare-footed, then why not you? Unless the air-conditioning is set to Arctic temperatures, you'll find that bare or stockinged feet are more comfortable. So **Ⓑ** or **Ⓓ** are your best options.

## SITUATION 2

It is Ramadhan, the Muslim fasting month, and it's lunchtime. You are out shopping with your pre-school children and they are hungry. It seems that all the restaurants are shut. What do you do?

**Ⓐ** Pop in a supermarket and buy some snacks.
**Ⓑ** Bang on the door of the nearest one and demand they open.
**Ⓒ** Tell your children to stop whining and to think of the millions of starving Ruritanians.
**Ⓓ** Find the nearest mall as they are never shut and you are bound to find a fast food place open.

## COMMENTS

Young children, along with menstruating and pregnant women, are not expected to fast. Nor are the 10 per cent of the population who are not Muslims. Many restaurants are shut during daylight, fasting hours and some, especially Padang, do shut for the month as the staff take their annual holidays back in their hometowns. Answers **Ⓐ** and **Ⓓ** are best. If 'forced' to eat in public, do it discreetly.

## SITUATION 3

After washing your hands in a public toilet, perhaps in an office building or mall, you discover that there is no towel or hot air drying machine. What do you do?

**Ⓐ** Shout loudly for someone in authority.
**Ⓑ** Berate the cleaner standing in the corner watching you.
**Ⓒ** Shake your hands until they're dry enough to wipe on your trousers.
**Ⓓ** Get some toilet tissue and use that.

## Comments

If there are no drying facilities, there are no drying facilities. The cleaner may be able to provide some tissue, but you should carry a stock so you are ready for this common situation. You are only likely to find toilet paper on your travels if you frequent four and five-star hotels. If you smile with recognition at **Ⓒ**, what are you doing reading this book? You're fully acclimatised.

## SITUATION 4
Which of the following is not acceptable behaviour?

Ⓐ You immediately go to the head of a queue.
Ⓑ Stopping at the bottom of the escalator to plan your day.
Ⓒ Punching all the buttons as you leave the lift.
Ⓓ Getting on the lift before anybody can get off.

### Comments
Indonesians will join a queue if it is marked out with railings, for example in hypermarkets and in some banks, which makes jumping to the front difficult. If there isn't one, then being first is a point of pride. Anyone of a frail disposition is advised to carry a walking stick or stout umbrella with which to thwack miscreants and to move folk standing at the top or bottom of escalators whilst speaking on both their cellphones. Getting on or off lifts is similarly fraught with difficulties, so option Ⓒ is the only one which will leave you feeling smug. And everyone else seriously pissed off.

If you really like queues, then open an account in a branch of Bank Central asia, popularly known as Bank Cinta Antri—the bank which loves queues. Great queues, lousy service.

## SITUATION 5
What kind of driver are you? (Hint: there is just one wrong answer.)

Ⓐ You obey the Highway Code.
Ⓑ You regard traffic signals and stop signs with indifference.
Ⓒ You travel everywhere by taxi.
Ⓓ You obey the traffic policemen.

The only wrong answer is Ⓐ because it doesn't exist as an enforceable body of regulations. Many street signs and traffic lights (Ⓑ) are obscured by trees or advertising hoardings or there are a few policemen standing around whose job is to over-ride these 'rules'. If you are a driver, obviously you should obey these policemen (Ⓓ), so make sure you have with you your ID (or scanned and laminated copies) as well as that of the vehicle at all times. Have a crisp banknote handy as well; ask around for the current rate of traffic 'fine'. Your best option is to not drive at all. Let someone else (**C**) take the strain.

## SITUATION 6

At a social gathering, someone makes a derogatory remark, in English, about *bules*—a word commonly used when talking about Caucasian expats. Its literal meaning is 'albino' and you are offended at differentiation based on skin colour. What do you do?

**A** Ignore it.
**B** Tell the speaker she/he is a racist.
**C** Ignore it, but vow not to socialise with this person again.
**D** Ask the speaker why Indonesians use skin whitening cream and tourists come to get a suntan on Bali's beaches.

## Comments

Most Indonesians will not have considered the power of language to offend, and few will understand Western culture, except as garnered from movies. Although the Dutch colonial era finished back in 1950, white folk are still viewed as 'rich' and, therefore, separate. Indeed many, but by no means all, are. The greeting "Hello, mister", tiresome though it can be in its frequency, and the word *bule* are rarely used with offensive intent.

For all the sloganeering about 'Unity In Diversity', since the Asian Economic meltdown of the late nineties and the beginning of *reformasi*, life has been a struggle for the majority of the population. A measure of self-governance, if not autonomy, has been 'granted' to the regions, thus enabling certain politicians and business people to enrich themselves, generally at the expense of the masses. Inevitably this has also given rise to numerous communal conflicts, often along religious fault lines which are, in themselves, a reflection of the country's ethnic diversity. White folk are but one more ethnic group.

If you respond **B**, i.e. aggressively, you will be reinforcing the stereotype and if you choose **C**, it could well be your loss. Depending on the circumstances, **D** is the best answer, but only if you expect a reasonably polite response. Otherwise **A**.

## SITUATION 7

It beggars belief the number of people who come to your front gate asking for money. They may be street musicians, collecting for their mosque, offering to spray your garden as a protection against mosquitoes or be obviously and abjectly poor. What do you do?

**A** Keep your front door shut.
**B** Empty your pockets of small change every time they call.
**C** Have a weekly budget for your charitable alms.
**D** Shout at them to go away.

### Comments

There is a fifth choice: live in an apartment. You'll miss out on some great street entertainment if you do, but you won't be bothered over much. There is, of course, no one right answer. If you can afford to come to Indonesia, then you can afford to give some small change to those less well off.

However, beware the con artists such as garden sprayers who use your water and charge the earth, if you'll excuse the pun. Many folk come equipped with a form which purports to come from a *yayasan* (charitable foundation); this will have a list of signatures, simplistic addresses and the amount supposedly donated. If in the five figure range, then be suspicious. Ask to see the *surat izin* (permission letter) from the local RT or RW, your community leaders.

If your visitors claim to be meter readers or other 'officials', for example those asking to check your gas cylinders, and you don't recognise them, make a great show of checking and writing down their ID details. And tell them to come back when you're not busy.

If you do decide to give some money, do it quietly and in small doses. The more you give, the more you'll be known as an easy mark. You may well find a better outlet for your altruism through volunteering. Check the 'Living In Indonesia' website (http://www.expat.or.id) for possibilities.

# DO'S AND DON'TS

## DO'S

- Say *selamat pagi, selamat siang, selamat soré* or *selamat malam* when greeting someone.
- Scan important documents or photocopy them, and keep them separate from the originals.
- Carry a stock of lesser value banknotes; then there's no excuse for anyone to tell you that they haven't got change. (*Tidak ada uang kecil, mister.*)
- Take normal precautions with your valuables.
- Remove your shoes when entering a mosque, temple or someone's house.
- Bring back small *oleh-oleh* (token gifts) if you leave Jakarta for a short while. Snacks for family, friends and colleagues are perfectly acceptable.
- Keep your 'alternative' lifestyle discreet.

## DON'TS

- Do not start eating before others or, if a guest, until invited to do so.
- Don't use your left hand to eat, give or receive anything.
- Do not stand with your hands on your hips however comfortable this feels as this gets interpreted as a sign of anger.
- Similarly, folded arms can also be misconstrued.
- Do not lose your temper unless you've tried everything else.
- Don't stroll around town as if you were on Kuta beach. Not even the poorest construction worker wears shorts, and you'll rarely see an Indonesian woman exposing her arms or legs. Unfortunately.
- Don't touch anyone but very young children on the head.
- Don't point with your feet. In fact, make every pointing action a little wavy.
- Don't display too much affection to anyone; in public, kiss your spouse discretely, if you must.
- Don't litter. Set an ostentatious example.

- Don't smoke without first asking if it is acceptable. It's not on public transport.
- Don't spit in public, even though Indonesians do. It's really disgusting.
- Don't photocopy this book. Please.

# GLOSSARY

## A

| Bahasa | Meaning |
|---|---|
| ada | there is, there are |
| aduh | oh dear, blimey, wow |
| air matang | clean, boiled water |
| air minum | drinking water |
| air putih | plain, 'white' water |
| anak | child |
| anda | you (polite form) |
| aneh | odd, weird |
| angkuh | arrogant |
| anjing | dog |
| antik | antique, ancient |
| apa | what |
| apotik | chemist, pharmacy |
| ari-ari | placenta, abdomen |
| arisan | social gathering, involves small-scale gambling |
| Arjuna | hero of the Mahabharata; also refers to a playboy |
| asal | origins, source, cause |
| Awas! | Watch out! Danger! |

## B

| Bahasa | Meaning |
|---|---|
| babi | pig |
| badut | clown |
| bahagia | happy |
| bahasa | language |
| bahasa | danger |

| Bahasa | Meaning |
|--------|---------|
| bajaj | moterised pedicab |
| baju-baju | clothes |
| bakmi goreng | fried noodles |
| bakso | meatballs, usually in soup |
| banci | transvestite |
| bandar | harbour, port |
| bangun | tidur, wake up |
| banjir | flood |
| bapak | father, father figure |
| baru | new |
| basa-basi | good manners, courteous small-talk |
| Batak | native of North Sumatra |
| batik | printed pattern |
| bau | smell (aften—bad smell) |
| bayi | baby |
| belimbing | starfruit |
| bemo | motorised public transport vehicle |
| bengkel | workshop (often for cars) |
| beras hitam | uncooked black rice |
| beras merah | uncooked 'red' (or brown) rice |
| berwarna | coloured |
| besok | tomorrow |
| Betawi | person native to Jakarta |
| biji | seed |
| binatang | animal |
| bingung | confused, puzzled, bewildered |
| bintang | star (also brand name of beer) |
| bir | beer |
| bisa | can, be able to, could |
| bodoh | dumb, stupid |
| bubur | porridge, general mush |

| Bahasa | Meaning |
|--------|---------|
| bukan | not, no |
| bule | white person, albino, pale |
| bumi | earth |
| bunga | flower |
| burung | bird |

## C

| Bahasa | Meaning |
|--------|---------|
| campur | mixed, blended |
| cantik | pretty |
| cari | look for |
| cerewet | talkative, fussy |
| cetak | print |
| cewek | girl |
| cicak | house lizard |
| cinta | love |
| cium | kiss, smell |
| coba | try, attempt |
| cocok | suitable, agreeable |
| contoh | example, specimen |
| cowok | boy, lad |
| cuci | wash |
| cuci-mata | window-shopping, girl-watching |
| cukup | enough |

## D

| Bahasa | Meaning |
|--------|---------|
| dengan | with |
| dijual | for sale |
| disini | here |
| djarum | needle |

| Bahasa | Meaning |
|--------|---------|
| doctor umum | general practitioner |
| domestik | domestic |
| dua | two |
| duit | money, cash |
| dulu | previously |

## E

| Bahasa | Meaning |
|--------|---------|
| e'ek | poo-poo (child talk) |
| eksperimen | experiment |
| emas | gold |
| ember | bucket |

## G

| Bahasa | Meaning |
|--------|---------|
| gabah | unhulled raw rice |
| gado-gado | salad with peanut sauce |
| Gambang Kromong | Chinese-influenced, Jakartan gamelan music |
| gamelan | orchestra, 'classical' Indonesian music |
| gangguan | disturbances, hassle |
| ganja | marijuana |
| garam | salt |
| gatal | itchy |
| gila | mad, crazy, loopy, potty |
| gila uang | money-mad |
| goblok | really stupid |
| golok | machete |
| got | gutter; drain |
| gotong-royong | mutual cooperation |
| gudang | warehouse, storeroom |

| Bahasa | Meaning |
|--------|---------|
| gulai ayam | chicken curry |
| gulai kambing | lamb curry |
| guntur | thunder |
| gunung sampah | rubbish mountain |

## H

| Bahasa | Meaning |
|--------|---------|
| habis | finished, all gone |
| halilintar | lightning |
| hansip | neighbourhood watchman |
| hatu | ghost |
| Hanuman | monkey hero in the Ramayana epic |
| hanya | only, just |
| harum | nice-smelling, fragrant |
| hati-hati | be careful |
| hidup | alive, on, e.g. lamp |
| hitam | black |
| hujan | rain |

## I

| Bahasa | Meaning |
|--------|---------|
| ibu | mother, older woman |
| ibu kota | capital city |
| ikan goreng | fried fish |
| Indomie | legendary local brand of instant noodles |
| ini | this |
| intan | diamond |
| itu | that |

# J

| Bahasa | Meaning |
|--------|---------|
| jahat | evil, nasty, horrible |
| jalan | road/street, to walk, to function |
| jam | hour, time |
| jambu air | rose-apple fruit |
| jamu | traditional tonic of medicinal herbs |
| jangan | don't |
| janur | palm leaves—usually arranged as wedding decoration |
| jauh | far |
| jilbab | Islamic female headgear |
| jongkok | squatting, crouching |
| jorok | rude, dirty-minded, slovenly |
| jus alpukat | avocado juice |

# K

| Bahasa | Meaning |
|--------|---------|
| kakak | older relative |
| kaki lima | street vendor's cart—'five legs' including the vendor's two |
| kalau | if, when |
| kamar kecil | small room, toilet |
| kambing | goat |
| kampung | village, lower-class residential area, slum |
| kampungan | uncool, unrefined, countrified |
| kamu | you |
| kanan | right (not left) |
| kancing | button |
| kantor | office, work place |
| Kapal Api | steam boat, brand name of local coffee |

| Bahasa | Meaning |
|--------|---------|
| kapur sirih | lime for chewing with betel nut |
| karet | rubber |
| kartu | card |
| kasih | give, love |
| kasihan | pity, sympathy, mercy |
| kau | you (informal) |
| kaya | rich |
| kayu manis | scented wood, cinnamon |
| ke | to |
| kebebasan pribadi | privacy |
| kebun | garden |
| kecoa | cockroach |
| kehormatan | respect |
| kemanusiaan | humanity |
| kemarin | yesterday, the day before |
| kenapa | why |
| keriting | curly |
| kerja keras | hard work |
| kerokan | painful massage with coin |
| kesabaran | patience |
| kesehatan | health |
| ketan | sticky rice |
| ketoprak | salad with tofu and peanut sauce |
| kijang | antelope, brand name for popular vehicle |
| kiri | left (not right) |
| kita | we (to include the person addressed) |
| konsultan | consultant |
| kontol | penis (very bad word) |
| kopi | coffee |
| kost | room and board |

| Bahasa | Meaning |
|--------|---------|
| kretek | clove cigarette |
| kroncong | Portuguese-influenced popular music |
| kuat | strong |
| kuching | cat |
| kue | cake |
| kuntilanak | evil child-hunting spirit in Javanese folklore |
| kunyit | turmeric |
| kuping-kuping | ears |

## L

| Bahasa | Meaning |
|--------|---------|
| lagi | again, more |
| lagu cinta | love song |
| laki-laki | men |
| lalapan sayur | dish of raw vegetables with hot sauce |
| lampu merah | red light, menstrual period (slang) |
| langsung | immediately, straight away |
| laten | latent |
| layang-layang | kite |
| lecek | dishevelled, worn out (Jakartan) |
| lelucon | joke |
| lem nasi | rice glue |
| lem tikus | rat glue |
| lengkuas | ginger plant variant |
| lewat | via, by way of |
| lihat | look |
| listrik | electricity |
| loe | you (very informal—Jakartan) |

# M

| Bahasa | Meaning |
|---|---|
| ma'af | sorry, excuse me |
| mabuk | drunk, delirious |
| macet | jammed, stuck |
| madu | honey |
| mainan | toy |
| makan | eat |
| maling | thief |
| malu | shy, bashful, reluctant |
| mandi | to bathe |
| mangga | mango |
| manggis | mangosteen |
| manis | sweet |
| martabak | thick crepe (sweet or savoury) |
| mas | older brother/relative, contemporary male (Javanese) |
| masak | cook |
| masuk angin | flu-like illness, 'entered wind' |
| matahari | sun |
| mau | want, desire |
| mbak | older sister/relative (like mas), contemporary female |
| mesjid | mosque |
| mie pangsit | ravioli-style noodles |
| mie rebus | boiled, plain noodles |
| mikrolet | localised public transport service |
| minum | drink |
| miskin | poor |
| Monas | national monument |
| monyet | monkey |
| mudah-mudahan | hopefully |
| mungkin | maybe, perhaps |

| Bahasa | Meaning |
|--------|---------|
| musholla | small mosque; praying room |
| musim hujan | wet, rainy season |
| musim kering | dry season |

## N

| Bahasa | Meaning |
|--------|---------|
| nanas | pineapple |
| nasi | cooked rice |
| nasi goreng | fried rice |
| nasi pulan | well-cooked rice |
| nasi putih | plain rice |
| nasi rawon | beef-stew with rice |
| nasi uduk | coconut-based rice dish |
| negara | state |
| nenek | grandma, any older woman |
| nggak | no (slang—Jakarta) |
| nyamuk | mosquito |

## O

| Bahasa | Meaning |
|--------|---------|
| obat | medicine |
| ojek | motorcycle and rider used as public transport |
| oleh-oleh | gift, present given as souvenir of one's holiday |
| operasi | operation |
| orang | person |
| orang Jawa | Javanese person |
| orang-orang | people |
| oseng-oseng | stir-fried dish with chilli |

## P

| Bahasa | Meaning |
| --- | --- |
| pak | shorter form of *bapak* |
| paling | most (general superlative form) |
| Pancasila | the state ideology |
| panggil | call, summon |
| panjang | long, lengthy |
| pantat | bottom, bum |
| Pasaraya | grand market, Jakarta's famous department store |
| payung | umbrella |
| peci | black rimless hat, usually black and worn by male Muslims |
| pelacur | prostitute |
| pelit | mean, stingy |
| pembantu | helper, servant, maid |
| pemulung | rubbish collector, scavenger |
| pendidikan | education |
| penduduk | citizen |
| penting | important |
| perempuan | woman |
| petani | farmer |
| pinang areca | nut |
| pisang | banana |
| polisi | police |
| polisi tidur | traffic hump, 'sleeping policeman' |
| preman | villain |
| puasa | fasting |
| pulang | go home |
| pulang kampung | go home (specifically to place of origin, especially village) |
| pusing | dizzy, lightheaded |

# R

| Bahasa | Meaning |
| --- | --- |
| rakyat | the masses, common populace |
| rambut | hair |
| rame | crowded, busy |
| rasa | taste, feeling, sensation, vibe |
| Rinso | legendary all-round local washing powder |
| ronggeng | performing dancing girl |
| rujak | fruit salad with spicy sauce |
| Rukun Tetangga (RT) | neighbourhood cooperative |
| Rukun Warga (RW) | administrative unit one level above RT |
| rumah | house |
| rumah makan | restaurant |
| rumah sakit | hospital |

# S

| Bahasa | Meaning |
| --- | --- |
| sakit flu | the common cold, perhaps influenza |
| sakit perut | stomachache |
| sama | the same as |
| sambal terasi | pungent fish-paste |
| sampah | rubbish |
| santai | relax |
| saron | xylophone-style instrument found in gamelan music |
| sarung | all-purpose wraparound cloth |
| sate | grilled meat on a stick, usually with peanut sauce |
| satu | one |
| selendang | sling scarf |

| Bahasa | Meaning |
|---|---|
| semampai | slender |
| semangat pemuda | spirit of youth, lust for life |
| semeter | one metre |
| senang | happy, content, pleased |
| sendiri | on your own |
| sering kebanjiran | prone to flooding |
| silakan | please, go ahead, 'be my guest' |
| sop ayam | chicken soup |
| sopir | driver |
| sudah | already, done |
| Sudah mandi? | Have you bathed yet? |
| suka | like |
| sulit | difficult, tricky |
| surya | sun |
| susah | difficult, hard |
| swalayan | self-service |

## T

| Bahasa | Meaning |
|---|---|
| tadi | earlier, just now |
| tahu goreng | fried tofu |
| tai | excrement (bad word) |
| tanda | sign |
| tanggal | date |
| teh | tea |
| teh manis | tea with sugar |
| teh pahit | tea without sugar |
| telor | egg |
| teman | friend, pal |
| tempat | place |
| tempat | tidur sleeping place, bed |
| tempe | fermented soya-bean cake |

| Bahasa | Meaning |
|---|---|
| terus | go on, straight ahead, continue |
| tetek | breast |
| tidak | no |
| tidak apa-apa | it doesn't matter, don't worry about it |
| tidur | sleep |
| tikus | rat |
| tingkat | floor, storey, level |
| tokek | gecko |
| toko | shop |
| tolong | please, *por favor* |
| tukang | tradesman/craftsman (very general) |
| tukang | *parkir* parking assistant |
| tukang sate | *sate* seller |

## U

| Bahasa | Meaning |
|---|---|
| uang | money |
| umbul-umbul | Betawi wedding decoration |
| untuk | for, e.g. *untuk apa?* (what for?) |

## W

| Bahasa | Meaning |
|---|---|
| warung | small shop or stall |
| waspada | beware of |
| wong Londo | foreign person (Javanese) |

## Y

| Bahasa | Meaning |
|---|---|
| yang | the one that/which/who, etc |
| yang dingin | a cold one, one which is cold |

# RESOURCE GUIDE

## EMBASSIES IN JAKARTA

You may wish to visit the embassies listed below to obtain a visa for entry to the respective countries. Alternatively, as a foreign resident in Indonesia, you need to be in touch with your embassy (*keduta'an besar*) for a variety of reasons such as passport renewal or trade. Most embassies advise resident expats that they register their presence in Indonesia with their consular office. Some embassies have consulates in other cities in Indonesia, usually Surabaya, Medan and/or Denpasar.

If the foreign government whose embassy you are looking for doesn't appear below, it may be because we haven't listed it or they don't actually have an embassy in Jakarta. Check on the foreign ministry website of the country concerned, and see which is their nearest embassy (to Indonesia) as it may have jurisdiction over requests coming from Indonesia. These embassies are often located in Singapore, Kuala Lumpur, Manila or Hong Kong.

Alternatively, call directory enquiries—108—and ask "*Minta tolong, nomor telpon keduta'an besar negara* (name of country)."

Please note that most embassies are in the central area (Golden Triangle) of Jakarta. If they are not housed in purpose-built structures (e.g. those of Australia, Malaysia, Russia and United States of America), they may move premises.

## North America

- **Embassy of Canada**
  World Trade Centre, 6th Floor
  Jl. Jend. Sudirman, Kav. 29
  Jakarta 12920
  Tel: (21) 2550-7800
  Fax: (21) 2550-7811
  Website: http://www.dfait-maeci.gc.ca/
  Email: jkrta@international.gc.ca

- **Embassy of the United States of America**
  Jl. Medan Merdeka Selatan No. 5
  Jakarta Pusat 10110
  Tel: (21) 3435-9000, 344-2211
  Fax: (21) 386-2259
  Email: jakconsul@state.gov (consular section)
  Website: http://www.usembassyjakarta.org

## Central America
- **Embassy of México**
  Menara Mulia Building, 23rd floor
  Jl. Jend. Gatot Subroto Kav. 9-11
  Jakarta Selatan 12930
  Tel: (21) 520-3980
  Fax: (21) 520-3978
  Email: embmexic@rad.net.id

## South America
- **Embassy of the Republic of Argentina**
  Menara Mulia Building, 19th floor
  Jl. Jend. Gatot Subroto Kav. 9-11
  Jakarta Selatan 12930
  Tel: (21) 526-5661, 526-5662
  Fax: (21) 526-5664
  Email: embargen@cbn.net.id
- **Embassy of the Federative Republic of Brazil**
  Menara Mulia Building, 16th floor
  Jl. Jend. Gatot Subroto Kav. 9-11
  Jakarta Selatan 12930
  Tel: (21) 526-5656, 526-5657, 526-5658
  Fax: (21) 526-5659
  Email: embrasil@cbn.net.id
- **Embassy of the Republic of Chile**
  Bina Mulia Building I, 7th floor
  Jl. H.R. Rasuna Said Kav. 10
  Kuningan, Jakarta Selatan 12950
  Tel: (21) 520-1131, 520-1132
  Fax: (21) 520-1955
  Email: emchijak@indosat.net.id

- **Embassy of Peru**
  Menara Rajawali 12th Fl
  Jl. Mega Kuningan Lot. # 5-1
  Jakarta Selatan 12950
  Tel: (21) 576-1820, 520-1866, 520-1176
  Fax: (21) 520-1932
  Email: embaperu@cbn.net.id
- **Embassy of the Republic of Venezuela**
  Menara Mulia, 20th floor
  Jl. Jend. Gatot Subroto Kav. 9-11
  Jakarta Selatan 12930
  Tel: (21) 522-7547, 522-7548
  Fax: (21) 522-7549
  Email: evenjakt@cbn.net.id

## Europe
- **Embassy of Austria**
  Jl. Diponegoro No. 44
  Menteng, Jakarta Pusat 10310
  Tel: (21) 338-090, 338-101
  Fax: (21) 390-4927
  Email: auambjak@rad.net.id
- **Royal Belgian Embassy**
  Deutsche Bank Building, 16th floor
  Jl. Imam Bonjol No. 80
  Menteng, Jakarta Pusat 10310
  Tel: (21) 316-2030
  Fax: (21) 316-2035
  Email: jakarta@diplobel.org, ambeljkt@rad.net.id
- **Royal Danish Embassy**
  Menara Rajawali, 25th Floor
  Jl. Mega Kuningan Lot #5.1
  Jakarta 12950
  Tel: (21) 576-1478
  Fax: (21) 576-1535
  Email: dkemb9@cbn.net.id, jktamb@um.dk
  Website: http://www.emb-denmark.or.id
- **Embassy of Greece**
  Plaza 89, 12th floor

Jl. H.R. Rasuna Said Kav. X-7 No. 6
Kuningan, Jakarta 12540
Tel: (21) 520-7776
Fax: (21) 520-7753
Email: grembas@cbn.net.id

- **Embassy of the Republic of Hungary**
Jl. H.R. Rasuna Said Kav. X-3
Kuningan, Jakarta Selatan 12950
Tel: (21) 520-3459, 520-3460
Fax: (21) 520-3461
Email: huembjkt@rad.net.id
Website: http://www.huembjkt.or.id

- **Embassy of the Republic of Italy**
Jl. Diponegoro No. 45
Menteng, Jakarta Pusat 10310
Tel: (21) 337-445
Fax: (21) 337-422
Email: embitaly@italambjkt.or.id
Website: http://www.italambjkt.or.id

- **Embassy of Finland**
Menara Rajawali, 9th floor
Jalan Mega Kuningan, Lot No. 5.1
Kawasan Mega Kuningan, Jakarta 12950
Tel: (21) 576-1650
Fax: (21) 576-1631
Email: sanomat.jak@formin.fi
Website: http://www.finland.or.id

- **Embassy of France**
20 Jalan Thamrin
Jakarta Pusat 10350
Phone: (21) 314-2807
Fax: (021) 392-9678
Website: http://www.ambafrance-id.org

- **Embassy of the Federative Republic of Germany**
Jl. M.H. Thamrin No. 1, Menteng, Jakarta Pusat 10310
Tel: (21) 390-1750
Fax: (21) 390-1757
Email: germany@rad.net.id
Website: http://www.germanembjak.or.id/

- **Royal Netherlands Embassy**
  Jl. H.R. Rasuna Said Kav. S-3
  Kuningan, Jakarta Selatan 12950
  Tel: (21) 525-1515
  Fax: (21) 570-0734
  Email: jak@minbuza.nl
  Website: http://www.netherlandsembassy.or.id
- **Embassy of the Kingdom of Norway**
  Menara Rajawali Building, 25th floor
  Kawasan Mega Kuningan Lot 5.1
  Jakarta Selatan 12950
  Tel: (21) 576-1523, 576-1524
  Fax: (21) 576-1537
  Email: emb.jakarta@mfa.no
  Website: http://www.norwayemb-indonesia.org
- **Embassy of the Republic of Poland**
  Jl. H.R. Rasuna Said Kav. X Blok IV3
  Kuningan, Jakarta 12950
  Tel: (21) 252-5938/9, 252-5940/42
  Fax: (21) 252-5958
  Email: plembjkt@rad.net.id
- **Embassy of Portugal**
  Jalan Indramayu No. 2 A
  Menteng, Jakarta 10310
  Tel: (21) 3190-8030
  Fax: (21) 3190-8031
  Email: porembjak@cbn.net.id
- **Embassy of the Kingdom of Spain**
  Jl. H. Agus Salim No. 61
  Menteng, Jakarta Pusat 10350
  Tel: (21) 335-0771, 335-940
  Fax: (21) 325-996, 335-134
  Email: embespid@mail.mae.es
- **Embassy of the Kingdom of Sweden**
  Menara Rajawali, 9th Floor
  Jl. Mega Kuningan Lot No. 5.1
  Jakarta Selatan 12950
  Tel: (21) 2553-5900
  Fax: (21) 576-2691

Email: ambassaden.jakarta@foreign.ministry.se
Website: http://www.swedenabroad.com/jakarta

- **Embassy of Switzerland**
Jl. H.R. Rasuna Said Kav. X3-2
Kuningan, Jakarta Selatan 12950
Tel: (21) 525-6061
Fax: (21) 520-2289
Email: vertretung@jak.rep.admin.ch
Website: http://www.eda.admin.ch/

- **Embassy of the Federal Republic of Yugoslavia**
Jl. H.O.S. Cokroaminoto No. 109
Menteng, Jakarta Pusat 10310
Tel: (21) 314-3560, 334-157
Fax: (21) 314-3613
Email: ambajaka@rad.net.id

- **Her Britannic Majesty's Embassy (UK)**
Jl. M.H. Thamrin No. 75
Menteng, Jakarta Pusat 10310
Tel: (21) 315-6264
Consular section: (21) 316-0858
Email: Consulate.Jakarta@fco.gov.uk
Website: http://www.britain-in-indonesia.or.id

## Arabia

- **Embassy of the State of Kuwait**
Jl. Teuku Umar No. 51
Menteng, Jakarta Pusat
Tel: (21) 391-2284, 391-2285, 391-9625
Fax: (21) 391-9472
Email: ami@kuwait-toplist.com

- **Embassy of the Kingdom of Morocco**
Kuningan Plaza South Tower, Suite 512
Jl. H.R. Rasuna Said Kav. C11-14
Jakarta Selatan 12940
Tel: (21) 520-0773, 520-0956
Fax: (21) 520-0586
Email: sifamajakar@cbn.net.id

- **Embassy of the Kingdom of Saudi Arabia**
Jl. M.T. Haryono Kav. 27

Cawang Atas, Jakarta Timur 13630
Tel: (21) 801-1536, 801-1537
Fax: (21) 801-1527

- **Embassy of the United Arab Emirates**
  Jl. Prof. Dr. Satrio No. 16-17
  Jakarta Selatan 12950
  Tel: (21) 520-6518, 520-6552
  Fax: (21) 520-6526
  Email: uaeemb@rad.net.id

## Africa

- **Embassy of the Federal Republic of Nigeria**
  Jl. Taman Patra XIV No. 11A
  Kuningan Timur, Jakarta Selatan 12950
  Tel: (21) 526-0922, 526-0923
  Fax: (21) 526-0924
- **Embassy of South Africa**
  Wisma GKBI, Suite 705
  Jl. Jend. Sudirman Kav. 28
  Jakarta Pusat 10210
  Tel: (21) 574-0660
  Fax: (21) 574-0661
  Email: saembassy@centrin.net.id
  Website: http://www.southafricanembassy-jakarta.or.id/

## Asia

- **Embassy of Australia**
  Jl. H.R. Rasuna Said Kav. C15-16
  Kuningan, Jakarta Selatan 12940
  Tel: (21) 2550-5555
  Fax: (21) 522-7101, 526-1690
  Email: public.affairsjakt@dfat.gov.au
  Website: http://www.austembjak.or.id
  AusAID: http://www.indo.ausaid.gov.au/
- **Embassy of India**
  Jl. H.R. Rasuna Said Kav. S-1
  Kuningan, Jakarta Selatan 12950
  Tel: (21) 520-4150, 520-4152, 520-4157
  Fax: (21) 520-4160

Email: eoiisi@indo.net.id
Website: http://www.embassyofindiajakarta.org

- **Embassy of Japan**
Jl. M.H. Thamrin 24
Jakarta Pusat 10350
Tel: (21) 3192-4308
Fax: (21) 3192-5460
Website: http://www.id.emb-japan.go.jp

- **Embassy of the Republic of Korea**
Jl. Jend. Gatot Subroto Kav. 57-58
Kuningan, Jakarta Selatan 12930
Tel: (21) 520-1915
Fax: (21) 525-4159

- **New Zealand Embassy**
Gedung BRI II, 23rd floor
Jl. Jend. Sudirman Kav. 44-46
Jakarta Pusat 10210
Tel: (21) 570-9460
Fax: (21) 570-9457
Email: nzembjak@cbn.net.id

- **Embassy of the Islamic Republic of Pakistan**
Jl. Teuku Umar No. 50
Menteng, Jakarta Pusat 10350
Tel: (21) 314-4008, 310-4009
Fax: (21) 310-3945
Email: parepjkt@rad.net.id
Website: http://www.pakistanembassyjakarta.com

- **Embassy of the Russian Federation**
Jl. H. R. Rasuna Said Kav. 7 No. 1-2
Kuningan, Jakarta Selatan 12950
Tel: (21) 522-2912, 522-2914
Fax: (21) 522-2916, 522-2915
Email: rusembjkt@dnet.net.id

- **Embassy of the Democratic Socialist Republic of Sri Lanka**
Jl. Diponegoro No. 70
Menteng, Jakarta Pusat 10310
Tel: (21) 314-1018, 3190-2389
Fax: (21) 310-7962

## South-East Asia

- **Embassy of the Lao People's Democratic Republic**
  Jl. Patra Kuningan XIV No. 1A
  Kuningan, Jakarta Selatan 12950
  Tel: (21) 522-9602, 522-7862
  Fax: (21) 522-9601
- **Embassy of Malaysia**
  Jl. H.R. Rasuna Said Kav. X-6 No. 1-3
  Kuningan, Jakarta Selatan 12950
  Tel: (21) 522-4947
  Fax: (21) 522-4974
  Email: mwjkarta@indosat.net.id
- **Embassy of the Republic of the Philippines**
  Jl. Imam Bonjol No. 6-8
  Menteng, Jakarta Pusat 10310
  Tel: (21) 315-5118, 3109-2789
  Fax: (21) 315-1167, 314-9773
  Email: phjkt@indo.net.id
- **Embassy of the Republic of Singapore**
  Jl. H.R. Rasuna Said Kav. X-4 No. 2
  Kuningan, Jakarta Selatan 12950
  Tel: (21) 520-1489, 5296-1433
  Fax: (21) 520-1486
  Consular Fax: (21) 520 2320
  Email: singemb_jkt@sgmfa.gov.sg
  Website: http://www.mfa.gov.sg/jkt/main.html
- **Royal Thai Embassy**
  Jl. Imam Bonjol No. 74
  Menteng, Jakarta Pusat 10310
  Tel: (21) 390-4052
  Fax: (21) 310-7469, 390-4055
  Email: thaijkt@indo.net.id
- **Embassy of the Socialist Republic of Vietnam**
  Jl. Teuku Umar No. 25
  Menteng, Jakarta Pusat 10350
  Tel: (21) 310-0357, 310-0358, 310-0359
  Fax: (21) 314-9615

## SCHOOLING

If you arrive in Jakarta on a sponsored expatriate package, you should be given all the help you need to secure good schooling for your children. Your company should pay for your children's education whilst here. There are some 15 international schools in Jakarta listed here which offer the curricula of your home country from pre-school up to internationally accepted schooling-leaving qualifications such as the International Baccalaureat (IB) and the International General Certificate in Secondary Education (IGCSE).

If you are recruited locally, you may not have the full expat package in which case the international schools fees could well be beyond your financial reach.

There are alternatives.

## Preschools

Within Jakarta you will find a wide variety of preschool options for your young children, from informal play groups with friends, to neighborhood kindergartens (*taman kanak-kanak* or TK), to international standard preschools.

Indonesian pre-schools (TK) are geared to a more academic approach, preparing children for entry to the school system, with an emphasis on writing skills. The language of tuition will generally be Indonesian.

You may prefer more creative play and social experiences for your youngsters, in which case consider the many franchise operations with international facilities and a curriculum overseen by expatriate 'consultants' with experience and qualifications in pre-school education. These will inevitably be more expensive as they have to pay franchise fees.

What is important is the quality of the teaching. Most pre-schools offer a 'free trial'; spend the time seeing how comfortable your child is with the adults and other children, compare facilities, ask about the curriculum and find out what is the main language of communication. You may find a mix of nationalities so your toddler could turn into a polyglot.

Observe the relationships children have with each other and the staff. How are problems dealt with? What are the disciplinary procedures? Harsh or kind words?

Although travel is a hassle in Jakarta, the nearest facility is not necessarily the best. But how easy is it to get to? Spending time in a traffic jam is no joy for anyone, let alone small children. Consider the school site and ask a few basic questions. Is it on a major road? How secure is it? Can strangers wander in or the kids get out?

## Indonesian 'National Plus' Schools

In the mid-1990s, the Indonesian Department of Education and Culture began to open opportunities for the development of what are termed 'national plus' schools. These schools are expected to offer international and Indonesian curricula in parallel. A major emphasis has also been tuition in English, so many employ expatriate teachers.

Admission is open to expatriate children as well as for the children of mixed Indonesian-expat marriages. They have become popular with the middle classes, particularly the Indonesian-Chinese, and many have an overtly evangelical Christian bias.

There are a few national plus schools with excellent facilities, well-qualified and experienced teachers and good results, not only in academic examinations but also in sports and the arts.

However, there are also many schools which appear to be 'profit centres' rather than education institutes. These have poor facilities, with no play areas, art rooms, inadequately equipped art rooms and science and computer laboratories. Staff turnover is high and teachers that you meet may well be under qualified, if at all.

No inference should be drawn from the inclusion or non-inclusion of a school listed here.

Only you can determine which school is the most appropriate for your child, if it will prepare your child for the next step in their education or if you feel comfortable with the staff and the philosophy of the school. Trust your overall impression of the school—the environment, the professionalism of the staff, the well-being of the children, and the activities—both in and out of the classroom. If something doesn't feel right, just keep looking.

Ultimately, the choice is up to you, so remember that school years are said to be the best years of one's life; don't make a choice that you may regret, and your children too, for the rest of their lives.

Finally, note that enrollment in most Indonesian schools and universities begins in April of each year for July admission.

## National Plus Schools

- **Binus High (SMU Bina Nusantara)**
  Jl. Sultan Iskandar Muda Kav. G-8
  Jakarta Selatan 12220
  Tel: (21) 724-3663
  Fax: (621) 7278-3939
  Email: contactus@binus-school-jkt.sch.id
  Website: http://www.binus-school-jkt.sch.id
  Grades: 1–12
- **P.S.K.D. Mandiri**
  Jl. Dr. GSSY Ratulagi No. 5
  Jakarta Pusat 10310
  Tel: (21) 392-4384
  Fax: (21) 392-4401
  Email: admin@pskd-mandiri-jkt.sch.id
- **Sekolah Cita Buana**
  Wisma Subud Complex
  Jl RS Fatmawati No. 52
  Cilandak, Jakarta Selatan
  Tel: (21) 769-6560
  Fax: (21) 750-2616
  Email: cita@cbn.net.id
- **Sekolah Djuwita (TK-6)**
  Puri Gardena, Jl. Gardena Utama, Jakarta Barat
  Tel: (21) 541-5501
  Email: sekolahdjuwita@yahoo.com
  Website: http://www.sekolahdjuwita.com
- **Sekolah Global Jaya**
  Bintaro Jaya, Sektor IX

Jl. Raya Jombang, Pondok Aren
Tel:. (21) 745-7562
Fax: (21) 745-7561
Email: sekolah@globaljaya.com
Website: http://www.globaljaya.com

- **Sekeloh IPEKA**
Perumahan Puri Indah Blok I
Jakarta Barat 11610
Tel: (21) 580-9003-6
Email: ipeka.puri@ipeka.org
Website: http://www.ipeka.org/default.asp

- **Sekolah Lentera Kasih**
Jl. Danau Asri Timur Blok C3 No. 3
Sunter Jaya, Jakarta Utara 14350
Tel: (21) 6530-1621
Fax: (21) 851-5809
Email: slk@cbn.net.id
Website: http://www.lenterakasih.com

- **Sekolah Lentera International**
Jl. Sultan Iskandar Muda No. 30
Pondok Indah, Jakarta 12120
Tel: (21) 725-2284 / 85
Email: sli-edu@centrin.net.id
Website: http://www.sli-edu.com

- **Sekolah Mentari**
Jl. H. Jian No. 6
Cipete Utara, Jakarta Selatan
Tel/Fax: (21) 725-5412
Email: office-staff@sekolahmentari.or.id
Website: http://www.sekolahmentari.or.id

- **Sekolah Pelita Harapan**
Lippo Karawaci (K1–Year 12)
2500 Palem Raya Boulevard, Lippo Karawaci, Tangerang
Tel: (21) 546-0234
Fax: (21) 546-0248
Email: info@sph.ac.id
Website: http://www.sph.edu

- **Sekolah Tiara Bangsa**
Perum Raffles Hills

Jl. Alternatif Cibubur
Cimanggis, Depok
Tel: (21) 844-7938/9
Fax: (21) 844-7940
Email: info@stbangsa.org
Website: http://www.stbangsa.org

## International Schools in Jakarta Area

The following schools accept children of all nationalities, with English the primary language of tuition.

- **ACG International School**
  Jl. Warung Jati Barat No.19
  Ragunan, South Jakarta
  Tel: (21)780-5636
  Fax: (21) 781-4827
  Email: barbara.burns@acgedu.com
  Website: http://www.acgedu.com
  Curriculum: International/British and New Zealand
  All levels: Kindergarten (three years old) to grade 13
- **Australian International School (AIS)**
  Pejaten Campus—Secondary
  Tel: (21) 782-1141, 782-4024
  Fax: (21) 782-7871
  Email: pejaten@ais-indonesia.com
- **Kemang Campus—Primary**
  Tel: (21) 7179-2949, 719-8856, 7179-0437
  Fax: (21) 7179-0937
  Email: kemang@ais-indonesia.com
  Website: http://www.ais-indonesia.com
  Curriculum: Australian
  Levels: Kindergarten through Year 12.
- **Superkids-Bayi Gemes**
  Tel: (21) 719-7319
  Fax: (21) 718-1245
  Email: admin@koleseaustralia.or.id
  Website: http://www.gemes.or.id
- **British International School (BIS)**
  Bintaro Jaya Sektor 9
  Jl. Raya Jombang

Tangerang 15227
Tel: (21) 745-1670
Fax: (21) 745-1671
Email: enquiries@bis.or.id
Website: http://www.bis.or.id/
Curriculum: UK National Curriculum, GCSE/(I)GCSE, IB
All levels: Pre-School to Year 13 (ages 3-18)

- **Gandhi Memorial International School**
  PRJ Kompleks Kemayoran Blok D Kav. No.1
  Jakarta Pusat, Indonesia
  Tel: (21) 658-6566/8/9
  Fax: (21) 658-65677
  Email: headmaster@gandhijkt.org
  Website: http://www.gandhijkt.org
  Curriculum: IB (Geneva) Authorised Primary Years
  Programme (PYP), Middle Years Programme (MYP) and
  IB Diploma Programme
  All Levels

- **Jakarta International Montessori School (JIMS)**
  Komplek ISCI
  Jalan Ciputat Raya No. 2
  Jakarta 12063
  Tel: (21) 741-1222 or 744-4864
  Fax: (21) 741-1222
  Email: khresna@bit.net.id, jims@bit.net.id
  Website: http://www.kiefschools.com/
  Curriculum: Montessori Method from Pre-School leading
  to IGCSE and AS Levels, Advanced Placement Test and
  Scholastic Aptitude Test

- **Jakarta International School (JIS)**
  Admissions Office
  P.O. Box 1078 JKS
  Jakarta 12010
  Tel: (21) 769-2555 ext. 16566
  Fax: (21) 750-7650
  Email: admissions@jisedu.or.id
  Website: http://www.jisedu.org/
  Curriculum: British/Australian/New Zealand kindergarten
  All levels on four campuses

- **New Zealand International School (NZIS)**
  Jalan Benda No. 78 (Main office, Kindergarten, Primary and Lower Secondary)
  Kemang Raya No. 35 (Senior Secondary Campus)
  Kemang, Jakarta Selatan 12710
  Tel: (21) 7884-1225/6/7
  Fax: (21) 780-5541
  Email: principal@nzis.net
  Website: http://www.nzis.net
  New Zealand Curriculum (Kindergarten to Year 8)
  Curriculum: Cambridge University International Examinations (Secondary)
  Levels: Kindergarten to Year 13
- **North Jakarta International School (NJIS)**
  Jl. Raya Kelapa Nias
  Kelapa Gading Permai
  Jakarta Utara 14250
  Tel: (21) 450-0683
  Fax: (21) 450-0682
  Email: info@njis.or.id
  Website: http://www.njis.org
  Curriculum: American, assisted within an international framework with streaming towards IB and AP programmes for Senior High School
  Levels: Elementary, middle, and junior high school

The following schools primarily cater for children of a specific nationality with the language of tuition being that of the 'home' country.

- **Al-Haraman Al-Saudiah Academy**
  Jl. Cipinang Cempedak No. 25
  Jakarta Timur
  Tel: (21) 819-1254
  Fax: (21) 851-5154
  Email: saschool@centrin.net.id
  Curriculum: Saudi
  Levels: Elementary and junior high school
- **Deutsche Internationale Schule Jakarta**
  Jl. Puspa Widya No. 8

Bumi Serpong Damai
Tangerang 15322
Tel: (21) 537-8080
Fax: (21) 537-5102
Email: sekretariat@dis.or.id
Website: http://www.dis.or.id
Curriculum: German
Levels: Elementary and junior high school

- **Jakarta Japanese School**
Jl. Elang
Bintaro Jaya Sektor 9
Tel: (21) 745-4130
Fax: (21) 745-4140
Email: jakarta@jjs.or.id
Website: http://www.jjs.or.id
Curriculum: Japanese
Levels: Elementary and junior high school

- **Jakarta International Korean School**
Jl. Bina Marga No. 56
Ceger Timur, Jakarta Selatan
Tel: (21) 844-4958-61
Fax: (21) 844-4927
Email: jiks@jiks.com
Website: http://www.jiks.com
Curriculum: Korean
Levels: Elementary to senior high school

- **Jakarta Taipei School**
Jl. Raya Kelapa Hybrida Blok QH
Kelapa Gading Permai, Jakarta Timur 14240
Tel: (21) 452-3273
Fax: (62-21) 452-3272
Email: jts71568@rad.net.id
Curriculum: Taiwanese
Levels: Elementary and junior high school

- **Lycée International Français**
Jl. Cipete Dalam No. 32
Cipete, Jakarta Selatan 12410
Tel: (21) 750-3062
Fax: (21) 750-3624

Email: secretaire@lifdejakarta.org
Website: http://www.lifdejakarta.org
Curriculum: French
Levels: Elementary to senior high school
- **Nederlandse International School**
Jl. Jeruk Purut
Cilandak Timur, Jakarta Selatan 12560
Tel: (21) 782-3930
Fax: (21) 782-3929
Email: nisjak@cbn.net.id
Website: http://www.nis.or.id/
Curriculum: Dutch
Levels: Elementary to senior high school
- **Pakistan Embassy School**
Jl. Dempo Matraman Dalam II No.1
Matraman, Jakarta Pusat
Tel: (21) 390-4137, 390-4138
Email: pesjak@cbn.net.id
Website: http://www.geocities.com/pes_us/
Curriculum: Pakistani
Levels: Elementary and junior high school
- **Singapore International School**
Bona Vista Complex
Jl. Bona Vista Raya
Lebak Bulus, Jakarta Selatan 12440
Tel: (21) 7591-4414
Fax: (21) 7591-4418
Email: sisjkt@sisjakarta.com
Website: http://www.sisjakarta.com
Curriculum: Singaporean
All levels: Pre-Primary, Primary and Secondary

# FURTHER READING

Those wishing to delve into academia will find a myriad of theses and articles published by universities and smaller publishing houses. You can read about the history, geography, ecology, culture and more of the archipelago from pre-historic times to the current reformasi era.

The following list is of what is on my bookshelves or those of friends. I don't have any 'coffee table' tomes, but would if I didn't live within easy range of incredibly photogenic sights—TC.

## NOVELS

*Ups and Downs of Life In The Indies*. P A Daum. Singapore: Periplus, 1999.
- Dutch colonial life in the 19th century.

*A Gentle Occupation*. Dirk Bogarde. London, UK: Triad Granada, 1980.
- The war in the Dutch East Indies in 1945 after the Japanese left. Semi-autobiographical.

*The Year Of Living Dangerously*. C J Koch. New York, NY: Penguin, 1983.
- Journalists waiting for the revolution in 1965 which saw the downfall of President Sukarno.

*Monkeys In The Dark*. Blanche d'Alpuget. Sydney, Australia: Aurora, 1980.
- Life in Jakarta among expats in the inter-regnum between the 1965 coup and Sukarno's exile.

*Twilight In Djakarta*. Mochtar Lubis. OUP Australia and New Zealand, 1983.
- Life in the kampungs.

Anything by Pramoedya Ananta Toer.

## NON-FICTION

*A Short History of Indonesia: The Unlikely Nation.* Colin Brown.
New South Wales, Australia: Allen & Unwin, 2004.
- "Does exactly what it says on the tin, it provides a good readable summary of Indonesian history."—DJ

*Historical Sights of Jakarta.* Adolf Heuken. Singapore: Times Books International, 1989.
- Numerous maps and illustrations and details of little-known, and often neglected, historical places of interest.

*Nathaniel's Nutmeg: How One Man's Courage Changed the Course of History.* Giles Milton. London, UK: Sceptre, 2000.
- A galloping good jaunt through the early days of western interaction with the 'Spice Islands'.—Miko

*Sukarno: An Autobiography.* Sukarno and Cindy Adams. Indianapolis, Indiana: Bobbs-Merrill, 1965.
- "To the understanding of Sukarno and with that a better understanding of my Indonesia."

*The End of Sukarno: A Coup That Misfired, a Purge That Ran Wild.* John Hughes. Butterworth-Heinemann, 2003.
- The best insight into the tragic events of 1965 and reads like a political thriller.

*A Nation In Waiting.* Adam Swartz. New South Wales, Australia: Allen & Unwin, 1994.
- Indonesia in the 1990s before the 'abdication' of President Suharto.

*An Empire Of The East.* Norman Lewis. London. UK: Picador, 1995.
- Not about Jakarta, but a good writer casting his critical eye over Suharto's Indonesia.

*In The Time Of Madness.* Richard Lloyd Parry. London, UK: Jonathon Cape, 2005.

- A journalist witnesses the revolution in 1998 which saw the abdication of President Suharto.

## NEWSPAPERS AND MAGAZINES

*Jakarta Post*
- Daily except for public holidays. Regular listings of places to go plus classified ads, including vacancies. Sunday edition carries book reviews and accounts of gigs you'll have missed.

*Tempo Magazine*
- The English-language weekly magazine similar to *Time* and *Newsweek*.

*Inside Indonesia* (http://www.insideindonesia.org/index.htm)
- Quarterly: in-depth but readable articles about issues.

*Jakarta Java Kini* (http://www.jakartajavakini.com)
- Monthly glossy guide to posh restaurants, festivals and places to visit outside Jakarta.

# ABOUT THE AUTHORS

Derek Bacon was born in Staines, near Heathrow in London, in 1968. This was something he could do little about. But he made up for it at an early age by travelling, taking photographs and general larking about with people he met along the way. Some of this harmless larking involved settling in Jakarta for five years.

Currently living on England's south coast with one wife and one son, Derek is now a full-time illustrator and is determined not to go anywhere near Staines unless he really has to. Neither will he have any sort of mid-life crisis. You could see some of the work Derek does at his website: http://www.derekbacon.com.

# ABOUT THE AUTHORS

Terry Collins, the co-opted co-author, was born in London nine months after World War II ended. This makes him a bulge baby, although if he'd been born in the USA, he'd be a baby boomer.

Terry has had a varied career having at times been a teacher, a 'squatter's leader', a wallpaper hanger, a charity director, a leather worker, and on the dole. He has lived in France, Spain, Thailand and, since 1987, in Jakarta. Throughout this time, he has supported Charlton Athletic Football Club.

Terry has known Derek as a colleague and friend as long as he has known his wife, which is why he has lived in Jakarta for so long. It is a love-hate relationship—with the city that is. Since 2004, Terry has been the BBC's weblog correspondent in Jakarta, chiefly due to the writing on his website: http://jakartass.blogspot.com.

It is Terry's wish that by the time this book is revised, he'll be retired to the less-populated region of West Sumatra with wife Lily and son Jesse.

# INDEX

## K

*kaki lima* 164, 229, 230, 231, 232, 234

*kampung* 4, 5, 7, 15, 25–27, 28, 29, 34, 43, 47, 52, 53, 54, 68, 69, 71, 73, 88, 95, 99, 102, 107, 113, 127, 128, 132, 135, 138, 147, 178, 185, 186, 211, 219, 263, 288, 290, 307

kites 263

*kost* 71, 129

## L

language 273–281

local government 134–136

## M

*malu* 16, 58, 69, 85, 146

*mandi* 151–153

marriage 93–96

media 168–172

  newspapers and magazines 170–172

  radio 168

  TV 168–170

Monas 29–33

mosques 73–76

music 249–263

  crossover music 260

  *dangdut* 26, 95, 115, 168, 170, 185, 186, 249, 252–254, 256, 258, 260, 267

  *degung* 234, 254

  foreign acts 258–260

  *gamelan* 24, 54, 94, 250–252, 254, 255, 257, 261

  Indonesian musicians with a foreign following 260–263

  *jaipongan* 254–255

  *keroncong* 255

  pop music 257–258

## N

national anthem 304

national holidays 265–269

national motto 304

non-Indonesian food 234–235

non-verbal communication 283–286

## O

*ojek* 6, 131, 184, 194, 208, 211, 214

## P

*pembantu* 67–71

photography 270–271

police 60–65

  amateur police 60–62

  real police 62–65

population 305

privacy 105–107

## R

recommended restaurants 235–236

religions 305

rice 219–223

rubbish 176–178

rupiah 3, 6, 8, 41, 42, 61, 62, 67, 68, 146, 154, 155, 157, 162, 170, 174, 176, 189, 190, 191, 289

## S

*sate* 65, 72, 188, 230, 234

satellite towns 134

sex 96–99

shopping 161–168

*sinetron* 169, 244

smells 187–189

smoking 238–239

  *kretek* 9, 95, 105, 187, 188, 196, 238, 239

social etiquette 85–91

Soekarno-Hatta Airport 2, 9, 11, 118, 125, 153, 216, 306

sounds 184–187

statues 248–249

stress relief 146–147

Suharto 29, 32, 33, 36, 37, 38, 39, 40, 41, 43, 45, 46, 47, 48, 49, 57, 79, 80, 81, 93, 139, 142, 169, 171, 222, 245, 248, 254, 264, 276, 284, 289, 299

Sukarno 1, 25, 28, 29, 32, 38, 43, 47, 49, 75, 139, 140, 162, 258, 268, 269, 275, 289

superstitions 80–83

swearing 282

## T

tailors 166

telephones 172–173

telephone codes 305

time 76

toilets 153–154

Titles in the CULTURE**SHOCK!** series:

| | | |
|---|---|---|
| Argentina | Hawaii | Paris |
| Australia | Hong Kong | Philippines |
| Austria | Hungary | Portugal |
| Bahrain | India | Russia |
| Barcelona | Indonesia | San Francisco |
| Beijing | Iran | Saudi Arabia |
| Belgium | Ireland | Scotland |
| Bolivia | Israel | Sri Lanka |
| Borneo | Italy | Shanghai |
| Brazil | Jakarta | Singapore |
| Britain | Japan | South Africa |
| Cambodia | Korea | Spain |
| Canada | Laos | Sweden |
| Chicago | London | Switzerland |
| Chile | Malaysia | Syria |
| China | Mauritius | Taiwan |
| Costa Rica | Mexico | Thailand |
| Cuba | Morocco | Tokyo |
| Czech Republic | Munich | Turkey |
| Denmark | Myanmar | Ukraine |
| Ecuador | Nepal | United Arab |
| Egypt | Netherlands | Emirates |
| Finland | New York | USA |
| France | New Zealand | Vancouver |
| Germany | Norway | Venezuela |
| Greece | Pakistan | Vietnam |

For more information about any of these titles, please contact any of our Marshall Cavendish offices around the world (listed on page ii) or visit our website at:

www.marshallcavendish.com/genref